Due Return		Due Return	
Date	Date	Date	Date

INTERNATIONAL POLITICS

Foundations of the System

*Publication of this book was assisted
by the John K. Fesler Memorial Fund to promote
greater understanding of law, business,
and public affairs, a cause to which
John K. Fesler was deeply committed.*

INTERNATIONAL POLITICS

Foundations of the System

WERNER LEVI

UNIVERSITY OF MINNESOTA PRESS

MINNEAPOLIS

Library of Congress Catalog Card Number: 73-84786
ISBN 0-8166-0703-6

Contents

INTERNATIONAL POLITICS

Foundations of the System

Introduction

MAN IS DRIVEN, perhaps by instinct and certainly by necessity, to exist in groups. He cannot survive alone. Inevitable membership in his society enables him to live, but also forces him to forgo the fullest satisfaction of all his interests. Group existence increases available resources and at the same time compels their sharing. Absolute needs, conflicting goals, and a great diversity in the conditions of life assure cooperation as well as conflict for a minimal satisfaction of the members' interests. Their overriding concern with survival induces them, out of selfishness or sometimes humaneness, to behave so that peaceful coexistence becomes possible. Man must therefore find ways to solve disagreements and encourage cooperation with others. These must be social ways. For the more complex a society becomes, the less can men rely for existence upon the spontaneous or rational decisions of each member.[1]

Even the most intelligent pursuit of interests or the most altruistic contribution to the needs of his society cannot make up for the inability of any one man to foresee all the knowable consequence of his own behavior for the whole society. He has no overview. He lacks the ability to anticipate the reaction of fellow members to his actions, or his reaction to their actions. There are, then, several reasons why he must rely on organized social rather than private individual decisions. They are ultimately the only safeguard of his own existence because they alone can safeguard the society. They are the most efficient protection against the actions of asocial or antisocial members. Very likely also they can most adequately resolve disagreements and produce cooperation for the largest number of members on most occasions. Moreover, behind all human behavior is a nonrational and often

3

unreasonable element. It leads to unpredictable actions. Yet erratic behavior is anathema to the social order. It represents a problem which society tries to solve, partially, by guiding behavior into established channels and reg- ularizing it. Among the variety of means every society develops to provide such guidance and regulation, politics is the most directly relevant.

The Task of Politics

For all these reasons, social organization is inevitable and politics is present where there is social organization. Because the society's members have survi- val as their foremost expectation, every society must arrange for the authorita- tive regulation of social behavior to achieve regularity and predictability. This is the essence of social order, and a minimum of social order is the crucial prerequisite of social coexistence and an important condition for reli- able peace. Politics aims at creating and maintaining that order, whether it be in the city, the state, or the world. It accomplishes this, its major task, through actions, processes, institutions, and their organization compos- ing in their totality the form and substance of the political system.

The political system is created, controlled, and borne by men. The carriers of politics are human beings. Politics is a form of human behavior. It cannot be understood without attention to its human foundations. The choices men can make are of course not entirely free. Human nature, a given environment, the sluggishness of social change are restraints. But within the framework of these limitations human wills have great influence upon the nature of their society and its politics, including the international.

As human institutions, societies differ in their objective and subjective properties. They vary in the degree of prevalent violence or the benefits they bestow upon their members. Social relationships may be intense and voluminous or irregular and unequally distributed among the membership. Structures can be rigid or flexible. Politics can assume many different forms and serve many different purposes. The attitudes of the members toward the society, their sentiments, their identification with it, and their expectations from it can differ so much that it becomes possible to speak of two subtypes of the universal, generic society: the society in the narrower sense ("Gesellschaft") and the community ("Gemeinschaft"), depending upon the members' emotions toward their collectivity.*

*The distinction between the two types of society follows Ferdinand Tönnies well-known ideas. It will be much elaborated on in Chapter 5 and very important conclusions will be

4

Introduction

Human choices affect the nature of their society: the functions it is to perform, the social order that is to prevail, the means that are to be used and the tasks its politics are to fulfill. These choices very much reflect the interests of those in control of the political system. They may or may not be shared by other members of the society. Who wants to change and who maintain the system depends largely upon the degree of satisfactions obtained. Because these are unequally distributed and, moreover, since needs change, pressures develop for the transformation of the society and tensions arise, more often in unstable societies — societies whose processes are insecurely established and whose social behavior is quite unpredictable. The international society falls into this category.

Its nature, especially the substance of relations between states, has probably undergone more radical transformations in the last one hundred years than that of any other society. Beyond a rather high level of abstraction any description or analysis of this society is valid only for a limited period of time and never quite correct unless qualified by at least a reminder of its extremely dynamic character. For instance, the concept of sovereignty has endured in principle for several hundred years, but with its substance constantly changing. The nature of alliances has varied from simple promises of mutual support by states to complex coordination of industrial production of matériel. The drive for national grandeur as a base of international politics is giving way to economic growth. What seems to be in general true of so-called premodern societies — namely a very slow, almost imperceptible transformation over lengthy periods of time changing to rapid and rather fundamental change once they adopt modern technology — is true of many contemporary new states and the international society.

The international society is young. Its membership is constantly growing. Its structure is adapting to ever-new conditions. Its functions are changing and growing in volume in response to increasing needs and demands. It has few traditions, few routines, and few set forms. The increasing number of international organizations and the dynamics of existing ones are part of the evidence that the members of this society are not at all firm about all the tasks they want their politics to perform. Not surprisingly, therefore, the international society and its politics are subject to perpetual change and

drawn from it. For the time being, society will be used in its broadest, generic sense as comprising both a society in the narrower sense (loosely knit and lacking the emotional support of its members) and a community (a solidary group invested with its members' supportive sentiments).

5

to a great variety of vastly different value judgments as new purposes and methods are added. Controversy rages around the structure as well as the functioning. Many "have" nations, for instance, are more satisfied with the status quo than many "have not" states. The subjectivity of these judgments creates difficulties for the social order of the society. With only limited or very general agreement upon the tasks of the system and how they are to be performed, the efficacy of the international political system is reduced. It lacks support for making its growth peaceful and the direction of its evolution uniform. Bending the task of the system toward specific national purposes (rather than the common weal) by exploiting the existing system or restructuring it, is a major subject of international politics and an important cause of the conflicts bedeviling the international society.

For the statesman and student interested in finding a common ground for judging the performance of the political system and pointing to possible improvements, there is a way of coping with the welter of national criteria. Besides all the different expectations states have from international politics, there is one general result which all states expect, at least officially. It is the continuing peaceful existence of the international society. All states expressly value it. They have so stated in the preamble and purposes of the United Nations Charter. This universal confession, taken at face value, can serve as a standard by which to measure the quality of the international society's characteristics. To the extent that the political system fails to produce reliable social order and permits violence destructive of the international society, it qualifies as ineffective or inadequate. This standard of peaceful survival is still subjective and general. It would probably be difficult to find a definition of either peace or survival on which all men could agree. But in its most general meaning, peaceful survival is a common choice of states suitable to serve as a standard for the evaluation of the political system's quality.

In brief, the differing character of societies, the variety of men's expectations from their political systems, the choices of tasks for the political system available to men, the diversity and transformations of the institutions and structures they can give their society all indicate that the international political system is an eminently human system. This recognition must affect the study of its nature and quality. In the investigation which follows, the character of the enquiry, the topics to be treated, the aspects to be considered, the knowledge to be applied, and the methods to be used will be determined by this recognition. At all times, the objective existential facts of international

6

politics — such elements as nationalism, sovereignty, balance of power, alliances, war — will be related to their subjective, psychological bases. For these facets of politics do not have an existence independent of men. Their nature and its changes cannot be understood without reference to men.

Because of the intimate relationship between the characteristics of a society and the psyche of its members, it is advisable for an understanding of its political system and its politics that there be an analysis of the objective features as well as of the human sources from which these features spring. A study of the objective features alone, so often undertaken, could at best tell what exists but neither why it exists nor why it changes and how. The full meaning of international politics — what its aims are, what its strengths and weaknesses are, how it functions, and above all how it may be changed — can be discovered only with the help of this dual approach. It alone holds promise for pinpointing reasons for the inadequacy of the international political system and therewith for the causes of war and conditions of peace. When this promise has been fulfilled, it becomes possible on grounds more substantial than wishful thinking to propose and perhaps bring about changes toward greater adequacy for the political system and thereby improved prospects for reliable social order and peace.

In this study the first step is toward an overview of the international political system: what it is and what it does, how it can be identified, and how adequately it appears to be fulfilling its task. The next step is to clarify the human environment in which the political system is operating and to examine how the features of the international society may foster or hinder the functioning of the system. The third step is to analyze the political system itself and more specifically to examine the character of political power since it plays an unusually prominent role in international politics. When all these steps have been taken, a picture of the essentially objective characteristics of international politics will emerge, showing that the fulfillment of its task is quite unsatisfactory. This is so not only from the standpoint of an idealist hoping for eternal peace, but also as measured against the normal goals of the political system itself: the production of reliable social order and of behavior safeguarding the continuing existence of the society. In contrast to the frequent practice of proceeding to design blueprints and constitutions for a "better" international system which disregard the human factors responsible for the faulty system, an attempt will be made here to identify these factors. Possible improvements may then be related to the human condition on which they must rest.

7

INTERNATIONAL POLITICS

The next step in the investigation must therefore be to discover what the psychological foundations of the international political system are: why the system is wanted and receives such strong support, why it is maintained in spite of widespread criticism, and why there is so much resistance to deliberate change. Thereafter the various political processes and the political behavior of states can be examined in the light of the objective and subjective nature of the international political system. This examination will provide a clue to unraveling the intricate nature of the causes of war and conditions of peace. Finally, some trends will become discernible of the direction in which the evolution of the international system is moving. Their projection into a foreseeable future might disclose what the chances are for the growth of a more nearly adequate international political system.

These results could not be achieved by merely studying international organization, on the ground, for instance, that it represents the constitutional or political framework for international politics. Such a study would be quite incomplete for two main reasons. The first, already alluded to, is that the objective, visible phenomena of international politics permit only limited conclusions regarding its nature. The second is that international organization and the international political system overlap but are not coterminal. Each covers an area of international behavior not covered by the other. This is true even though the United Nations is very comprehensive in both space and subject matter and even though the intention has been to assign primarily political tasks to it. An overlap occurs because politics and organization aim at ordering the functions of human interrelations, at providing consistent and dependable methods of interaction and schemes for routine behavior. An individual sphere of application occurs because not all activities of international organization are necessarily political and, more important, because potentially politics so penetrates and permeates all social behavior that it cannot be delimited to an organization with formal structures and defined boundaries.

This argument is perhaps more readily admitted for national than for international politics. In the international society human behavior does not seem to be very well ordered. Coexistence of peoples, organized in states, appears often to be so fragile as to endanger the international society. Social order seems much of the time most precariously maintained or in times of war nonexistent. The image is therefore widespread that international relations is chaotic; that effective rules of international behavior are absent; that arbitrariness in state actions is endemic. Quite logically therefore the existence of an international political system has been denied, although few would deny the existence of international politics.

These erroneous impressions are understandable. Disorder attracts attention. Order is taken for granted and its existence passes unnoticed. Yet paradoxically the international order is so unreliable and the potential for disorder so great, that at all times a sense of insecurity overshadows all international behavior. When disorder actually occurs it tends to confirm long-nurtured fears and the impression that disorder is the normal state of affairs in international politics. The obvious differences between the international and national political systems then seem to provide explanative support for the popular notion that the international society is anarchistic.

Many of these impressions are based upon deceiving appearances. There is much order in the international society, even in times of war. Numerous contacts, transactions, and relations between states are routinized. They are ordered by well-established, well-understood, and well-obeyed rules. States habitually solve problems arising from overlapping, common, or conflicting interests in an orderly fashion. Diplomacy developed from the desire for the orderly conduct of relations between peoples alien to each other (as Harold Nicolson pointed out) and it has fulfilled this function well. Since its birth (in modern form) it has been supplemented by the institutionalization of much international behavior for the sake of social order: public and private international organizations; foreign office staffs and diplomatic agencies, regional arrangements.[2] These institutions were often a response to popular demands that technological progress should mean a better life and a corollary expanding network of international relations across the globe. These proliferating contacts among states mean a greater potential for international order, though possibly also for disorder. They mean, in any case, an augmented "amount" of politics. The new institutions are relevant to politics, either as an integral part of the political system or as the environment in which the system must function.

But putting the problem of international social order into a proper perspective is not the same as denying that the quality of that order leaves much to be desired. The low efficacy of the international political system in maintaining social order or providing justice becomes quite apparent when it is compared with that of many national political systems. In trying to find the causes for the inadequacy of the international political system and means for their remedy, attention will be paid in this study, whenever useful, to those political systems which seem to achieve their tasks more effectively.

9

INTERNATIONAL POLITICS

In addition to suggesting solutions to international problems, this approach will also prevent despair, for it will demonstrate that men have the capacity to create peaceful and orderly societies if they have the will to do so; or that, lacking this will, new and expanding mutual dependencies will force them into social order.

1 International Politics and the International Political System: An Overview

THE STUDY of international politics and the political system focuses on a single aspect of the international society. There is artificiality in such an enterprise. A society is an integrated, whole social group. Each part is related to every other, especially when the reality of the group is considered to lie in the network of the interactions and interrelations among its members. It would be unsound and really quite impossible to ignore all other aspects of the society. The problem — if an understanding rather than merely a description is desired — is that the study of the whole is only a little less unfeasible than the study of its parts. To some extent, the problem dissolves when the emphasis is on the individual as the vital center of the society. He represents the link with all its aspects. But difficulties remain. A compromise becomes necessary. Those other aspects of the international society likely to add to an understanding of politics must be drawn in. For this reason an overview will now be taken to clarify what politics and the political system are and where or how they fit into the total international society.

The Ubiquity of Politics

Maintaining order in a society means that the political system's concern with the form and manner of behavior is primary, but not necessarily exclusive. In fulfilling its task, the system becomes inevitably involved also in the content, goals, and substantive results of behavior, mainly for two reasons.

The first reason is that by the nature of social order the political subsystem of the society must deal with all social behavior, in whatever subsystem it takes place. Obviously, murder cannot be allowed in the economic subsystem without affecting the social order in general. Social order relates to the totality of social behavior. Politics permeates therefore all subsystems of the society. It is omnipresent. Even if the political system's task were reduced to a minimum, as for instance the "nightwatchman" function in the ideal capitalist system, it would still be concerned with economic, religious, and other forms of behavior. It would, in any case, be interested in the manner of behavior even if it should want to remain aloof from the substance. Orderly or disorderly (that is to say, regular and predictable versus irregular and unpredictable) behavior is the object of the political system's preoccupation no matter in which subsystem the behavior occurs.

The second reason for the political system's involvement in all subsystems of a society is that the form and manner of behavior inevitably determine some of its substance. Regulating a person's (or state's) social behavior includes a decision on how and whether an interest may be satisfied. If the interest is to obtain money, working for wages may be allowed but not stealing. Control over the form of behavior thus also means control over its goals. The political system in practice takes advantage of this relationship between form and substance by trying to maintain social order through either the regulation of behavior (e.g.: stealing is forbidden; no state may interfere in the internal affairs of another) or the regulation of goals (nobody may have two wives; no state may own the open sea).

This expansion of the area of relevance for politics shows that politics is not an end in itself. There may be individuals for whom "playing politics" has an inherent satisfaction. More normally, politics ultimately relates to human survival by affecting most of the conditions that make survival possible. Politics is a method for promoting the entire society. It is therefore not a conspiracy of evil men — as some critics of society would have the world believe — when politics is used to advance the interests of the economy, religion, art, education, or what not. This is the stuff politics has to deal with by its very nature. Moral questions can be raised not so much about what politics is dealing with as about how it is dealing with it.

It is quite legitimate for any political system to expand its concerns beyond the form and manner of social behavior. It must inevitably enter the realm of social decisions concerning the substance of international cooperation and conflict. The political system must become involved in the creation and allocation of rewards and sacrifices, advantages and disadvantages. Thus the opportunity of the state to shape the society and reap great benefits by political means presents a great temptation to gain control over the political system and, having gained it, to enlarge its jurisdiction far beyond the needs of maintaining social order. In the international society, imperialism is an outstanding example of what governments can achieve through the control of the political system.

But it would be erroneous to ascribe every enlargement of the political system's jurisdiction to greed. It also results from a growing complexity of the international society. Increasing contacts require more regulations; man's entry into space necessitates political agreements; growing economic interaction introduces their political ordering, to name a few examples. There are, in short, many roots for the enlargement of the political system's expanding jurisdiction and functions.

The Identification of the Political System

The pervasiveness and omnipresence of the political system blurs its boundaries with the economic, religious, and other subsystems of the society. Identifying the political system is made difficult chiefly by two consequences of the system's functioning within all other subsystems. One is that those operations indispensable and typical for the political system can be separated from those which are not only, on the basis of what maintenance of the social order requires at a given point in time. This requirement may depend both upon secular changes in the society and upon temporary conditions. For instance, behavior tolerable, even desirable, in time of peace may no longer be so in time of war and then needs to be controlled politically.

The other consequence is the mutuality of the interpenetration of the various subsystems. The boundary of the political system does not run, so to speak, outside all the other subsystems, which means, of course, that their boundaries also do not run outside the political subsystem. They all overlap. Each subsystem (including the political) exists partly within every other subsystem, with the area of overlap varying as changes occur in each one. The interpenetration occurs because the social issues and the public social policies of concern to the political system may arise in the various other systems of the society according to their subject matter (i.e., economic, educational, religious, and so on). The interpenetration and interaction happen because the systems overlap in operation — if not manifestly, then most certainly latently — and because an action may be both political and something else.

13

INTERNATIONAL POLITICS

The practical importance of distinguishing the political from the various other subsystems of a society has to do with the improvement of the international political system. Its present inadequacy can be changed only if the system and the causes of its weakness are recognized and analyzed. Such knowledge is all the more important because there is at most a vague understanding of the international political system and the nature of international politics. The system differs in so many respects from better defined national political systems and is so much less efficacious than most of them that its very nature has remained largely enigmatic, to the point where its very existence has been denied. Yet inadequacy or obscurity is not synonymous with absence. But there may be a relationship between the inadequacy and the obscurity so that illumination may also lead to improvement. In making such an analysis, terms and concepts commonly used for political systems may be employed, both because of their familiar connotations and because the special characteristics of the international political system will emerge more clearly.

From what has been said so far about international politics and the political system, politics turns out to be the authoritative regulation of social behavior for the creation and preservation of social order with a view to the continuing existence of the society. Included in this regulation — and limited to its purpose — are authoritative decisions on social issues and policies. Social order as the resultant of the political processes, activities, and operations (i.e., what politics is doing) is the functional part of the political system. The particular way of performing the functions (how politics is doing it) is the procedural part of the political system. The regularities (the usual practices and patterns) in which political acts are performed are the political institutions. The enduring relationships created by regular and repeated types of interaction in their totality compose the structure of the system. All these components — the processes, the structure, the institutions, the organization of the relationships — become real in the behavior of people. For instance, the reality of "a government" (a logical abstraction) is in the particular behavior of certain men and the particular behavior it produces in other men, such as assembling information on a social problem, debating alternative solutions, choosing among them and making a decision, announcing a policy and expecting requisite behavior by those affected, having policemen and judges act to enforce behavior.

The need to discover and analyze these components arises from the fact that a political system cannot be defined only by its task or what it does.

14

There are other subsystems sharing at least incidentally in this task. The religious system, for instance, is also contributing to the maintenance of social order. The definition must focus in addition on what the system is: its structure, institutions, activities, means and methods. These are peculiarly its own, distinguishing it from other systems performing similar tasks — even if they do so secondarily.

The term *system* is here to be understood simply as a combination of parts so interrelated that a goal is reached or a unit is formed. This unit is characterized by structures and functions directed toward some purpose. System must be understood as a logical concept and as a device for ordering and relating phenomena. All the essential elements of a political system — its goals, its structures, its functions — are in their specific form subject to change by human will and manipulation. This is so because the essence and reality of the political system, as of all social in contrast to mechanical systems, are human actions. Each particular system becomes thereby relatively unique. The social system is what the people composing and sharing it make of it. The widespread assumption that social and political systems are functioning through some automatism beyond the reach of human will is not shared here. (And if it were to be argued that human will and the changes it produces in the system are themselves integral parts of the system, in some way preordained, and hence themselves part of the automatism, it would ruin both the explanatory power of assuming some automatism and the descriptive power of assuming a system.)

Admittedly human will is in practice not all powerful in regard to forming social systems. There are continuities which it cannot affect at a given moment. The reason is threefold. The given environment to which a system must adapt does not change abruptly. Most individuals behave incrementally. And collective wisdom and experience is not only transmitted from generation to generation, but generations overlap so that at no point in time does a society ever start with a clean table. The larger the population of a system and the more involved the network of social relationships, the more cumbersome becomes the manipulation of the system. Deliberate changes in the system at any point in time or in substance can be only limited, albeit important.

The point is that any one group of people may not be able to re-form or change a system in its entirety; that some parts of a system may be more easily manipulable than others; and that over the long run any kind of social system is greatly affected by human influence. Thus, while social behavior is to some extent conditioned by the influences of "the system" (which really means that some social behavior must be what it is because other social behavior is rigid), to some extent it can also escape these influences by changing the system. Fundamentally, therefore, the nature of any social system is the result of human wills — past and present. It cannot be fully explained by the abstracted and generalized analogies between social, or specifically political, systems and all other systems, as general systems theory is attempting to do. Nor can it be explained as products of given environments either by disregarding the human element or by so pre-programming human behavior that what happens is bound to happen — particularly that the system's members will always behave in such a way as to maintain the system. They may be unaware of the behavior required to this end. There is nothing in any social system to make them automatically aware. At best the continuities allow for some probability of behavior and establish limits. With the network of its members' actions as the substance of a social system, the members have control over the nature and, possibly, the existence of the system to the extent that they have control over their actions.

Such an understanding of a social system has at least limited conceptual utility in clarifying what parts compose the system and what relationships exist between its component parts. An analysis of the system may then not only disclose how it functions but also, by paying proper attention to the people in the system, why it functions as it does and why it changes. An indispensable prerequisite for taking advantage of the system concept in this sense, and indeed a consequence of using this concept, is the proper identification of the political system.

Criteria of a Political System: The Function

The primary task of a subsystem together with its mode of operation provides one means of identification. When this is understood, apparently overlapping concerns about the same social issue among several subsystems will turn out to be rooted in differing viewpoints and primary purposes, though these may be complementary from the society's standpoint. The primary task of the political system is the authoritative maintenance of social order and deciding social issues for the sake of order. The primary task of the economic system, by contrast, is the satisfaction of material needs, of the religious system that of spiritual needs. For both systems social order is vital but incidental. They rely upon the political system to secure it as a prerequisite of their own proper performance. In turn, the political system can operate more effectively if the other systems perform their tasks well. An economic system can contribute to social order by satisfying needs, creating sets of mutualities and interdependencies through a division of labor. Religious systems can make their contribution by urging ethical behavior and mobilizing man's conscience. Membership of the same individual in a variety of these systems produces the favorable effects of pluralism. When everybody and everything depend upon someone or something else for greatest self-realization, there arise incentives for cooperation and limits to conflicting behavior. Social order becomes a cherished objective even though every member of the society may have different reasons. Each subsystem of the social system assists in the fulfillment of every other's task. The value of each to the members of the society is enhanced and their willingness to support an integrated social system overall, i.e., a society, is thereby increased. The social reality is, of course, that largely because of the overall and integrative effects of these subsystems a strict separation between them functionally is very difficult and sometimes impossible. Nevertheless, these effects should not be permitted to obscure the identity in principle of each of these subsystems.

Criteria of a Political System: The Bailiwick

An important mark of the political system is that the whole society is its bailiwick. It is central to the international social system. Unlike other subsystems it can never relate to only one part of the society. The order-preserving function makes the system coterminous with the whole society, i.e., mankind in the case of the international society. It coordinates and permeates all behavior to produce orderliness toward the continued existence of the society. There is no way of preventing political consideration of all social behavior since the regulation of all social action is subject to politics. When, for instance, during international conferences on economic or cultural matters statesmen call for the treatment of the subject "apart from politics," when they urge their colleagues not to let "politics interfere" with the success of the conference, they are asking the impossible. This is true on at least two counts: all international behavior, even in the so-called nonpolitical functional agencies, is subject to the scrutiny and rules of the political system; and, especially in the international system, for reasons yet to be discussed, all matters are politicized to an utmost degree.

The inevitable comprehensiveness and pervasiveness of the political system, because of its "nightwatchman" function, touches all behavior actually or potentially affecting the order of the international society. This is inherent in the system's nature and no particular problem in itself. But the possibility that the system may affect directly only a section of the society in any given actual political operation has raised the question whether the system really is a global system. When, for instance, the issue is coastlines and their relations to frontiers, Switzerland, Bolivia, and Nepal are unlikely to have much of an interest to be affected. Or, when three states in South America conclude an alliance aimed at their region, states in Southeast Asia may not feel that they are affected politically.

Such situations may seem to illustrate a system so different from the more customary political systems within modern states as to make the two types incomparable. But this would be an erroneous conclusion. In the first place, the problem really relates more to the nature of the international society than the international political system. In the second place any political system in directing behavior most rarely addresses itself simultaneously to the totality of the members. It addresses itself only to those who engage in a given behavior which the political system wishes to control. Members of a society, whether acting individually or collectively, are almost never relevant as human beings in general (and the same goes for states as acting units). They are relevant as actors of specific roles: father, businessman, teacher. The social behavior representing the abstraction *society* is the resultant of all roles and all players. It is a composite, emerging from the network of interrelated actions by the members. The majority of social policies, allocations of benefits or distribution of sacrifices, demands for actions or their suppression, are decided by the political system for groups of the society's membership. Social order most often threatens from the behavior of a limited group. The enforcement of social behavior takes place under defined circumstances in given situations rarely shared by all members of the society. The political system achieves its tasks through the harmonization of many diverse behaviors — whatever their immediate individual goals may be. The order resulting overall for the whole society provides the connection between each separate operation of the political system and every other of its separate manifold operations. It is the rationale and the integrative force for all the

18

political operations of the system. There is, in principle, no difference here between national and the international political systems.

Criteria of a Political System: The Locus of Decision-Making

The absence of a central government in the contemporary international political system sharply distinguishes it from national political systems. But the impression that this difference converts the international political system into one sui generis or demonstrates its nonexistence is erroneous. The locus of decision-making is presently more diffused in the international than in national societies. But the difference does not necessarily rob the system of its political character, although it may greatly diminish its efficiency. In a society of sovereign states order is maintained by the decisions of different states on different occasions. When a state has made a decision for the international society (e.g., that no outside state can establish missile bases in Central America) which is accepted as authoritative by other states, it has made a "governmental" decision. Any state can potentially undertake political actions and make political decisions for the international society upon its own initiative. This is unlike the situation in national societies where the performance of some political acts, especially the making of authoritative decisions, is reserved to specific organs. The state (in the narrower, legal sense) is usually considered to represent the essence of the political system, with the government as the main operating organ. But it is quite possible that the government may itself be the composite of several organs in each of which decision-making power is located. The United States Congress, the president, the Supreme Court, the political parties, even numerous so-called administrative agencies could be considered as independent organs performing authoritative order-preserving tasks independently within their respective bailiwicks (although they are construed to derive their authority from "the people"). To subsume them all under the "United States government" and claim them to be one centralized locus of political decision-making could be considered a fiction.

There are other types of societies in which a variety of organizationally independent organs can be charged with performing order-preserving tasks. A society in which the elders, a chief, a medicineman, or a priest perform these tasks has a political system. These men are, so far as they are aware, most tenuously related organizationally. They are, however, most closely related through the overall social function which integrates their separate

19

activities. In short, the reality of a system is in the complementary tasks which in their integration form parts of the system. It does not reside in logical concepts which describe the system. The point is that though structurally a variety of independent organs perform operations for the maintenance of social order, their functional integration toward the end of social order combines these organs and their operations into a political system.

In the contemporary international society — to use the analogy from modern national societies — the "government" is represented by the sum total of the states in which the power to make political decisions is located. There is no need to •belabor the inefficiency of such a system or the anxieties it causes. The League of Nations and the United Nations, together with other international organizations, have been the evidence of attempts at improvement. More specifically, the creation of these organizations can be understood as attempts to replicate "government" by concentrating the making of political decisions and eliminating its arbitrariness. But they were meant as an improvement of an existing political system, not the creation of one where there was none before.

Criteria of a Political System: The Subject Matter

A corollary to the universality of the political system is the limitation of its concern, in principle, to social order. This order is created by the regulation of social behavior either directly or through authoritative decisions on social issues and social policies. There is the further limitation that within social affairs the political system typically is concerned only with those affecting social order. The international society presents a special situation in this respect. All international affairs tend to be social affairs because in the vast bulk of relationships within the international society collectivities, mostly states, remain a relevant part. Whether these social affairs are also relevant to social order is more problematical and never quite certain because the conditions of order change. In any case, just because under the international social system governments are usually the actors, it does not follow that the subjects they are dealing with are relevant to social order and hence political. The international control of epidemics, for instance, is not necessarily a political matter, even though governments handle it. Yet the very fact that governments are always involved is a reflection of the extreme politicization of the international society. In international relations every matter can potentially become a political matter, much more so than in national societies.

20

Governments therefore keep an eye on any aspect of international relations with a view to its possible relevance to social order. This practice tends to make all matters political.

An additional reason for the expanding range of political matters in international affairs is the trend, discoverable in all political systems, of expanding the function of political systems beyond the task of "nightwatchman." This can also be expressed in reverse: to be an effective nightwatchman in an increasingly complex society requires the assumption of an increasing number of functions! The larger the number of functions assumed by the political system the more the system is obliged to deal with the substance instead of merely the form of social behavior. The growth of international organizations reflects the enormous growth in the scope of the international political system. Virtually every conceivable subject can be a matter of international concern (though not of regulation). A good example of the trend and the necessity of expanding the political system's scope is the endeavor to prevent international conflicts from deteriorating into violence. At the Hague Conferences of 1899 and 1907 agreement was reached on methods for the peaceful solution of international conflicts. The substance of conflicts, the stakes involved in conflicts were left out of consideration. Progressing division of labor among nations demonstrated the incompleteness of such an approach to the settlement of conflicts. During the era of the League of Nations numerous international organizations were created (economic, health, intellectual, communications, etc.) in the recognition that the settlement of conflicts also required dealing with their causes and substance. With the arrival of the United Nations and its specialized agencies a yet vaster network of political enterprises was created for the purpose of anticipating conflicts or dissolving them in their incipient stages. Some of this expansion in the scope of the political system was deliberate. Some resulted from the increasing interaction among states. In many cases it merely made explicit what was implicit in an effective order-preserving function. But whatever the reasons for this development, it is indicative of the social nature of international affairs and, more important, of the relevance of most of them for the political system.

Criteria of a Political System: Authority

For the political system to be effective, its decisions must be authoritative. This means they must be binding upon those for whom they are destined; they must command obedience. The universal and pervasive nature of the

21

political system makes its decisions binding regardless of their substantive content. The borderlines between the substance of political and other subsystems of the international society are therefore no boundaries to the authoritative nature and effect of the political system's decisions. In case of discrepancies, the decisions originating in the political system always prevail. Why they have this quality and what their moral basis may be is irrelevant to the objective fact of their binding force — though authority would have a better standing and a greater efficiency if it could claim legitimacy.

Probably for this utilitarian reason, legitimacy has been claimed to be an integral part of authority. To make inevitable authority more palatable, it has been separated from power and defined in the terms of a legal tradition which admits of legitimacy. In this way authority and its quality of making decisions binding upon people took on the aura of something not coercive but voluntarily accepted. Such persuasion of those subject to authority could be particularly effective when legitimacy was — very convincingly — defined subjectively as the feeling that political decisions are acceptable because they are right and moral in their source of authority. This subjective definition of legitimacy helps to strengthen authority because people are more likely to be obedient when they are persuaded that they ought to be. One may readily grant that legitimacy would embellish and improve a political system's efficacy. Rulers have recognized this for their own benefit. They never tire of pointing to the source of their authority, be it the mandate of heaven, racial superiority, or the will of the people. All these arguments aim, expediently, at strengthening authority. They hardly relate to the concept of authority. A gang controlling a village and commanding obedience from the villagers could represent a political system (if the other criteria of such a system were fulfilled). Comparable situations exist in states where "revolutionary" regimes follow each other in quick succession, gaining their position by force of arms. Again, an authoritarian or totalitarian regime is no less a part of a political system because many of its subjects are not likely to be loyal or because they deny its legitimacy. Similarly decisions by powerful states for the international society may not have sentimental agreement by weaker states. But the latter obey nevertheless. Indeed, one of the practical reasons — if expediency is to be relevant — why a forced peace treaty is legal though not necessarily legitimate is that the defeated state would probably be totally destroyed if the victorious state could not count on the validity of the treaty. The demand for legitimacy as an integral part of the concept of authority stems from the assumption that society is

22

based upon a normative order. If this means that the norms are generally accepted by all the members, it is an assumption that in most cases is partially true at best and not at all true at worst. Most societies are based also, at least in part, on coercion. The international society is one of them. In such societies authority may still prevail although legitimacy has become irrelevant.

The complaint has often been heard that in the international society might makes right. The reference is to the fact that powerful states can make and enforce political decisions without legitimization of their power. This possibility is, however, a consequence of the political system which states themselves have established. In this system the sovereign right of each state to make its own political decisions is generally acknowledged. This consensus can serve as legitimization for the unilateral activities of states. But the legitimacy to make a decision does not necessarily include its content. The need also exists to legitimize the content of a particular decision. There is very little agreement among states on this aspect of legitimacy! In some respects, this situation can also be found within even the best of democratic states. A citizen may grant that it is moral and right for a properly elected legislature to pass laws. He may nevertheless deny legitimacy to a particular law. However, the validity of the law may be based more on an effective constitutional machinery than on agreement among citizens on what is moral and right, and the disagreeing citizen is bound! Similarly with states. The wish for (subjectively defined) legitimacy exists. International law prescribes that states cannot be bound against their will. If states disagree with a decision, they need not accept it. Formally they are better off than a citizen in a democracy. In practice, the rule is made ineffective by the uneven capabilities of states either to command obedience for their political decisions or to refuse obedience to the decisions of others. In the face of these realities, legitimacy is applied by states when it is compatible with their interests.

States have occasionally invoked higher authority, such as God or the common will, to legitimize their political decisions. More often (together with the legal positivists) they have argued that the effectiveness of political decisions proves their legitimacy. This understanding of legitimacy has little to do with any belief that the source of authority for making political decisions is moral or right. But it is a realistic definition, reflecting not only the controversial interpretation of moral norms in the international society but also their relative irrelevance. The realism of this objective or positivist definition of legitimacy is based on the absence of any subjective foundation. States are far from any concord on a higher authority from which legitimacy for the content of political decisions could be derived (something akin to it existed when international law applied only to the states of Christendom). There is not even assured agreement upon the maintenance of the international society as a desirable goal which could serve as the ultimate source for validating international norms and legitimizing political decisions. Among states there exist more and more supplementary or like self-interests producing common action. But a sense of community is at best in an embryonic condition. States have no loyalty binding them to any international political organ. No fellow feeling ties them together. No sense of mutual responsibility makes them rush to each other's rescue in case of need. On the contrary, citizens are rarely aware of benefits to be derived from membership in the international society while the costs are usually fully realized. There is a tendency for them to consider the outside world basically hostile and potentially dangerous. These sentiments alone can explain the absence of legitimacy understood as a belief that political decisions are right and moral in the source of their authority.

Since "legitimacy" is interpreted as justifying that which is accepted by states, legitimacy in international politics is merely a matter of acting in a formally correct manner or of successfully enforcing obedience to a decision. The political system therefore has to rely heavily upon (usually enforced) acquiescence for its proper functioning. Hence the criticism that international politics is "power politics." So, of course, is national politics. The uneven capabilities of citizens to exert "legitimate" or "illegitimate" extralegal influence enhance the political power of some of them. It is a fact, however, that the international society rests more openly and crudely on power and some of its worst tools, force foremost among them. States often accept unfavorable decisions because other alternatives would be too costly. Acceptance rarely contains that element of consent to be found among citizens of a free society who often accept an unfavorable decision because they feel that the decision was at least made legitimately. In the international society this consent is frequently replaced by the threat of force which is not supplemental, as it tends to be in national societies, but elemental. The international political system is little tempered and assisted by either the fiction or the reality of legitimacy in the subjective sense and the voluntary restrictions upon behavior to which it gives rise.

Increasing mass involvement in international affairs has caused governments to pretend more and more legitimacy for their international actions.

They insist that their decisions conform to generally accepted and valid princi-ples of international law. They claim that their (selfish) pursuit of national interests happens also to benefit the interests of mankind. They hope thereby to demonstrate the highest welfare of mankind as the source of their own nations' welfare and legitimize their national political decisions. Imperialism in the name of the White Man's Burden or warfare to spread the Word of God are examples of what can be done with the aid of such subterfuge. De facto, states grant each other the right to engage in any behavior justified by the actor as the pursuit of vital national interests. In this manner power becomes the source of legitimacy.

The Efficacy of the Political System

The question was raised earlier whether in the light of so much international disorder there really exists an international political system. The analytical overview so far should make clear that there is a system but that by its nature it is unable to fulfill its tasks or reach its goal adequately. It is often saved from complete disappearance only because states can neither wither away nor isolate themselves. Until transformed, the system will linger on, incapable either of reliably achieving social order or of preventing a quasi breakdown of the international society. The judgment that it is inadequate can be made on the ground that it does not safeguard the peaceful survival of the international society. Beyond this minimum achievement, the system's ability to establish reliably any kind of specific order is even more doubtful. But this failure is not alone due to an inherent "natural" weakness. It is due mainly to an unwillingness of states either to specify an order with sufficient detail and conviction to give the system a decisive direction of development, or to implement whatever order states may have agreed upon in the abstract.

Statesmen have reached such agreements on many occasions and incor-porated them in preambles to treaties and other international documents where their binding force is nearly nil. The preamble of the United Nations Charter, for instance, sums up fairly completely what states expect from an interna-tional order. It is a peaceful world in which human rights, the dignity of the individual, and equal rights for all men and states are valued, and in which conditions are created that allow justice, respect for obligations, social progress, and high standards of living to flourish. The generality of these goals is a direct consequence of the need to make them acceptable to all the states of the earth, individually acceptable. For, as has just been pointed out, states can be bound legally only with their agreement. There can be no majority or minority as far as the goals of an international organization are concerned. A disagreeing state need simply not join, or can leave. It can thereby express the egocentrism of states which dominates the international society. Every state tends to consider itself the center of its universe, with the international society and its organizations subservient to its own, not any common welfare. From the state's standpoint, the linkage it establishes with the outside is generated by its own goals, not to serve some internationally determined goals. The specifics of an international order are therefore difficult to reach agreement upon. That every state wants to survive and hopes to benefit from the international order in this respect is the one item on which there is consensus. Beyond this minimum, there is very little agreement among states which could serve as an indicator of the shape the international order should take.

Even peace is desired only with qualifications, such as "honorable" or "just." A powerless, poor state may not agree that peace exists when violence is absent. Conceivably, also, states may want peace only for themselves, not for other states. When it comes to the means for reaching goals, disagreements are usually more numerous because the choice of means is greater than that of goals. Adequacy of a political system will be defined differently by different states and by different groups within states. What a nationalist-minded person may find wholly acceptable may be totally unacceptable to an internationalist-minded person. And when two governments agree on a desirable goal they may still disagree on the means to reach it. There is widespread agreement among foreign policy makers on the need for improving the international political system to achieve a more reliable social order. There is even widespread agreement among them that such a fundamental feature of the system as independent sovereign states cannot be blamed for the unreliability.[3] From that point on, however, they differ widely regarding its causes. Some blame another state's predominant ideology, others blame another state's political or economic system. Reaching agreement is made difficult by the fact that many states are not clear what they themselves consider minimal conditions. Concepts of independence, for instance, can range from territorial inviolability to comprehensive autonomy over political, economic, and cultural affairs. Beyond these minimums the sky used to be the limit of the goals states tried to pursue and expected the international society to help them pursue; but even that limit has now been transgressed.

26

The International Political System: An Overview

In principle, differing, divergent goal orientations are quite compatible with any single social organization. Social order does not mean complete agreement on all social goals or an absence of conflict. The point is, however, that the political system of the society must be able to handle the consequences of such differences and conflicts so that the orderly existence of the society is not endangered. The general reasons why the international political system seems unable to achieve this ability are, first, that the extreme politicization of the society endows each goal with the potential quality of becoming a matter of life and death; and that, second, the principle of tolerance for diverging goal orientations is corrupted when there is *only* divergency of goals, unbalanced by the convergence of some goals and especially the goal of maintaining the society.

The political system cannot reliably create or maintain social order. It can neither prevent nor stop arbitrary behavior by states. Any sufficiently capable state can (although it may not) decide unilaterally upon making war or creating disruptive disturbances to reach self-chosen, self-serving ends. Nothing more is needed to demonstrate the inadequacy of the international political system. The source of this inadequacy can be discovered in some of the consequences of the major features — previously mentioned — which determine the general character of the international political system.

Some Objective Sources of the Political System's Inefficiency

The impressive growth of interaction in volume and types among states would require a broadening jurisdiction of the political system. Yet, while the international organs with advisory power have increased in number, the decision-making power of a common international organ remains nil. As the volume of interaction augments, this situation becomes relatively worse in the same proportion.[4]

Second, the absence of a central government obliges the member states individually to perform the order-preserving tasks. A premium is placed upon a state's capability to do so. A biased performance in favor of the capable state is thereby virtually guaranteed. The few constraints which exist to limit selfishness in decision-making are themselves most effective when based upon selfishness. Norms will be obeyed when they are thought to be useful in a given situation; international organizations will be used when they are likely to advance the state's interests; peaceful behavior will be chosen when the interests at stake do not warrant violent behavior. These

27

are weak controls though their strength is growing as the occasions inducing their application become more frequent. The basis of their effectiveness is the mainly subjectively formed perceptions of those charged with defining the national interests. The temptation for any state is always great to exploit its national power to the utmost in pursuit of its own interest and at the expense of international order.

The diffusion of decision-making results almost inevitably in the dissatisfaction of some states — those most disfavored by the bias of the decision-maker. Small and weak states are likely to be permanently among this group. Hence their usually enthusiastic support of international organizations and collective action as a means for reducing bias in international decisions. Powerful states find it more feasible to counteract bias by their own means alone. They are enabled by the international political system to engage in violent dissent if they so choose and thereby to create international disorder. In contrast to national societies, where conflicts over clashing interests are normally prevented by the government from threatening the order of the society, in the international society such conflicts may be solved by those member states capable of solving them with possible disregard for the society's order. Thus the effectiveness of the international political system becomes weakest when a member state chooses to create disorder, while the effectiveness of national political systems normally becomes greatest at that point.

Third, the necessity of states to implement their own political decisions by their own self-chosen means diminishes the value of formal peaceful, more orderly means for the solution of conflicts (diplomacy, international organizations, international law) and enhances the value of violent means (force, subversion). The political processes thus become a continuous threat to international order. They also become enormously wasteful. The parsimonious (and effective) arrangement of concentrating within a central government a power potential sufficient to guarantee the citizen at least his survival, so that he can devote more resources to other pursuits, is not repeated in the international society. Since every state must protect its own interests, an enormous proportion of national resources has to be marshaled for the realization of political decisions or for opposition to them.

Means are enlisted for international political purposes, such as cultural and religious matters, which could otherwise remain beyond the bounds of the political. Almost every object of human interest becomes potentially and all too often in fact a political tool. The color of a man's skin or a cultural achievement turns into a political instrument for the expansion or undermining of empires. All behavior on the international scene becomes extremely politicized. A state's essentially internal affairs are bent to the ends of foreign policy, while all international events are examined for their impact upon internal affairs. Any separating line between internal and external policies becomes blurred. The linkage between the two is so close as to make them practically inseparable in their effects. Everyone and everything is scrutinized by governments for any possible implication, however slight, for international politics. Everyone and everything are permitted to be their inherent selves only after governments have determined them to be irrelevant to the state's national interests. The nonpolitical realm in the international society is greatly reduced. One immediate consequence is the virtual insignificance of the normally very beneficial informal adjustments and accommodations that result from the interplay of groups in a society. They have, in every society, their political importance, but mainly in the sense of easing the burden of the political institutions and increasing the sense of community. They reduce the arbitrating functions of the government. The politicization of the international society has the opposite effect, and that just when the political institutions are least able to carry the extra burden. Every move of states on the international scene or any action that has relevance for the international scene is carefully calculated. Unexpected moves or events or consequences of actions are quickly brought under control. Governments try to leave as little to chance or informality as possible.

Fourth, the benefits of pluralism and interdependence, so useful in securing national societies, are largely denied the international society. This is so for several reasons. The interdependence may not be sufficiently weighty to overcome contrary effects, such as nationalism. Nations will do without that upon which they are dependent for the sake of higher national values. Again, the interdependence may be very unevenly distributed among states and of very uneven significance for those states which are interdependent in some items. Altogether there is a tendency either to confuse interaction with interdependence, or to draw pollyannic conclusions from existing interdependence for the international political system or to exaggerate the extent of interdependence. Finally, the pluralism is not allowed to lighten the burden upon the political system but is rather turned into its integral part. The point has been reached where the political struggle for power and prestige is increasingly conducted with economic and cultural weapons, replacing traditional, especially military weapons (and more will be said later on these important points).

Another reason is that extreme politicization undoes the favorable effects derived from interweaving and overlapping of many diverse interests among the members of a society and emphasizes the separation based on political differences. When members — whether individuals or collectivities — of a society relate to each other first and foremost in their political capacity even when they are substantively engaged in religious, cultural, or similar activities, their interdependence and mutual needs have little leeway to soften political conflicts. When, for instance, the spectators of the Bolshoi Ballet's performance in New York or the Moscow audience of the New York Philharmonic's concert in the Soviet Union are never quite allowed to forget the political purposes of these "cultural" exchanges, the end effect of the enterprise tends to be as much political as aesthetic. Most interests and almost all behavior are subordinated to often dichotomous and always dominant political interests. Wherever they originate and whatever their nature, they always become tainted in the international society by politics.

The final reason for the weak influence of pluralism is the underdevelopment of the nonpolitical subsystems of the international society, coupled with a lack of awareness of such development as does exist on the part of large sections of the population in every state. When people ignore the importance of international activities to them, they do not develop any interest in them or the system within which they take place.[5] And, as investigations have shown, such ignorance is widespread, not only in newer countries whose involvement in world affairs is of very recent date, but also in long-established states whose international activities are essential to the welfare of their citizens. The direct international interests of very many people — economic or otherwise — are mediated by relatively few individuals (officials, exporters, bankers) so that the objective existence of these interests does little to affect the often hostile or at least indifferent feelings of these people based upon their impression of the almost exclusive political nature of their country's international relations.

Finally, a fifth source for the inadequacy of the political system can be discovered in the lack of legitimacy supporting the authority of decision-making states. A command issued with authority so that it must be obeyed, arouses psychological resistance and resentment if it is considered unsanctified by legitimacy. When a whole political system is based upon this principle, resistance and resentment will be transferred to it. There can hardly be enthusiastic support, let alone loyalty, for such a system. Yet, without them, the necessary changes to make the system more adequate are not likely to occur. A vicious circle develops, in which the inadequacy of the system repels its members and the repulsion then prevents improvement of the system.

The inadequacy of the international political system is, of course, not a discrete phenomenon in an otherwise more perfect international society. It is, rather, a reflection and a part of a society which is altogether weak and deficient in cohesion, mutualities, and stability. For a fuller understanding of the political system, an examination of the international society in which the system functions must therefore be helpful.

2 The Nature of the International Society

THE RAW MATERIAL of the international political system is the international society. The task of the system is to maintain order and assure peaceful behavior among men across the globe. To some extent, therefore, the nature of the international society is determined by the influence of the political system. To an even larger extent, however, the political system is influenced by the nature of the international society. There is an interaction between the two. If the political system performs its task only inadequately, some of the reasons are to be found in the overall nature of the international society.

The precise nature of mankind as a social group is a much debated topic. There have even been denials that mankind could be called a society. The argument has been that all societies (in the generic sense) share certain universal similarities, such as status, role, and territory, which in their interrelations constitute the social system. Mankind, so it is claimed, is constituted quite differently and to extend the concept of society to it makes the concept meaningless. Much of the debate is a matter of definition. It would have greater relevance if, after the concept of society has been clarified successfully, there would emerge greater knowledge about the nature of a society. This is unfortunately not yet the case. It remains, therefore, necessary to establish first what in general is meant by the concept society and thereafter to examine some of the important aspects of the international society. Some conclusions can then be drawn regarding the mutual effect of the international society and the international political system upon each other.

Society, in its most general, generic meaning, as so far employed here, refers to a group whose members are connected by a network of behavioral relationships. A society is distinguished from a mob by the meaningful orientation of one member's behavior toward another's for the fulfillment of some purpose. It is further distinguished from a mob or any temporary, spontaneous gathering of people by the regularity of the behavioral relationship and the durable nature of the social purposes to be fulfilled. A society's character as a distinct social unit is shaped by the functions which it performs regularly over a period of time, the patterns by which the members' relationships are ordered and interconnected, and a structure into which the collective behavior is organized and integrated toward the fulfillment of the society's purposes.

These are conditions of a very general nature. For this reason, presumably, they are widely accepted as representing at least the minimum ingredients for a definition of society. Disagreements arise about the particulars of these conditions and possibly additional conditions. But these disagreements are largely of a semantic nature. It is more profitable to proceed to an examination of some fundamental aspects of the international society in order to discover the special nature of this social unit and how it may help to explain the nature of the international political system.

The Relationships between States

The mutual needs, problems, and sensitivities of all states have become a matter of record. References to them in public documents abound to the point of triteness. The prospect is that they will increase as global division of labor advances, standards of living across the globe rise, consumption reaches a higher volume, and withal as man endangers his environment. During modern times every step in the growth of man's needs (real or imagined) has had international effects. They have not always been happy ones. On the contrary. Very frequently the sequence of events has been that they led first to internal national adjustments, then became the cause of international competition and conflicts (e.g., imperialism), thereafter induced international cooperation (e.g., international river control), and only finally ended in international organization. An especially unfortunate experience has been that all too often the lessons learned from one case are not transferred to newly arising situations, but that instead states go through this sequence all over again. The latest examples are problems of ecology, most of which are by their nature international, yet whose attempted solution on an international basis is still in the distant future.

A number of reasons for this approach can be found easily enough: some of these problems are more acute for some states than for others; some states are not affected at all by these problems; some states are in a better position than others to do something about them; some states think they can export the difficulties created by these problems to other states; and some states blame other states for the creation of the problems. Underlying this situation is the very unequal involvement of different states in global problems as a result either of their inequalities or of their unequal involvement in the problems at hand. The consequence is that the relationships tying individuals, groups, and states internationally are not evenly distributed across the globe. They are not everywhere of the same volume of significance. Some states exist detachedly and remotely from the life of the international society. Burma, Nepal, Bhutan have tried to isolate themselves. Other states try to confine their relationships to neighboring states. Or else they confine their relationships essentially to a group of other states, for example, former French colonies which relate mainly to the European Economic Community. Some states, at least for a time, maintain relations with states with which they have had traditional ties, such as colonies with the metropolitan powers (e.g., Indonesia and the Netherlands, Malaya and Great Britain). Finally, there are states, mainly the largest, relating to each other across the globe, relating with other regions, and often even with isolated states. They are the major links of the international society because through their universal relationships they also mediate relations among other states otherwise in meager contacts.[6] They make the world politically One.

The omnipresence of the few major nations forces every state everywhere to take into account the possible reaction of these powers to whatever it does. There is now no way realistically to separate out geographically defined areas of the globe and treat them as independent or quasi-independent systems or subsystems in their own right. The mere existence of the major nations with their ubiquitous interests makes them active participants in all parts of the globe. It would be misleading, or at any rate rather meaningless, to separate a "center" of world politics from "peripheral" world politics. States may be important or less important for world politics, but their interconnection is complete. For this reason it becomes little more than a semantic effort to try to divide the globe into regions or subsystems; to endow these with some autonomous existence; and to define the inevitable presence of the major nations in such terms as "penetrants" or "environment." International politics is indeed world politics and there are no outsiders. Moreover, there is no evidence that the international politics within so-called regions differ at all in principle from those of the global system.[7]

Even if agreement could be reached on how a region should be defined, its close study would very likely show nothing much more than that states located contiguously can do things to and with each other which states widely separated geographically cannot or need not do. Even this showing is becoming increasingly unimpressive as improving technology diminishes the significance of physical distance. As far as international politics are concerned, every factor or combination of factors that has been thought to produce a new international behavior in principle, peculiar to regions, can be found in nonregional combinations of states without producing such effects. The reverse is true as well. Thus, for instance, feelings of solidarity can be found or not found within regions just as readily as between states thousands of miles apart and the same is true of hostilities; voluminous trade is no monopoly of neighboring states; wars are being fought between near and distant states; the states of the European Economic Community are accepting common laws, but then Japan adopted Western laws in the nineteenth century. The conclusion seems inescapable that international politics do not differ in essence within regions from what they are globally. They are what the individual nations choose to make them. Cooperation will be a source of strength for regions, nationalism and national individualism will be a source of weakness. There is no evidence that cooperation, competition, conflict are caused or shaped differently in principle when they take place within regions than when they occur worldwide. Nor have states been willing to change or adjust the definition of their national interests, let alone the very basis upon which their individual nationhood is founded.[8] In sum, many states seem to be deeply immersed in the mainstream of international life. Others appear to exist outside of it. On cursory inspection the impression may well be gained that where so many states lack direct relationships — even though they interact occasionally — an international society does not exist. But this phenomenon can be found in national societies without making them any the less societies. All larger states have groups of citizens with different involvements in the national life. People in remote, rural areas often have less intense participation in the public affairs of their state than their fellow citizens in the larger cities and highly industrialized and densely populated regions. Division of labor leads different groups in a society to assume the performance of different funtions. In any case, direct, personal and above all face-to-face relationships are minute in most societies relative to the number of their members. Direct interrelationships based upon functions, mutual needs, and common interests can range from the most voluminous to the almost nonexistent. In many cases, only the single, though very important, interest of wanting to have their society is shared and provides the bond tying them together.

The size of modern societies makes it inevitable that interactions and interrelationships among the members are established mostly on an impersonal basis. The vast majority of the functional connections between members of large societies are mediated by a few individuals — union leaders, managers, parliamentary delegates — acting as representatives for collectivities. Technical achievements make the organization and bureaucratization, and therewith the depersonalization, of large societies necessary and possible. The broadening range of men's interests and their unequal capacities (e.g., between rich and poor, educated and uneducated) to satisfy them produces irregular transactions between individuals and groups (e.g., poor peasants may never see a stockbroker and their only contacts are vicarious ones through being citizens of the same state). In almost any modern society the point is quickly reached where the relationship among the mass of its members is most tenuous. Most members have little more than vague notions about their usually indirect or functional connections to some anonymous group of fellow members — if they have any notion about them at all. The differing intensities of the citizens' involvement in social relationships tends also to give them a different relevance for the political system. The legal equality of citizens in a democracy, for instance, tells little about any citizen's political importance.

On the international scene, similarly, governments or their agents act for the states they represent. The mediation principle is much more pronounced here than within states. The principle of the international system is that the state acts on behalf of its own citizens. With few exceptions, governments are the spokesmen for all their citizens and they address all the citizens of any other state with which they relate. They are assumed to represent and commit the whole population, even when only a part of it agrees with the government. Still, in principle (with some exceptions mainly in Western Europe) the individual has no standing before an international agency. This tenet is an outflow of sovereignty upon which all official international relations are based. It has led to the ascription of anthropomorphic and organismic qualities to the state and from there to wrong conclusions regarding the nature of the state, the international society, and the international political system.

There should at all times be a clear understanding that the concept "state" is a shorthand expression. The context in which it is used must make clear whether it stands for the collectivity of all citizens organized as a legal and political unit; for members of the government (in the narrower sense); or for other specific groups or individuals. But the fact remains that the bulk of relations between citizens of different states are mediated. Between some states, relations based on mutual, common interests are virtually nonexistent. Between other states, relations of many kinds exist in large volume. The different types of relationships reflect different types of involvements which states have in the international society. They can also be indicators of substantive differences in the stakes states have in international politics. But whatever the volume of relationships or their type, no state can any longer isolate itself from the international society. All states are related through their membership in international organizations. All states are functionally related, directly or indirectly, through international social issues affecting them all. All states are touched by ideas of whatever kind and origin. This innovation of recent date produces greater similarity between the international society and the more customary types of societies. Inescapable common problems or organizational memberships create contacts and the need to take positions regarding the interests of other states, for instance through votes in conferences. They produce an ordering of relationships which is political in nature, even though substantively these relationships may be very thin.

This last possibility is a reversal of the more customary course of events in the past. Then, expanding interests brought states into contacts which eventually needed political ordering. The history of international organizations demonstrates this chronology of events. With the present-day universality of membership in many international organizations, contacts between some states are created before any mutual interests bring them together. Indeed, there may be hardly any interests at all inducing states to join international organizations other than a prestige interest. To many new states membership in organizations is a confirmation of their existence and independence. It is as much a matter of psychological need as of material interest, or even more so. The relationship between such states with others may then be based on little more than common exploitation of the organizations for each to pursue its own, independent purposes. Such states may render each other mutual political help in order to exert pressures (e.g., by trading votes or logrolling) or set precedents in the hope for reciprocity at times of need (as when Columbia sent a frigate to South Korea during the Korean War). Quite possibly, this kind of relationship may be the only kind of relationship tying a number of states together when otherwise pluralistic and overlapping interests between them are poorly developed. Nevertheless, the world has become an "inclusive activity area" (to use Lasswell's term) and generates politics. But it also generates some characteristics endowing the international society with a special nature.

The first is that technology has been mainly responsible for enabling mankind to become a society and for turning international politics into global politics, or even world space politics. But technology is an expensive thing. Fewer and fewer nations can afford it sufficiently to participate actively and influentially in world politics. More than ever before in history, great inequality in developed national wealth means great inequality in political roles, mainly because economic capability is at least matching military capability in importance as a tool of statecraft. The danger becomes acute that ever-fewer nations will be able to afford political globalism.

The second characteristic is that the bonds holding states together are largely technical, functional. The international society lacks an integrating psychological dimension. There is little sympathy for the international society anywhere and much apathy. No strong drive is visible either to maintain or to disturb the prevailing order. The citizens' emotional investments in international relationships are minimal. Few vested interests would care about them. An incentive to develop loyalty to the international society matching, let alone replacing, loyalty to the nation is nonexistent. Without the mediating presence of the major nations, their worldwide interests, and their sponsorship of global organizations, relations between some of the smaller and newer states might have remained limited to their region. At most, they might have been selective with a few other states. The existence of an international society may indeed have been doubtful. As it is, the direct involvement of the major nations in every part of the globe has the effect of bringing smaller states directly or indirectly into relationships. The regularity and permanence of these relationships turns mankind into a social unit, even if in some substantive fields of interest or between some geographic areas the interactions may be sparse and relationships therefore weak. But this merely affects the quality, not the existence, of the social unit. The same

38

conclusion would be reached if one were to consider — as a Marxist would — the nation-state system as a system of domination and subordination in which the social nexus and the structure of the global society is exactly based upon the great inequalities among states — inequalities originating in colonialism and imperialism, perpetuated in neocolonialism and neo-imperialism, and symbolizing a kind of international division of labor between the rich and powerful on the one side, the poor and weak on the other.

From whatever angle one considers the relationships between states, their contemporary network justifies calling mankind an international society. By the same token the objective prerequisites are given for a political system to order these relationships, though subjectively many people in the world are unconvinced that their mutualities with citizens of other states are of sufficient volume to justify it — as their insistence upon the primacy of the "national interest" indicates.

The Stratification of the International Society

The density of a state's relationships with other states, the extent and intensity of its participation in the life of the international society are likely to reflect as well as affect its status as a member. This status is the position which the society of states gives every state in a rank ordering within the international society. It is related to the great inequalities among states and based upon the qualities a state possesses and their value in the eyes of the international society. The international society becomes stratified according to the differences distinguishing states from each other, and to the social esteem attached to these differences.

There are mainly two methods by which a state is assigned its rank. One is by ascription. Certain characteristics correlate in the esteem of the international society to a given position in the status hierarchy; historical record, traditions, and geographic location are factors of relevance here. The other method is achievement of rank by the state itself: educational level, economic development, political stability, military establishment. A variant of this achievement method is the assumption of a rank by a state through behaving in a manner typical for the assumed rank. An historical example would be Tsarist Russia during the late nineteenth and early twentieth century, when she was trying to play the role of a major power but lacked the where-withal to sustain it. For a while, though, she succeeded in bluffing her way

39

into a high rank, mainly by superficially developing qualities which are rated highly among states, such as maintaining a big military establishment and acquiring land.

In either of these two methods the evaluation by the international society remains crucial. The difference between them is that in the first the state to be ranked has no influence over the qualities forming the basis of its status, while in the second the state's efforts can affect its status. Which method is applied or in what mix they are applied depends, of course, upon what type of stratification is at issue.

The number of possible hierarchies of stratification matches the qualities that can be evaluated and compared. Stratification can be based upon size, economic strength, cultural achievements, and innumerable other qualities or combinations of them. Political stratification is based upon the relation of these qualities to the power potential of the state. The politicization of the international society makes this political stratification the most comprehensive one, since there is virtually no quality without political significance. When there is talk of big, middle, and small states, the reference is really to a sum of qualities in their endless variety making up a state's power potential.

Stratification is politically significant for several reasons. First, rank is a power factor. The argument has been made that rank ordering expresses nothing more than the assumed potential power ratio between states. Big, middle, or small states correspond to a big, middle, or small power potential. Rank would be nothing more than a synonym or symbol for a power relation. Rank is indeed such an indicator. But it is more; it has a significance of its own. Rank can do among states what charisma does among individuals. The fact of rank, beyond being the result of an estimated power potential, itself affects that potential. When a state is ranked highly, other states tend to act toward that state according to its high rank! A state is enabled to be influential by virtue of its ranking, to some extent regardless of the basis of the rank. Rank assumes an inherent value for states in their eternal quest for a power potential. It thereby becomes an objective of the national interest.

The second point making ranking significant for international politics follows from the first: achieving a certain rank in the international hierarchy becomes a foreign policy goal. The better the rank, the higher the prestige and status, the greater the power potential. Rank becomes an object of international competition and rivalry. Stratification causes tensions. Some smaller states, old and new, are reconciled to their lowly status. They have adjusted to having their political decisions made by other states. They may still marshal some of their resources to build up a power potential, but they have little ambition to change their ranking in the basic hierarchy. Other states feel frustration over their status. They are forever striving to improve it. The nearer they are to a higher rank, the more encouraged they appear to feel in their efforts to reach it. Tsarist Russia during the second half of the nineteenth century and Germany at the time of her unification are examples. The "biggest" states make every effort to retain their place or often to regain it when they have lost it (as General de Gaulle tried to do for France). The institution of ranking creates a sense of insecurity in the international society. Some states resent what they consider to be invidious distinctions. Others wish to improve their ranking or neutralize it through international maneuvering. Yet others simply resist the consequences of ranking. This class structure is perceived by some of the lower-ranked states as a system of domination regardless of the intentions of the higher-ranked states, even though they cannot change the situation. Herein may be found some compensation for the unrest created by attempts to alter the hierarchy. In complex society, the class and power structure determines who makes the necessary decisions for coordination. The structure promotes "law and order" (though not justice). Hence the claim of the biggest nations — embodied in their permanent membership in the Security Council — that they carry the major responsibility for international order, as indeed they do. Also, similar to the effects of a pecking order, a rank order may prevent violent fighting when each state learns not to challenge the stronger and to intimidate the weaker state. There is, for instance, a widespread assumption that after India's victory over Pakistan in 1971 and the likely superiority of India over Pakistan as a result, violent incidents between the two states will cease. Inasmuch as states adapt themselves to a hierarchy, the acceptance saves some effort needed to maintain it by force and reduces open conflict. But it does so, in many cases, at the expense of heightening dissatisfactions and possibly tensions among those obliged to adapt. The peacefulness and "integration" resulting from this acceptance of the rank system may be quite unstable and a surface phenomenon. The overall detrimental effect of the ranking system is certainly not balanced by the modicum of salutary effect it may produce.

The third point of significance about ranking is its great subjectivity. It is true that status, determining rank, is perceived more and more as a correlate of wealth, especially a state's gross national product.[9] The stage of economic

41

development seems to determine a state's status, rank, and role in international politics more than any other factor. Much of this factor is measurable and to that extent limits subjectivity and the uncertainty connected with it. But neither the evaluation of wealth elements nor most certainly the estimate of power potential is completely objective. Some of the evaluation is culture-bound, so that a change in the cultural context can bring about a change in rank without any change in the objective elements of the state's power base. Some elements of the power potential are wholly immeasurable, such as a people's morale and stamina, so that any evaluation is totally subjective. Altogether there has lately been a change in the importance of the whole ranking system. The demands upon statehood from national publics everywhere are increasingly for material satisfactions and less for psychic satisfactions. In many parts of the world people seem to be less concerned about their country's status than about what their country can do for their good life! At the same time these publics, especially in some of the newer countries, place more emphasis upon achievement than upon reputation and prestige. Status and rank are diminishing in importance. But this development has not yet gone far enough to affect the behavior of states very greatly. They are still tempted to discount both possible changes in general attitudes toward rank and possible changes in the value of factors determining rank by aiming at such a high rank that any likely change will not affect it. The chance of conflicts from the ranking system remains, with the political system carrying the greatest burden of solving them.

A fourth point of significance is the relativity of ranking in the hierarchy, especially in short-run considerations. From the standpoint of each state, except the highest and the lowest ranked, there are really two relevant hierarchies. One is a universal hierarchy in which all states are ranked by and for the international society. This ranking rests upon a comparison of all states. Since neither their qualities nor the international culture changes very rapidly in the normal course of events and increasingly less so under modern conditions (e.g., the rich growing richer, the poor growing poorer), the universal hierarchy is relatively enduring. The United States and the Soviet Union are likely to remain high, Tanzania and Mali low on the scale for some time to come.[10] The other hierarchy depends to some extent upon the specific, immediate context in which the qualities of states are evaluated for ranking. In an acute issue involving two states, the ranking of the two in relation to each other is of the essence to them and depends mainly upon their evaluations. It is part of trying to guess the other's power potential.

42

The Nature of the International Society

The resulting ad hoc hierarchy may differ from the position of these two states in the universal hierarchy (e.g., because in a bilateral relationship other factors may be relevant than those affecting their world relationship).

The overall importance of the fact of social stratification is its behavioral consequences. First, as has been pointed out, striving to achieve, improve, or deny rank leads to international tensions and conflict. And second, since it appears that certain behaviors, such as the volume of interaction, involvement in conflicts, participation in international organizations, support of or opposition to the status quo, are dependent upon the rank a state occupies, the place of a state in the hierarchy might permit prediction about its behavior. A certain type of behavior, it is argued, goes with high ranking, another type with low ranking. Or, expressed differently, the qualities of a state raising it to a high rank usually enable it to afford a behavior which the qualities giving a state low rank do not permit. But the possibility of prediction is ruined by the existence of two hierarchies or the relativity of ranking. In the concrete relations between two states, the ranking of each on the universal scale is far less important to either than how each ranks the other in relation to itself. A state is much less interested in whether another state is ranked large, medium, or small than in what that state can do to it! The possible truth that a certain behavior may go with a certain rank is of little practical consequence because in most international situations most states have no predictable given rank. One and the same state can exhibit all types of behavior depending upon which hierarchy is used for its ranking in the given situation. There can be a universal, multilateral, or bilateral hierarchy. India could behave like a "big" power toward Portugal in Goa, although her nonaligned posture globally corresponds more to a middle or small state behavior. Any "big" state is likely to behave like a "small" state when the use of its full power potential is practically impossible (the United States in Vietnam!).

States will behave in a manner they consider most effective. This could be "big" or "small" power behavior regardless of the rank of a state. Besides depending upon the hierarchy applied, a state may (relatively) have a different rank in different situations. This means that a "small" power is not always or predictably behaving like a small power, nor a "big" power like a big power. In a politically relevant sense, namely when states make and enforce political decisions, there is no one hierarchy for all states generally valid for all possible relations between states from which a "typical" behavior could be predicted.

In sum, the significance of social stratification in the international society for the political system lies in the heightened unpredictablility of behavior. It provides great incentives for arbitrary action. At the bottom of stratification is the inequality of states. Since attempts to eliminate it would be hopeless, the problem for the political system is to manage it for the preservation of social order. Various roads leading to this result have been proposed by different political systems. Democracy, for instance, attempts to limit the effects of inequality by granting legal equality and formally equal access to government. It also usually seeks to promote high social mobility and to guarantee a minimum satisfaction of everybody's interests. A fascist system makes a virtue of inequalities. It accepts and systematizes them, rewarding the elites and disadvantaging other sections of the population. The international political system is the most inefficient of all in reconciling the inequality of states with the maintenance of social order. The effect is all the more harmful because inequalities between states are enormous, social mobility (in the sense of compensating for imbalances) is limited, and relatively few qualities (in extreme cases merely physical strength) can define enormous inequalities. In the name of sovereignty the international system permits social stratification to run amok. Each state makes its own political decisions. In so doing it makes them for others as well. Every state must expect in any given situation to have its rules of behavior prescribed by the highest ranking state. The political system, far from smoothing or at least reliably regulating the political consequences of social stratification, grants them free rein. The unsettling consequences social stratification may have for any society are enhanced in the international society. Once high rank has itself become an element in a power potential, the "national interest" prescribes a striving for higher rank, even at the expense of social order.

The international society has developed a few measures to ameliorate the situation. As long as military and strategic considerations dominated world politics, alliances, military arrangements, collective security, and a balance of power were the main tools for evening out inequalities and preventing higher ranking states from exploiting those below them.[11] As economic manipulations began to compete with physical force as a political tool — mainly after World War II — economic arrangements were added to the more traditional tools.

Through mutual assistance and the aggregation of capabilities, states combine their power potentials to approach or match or surpass the power potential of an envisaged adversary. Occasionally an alliance may aim at balancing inequalities by keeping one of the partners under control (for instance, when Germany was to be included in the planned European Defense Community). The global collective security system of the United Nations tries to cancel all military inequalities by combining the strength of all states into one irresistible deterrent against any one aggressor. In its ideal form an international police force attempts to make inequalities in physical force irrelevant through its overpowering strength. The legal equality of states under the principle of sovereignty is intended to deny the benefits of inequality in all realms, military, political, or any other. The motivation behind common markets is, beyond the economic, also the desire to obtain political influence through economic capability. Finally, quite realistically, some arrangements take account of existing inequalities and attempt to soften their impact. The permanent seats of five nations, declared "major," in the Security Council is such an arrangement. Another is weighted voting in international organizations. The idea is that certain inequalities of states (size of population, extent of territory, volume of gross national product, financial strength, literacy rate, use made of an organization, either alone or in combination) in relation to the function of the particular organization cause states to have different stakes in the organization and therefore justify differential influence through weighted votes.

In all these cases the underlying principle is the same: to make up for perceived inequalities in power or any other relationships. The justification given is always the same: the peace and order of the international society are thereby better preserved. It may well be argued that recognition of inequalities and the organization of their consequences (as in the Security Council or in weighted voting) obviate the need for a state to demonstrate its superiority by a trial of strength every time a conflict arises. But it is very difficult to prove that these measures to overcome the inequality of states have fulfilled their mission with any reliability. They all leave sovereignty intact, and sovereignty is the best guarantor of inequality. It permits each state to use its own means and methods to change the basis of ranking and to deny such use to competing states. Herein lies the contribution of stratification to the insecurity of the international society. All measures to achieve equality among states are palliatives at best. At worst they confirm the more powerful states in their superiority.

INTERNATIONAL POLITICS

The Cultural Heterogeneity of the International Society

The difficulties created by the uneven network of relations between states and by the inequalities of states are rooted in part in cultural differences between states. This problem of cultural diversity has always attracted much attention because it is very visible. For this reason, probably, its importance has been greatly exaggerated. The argument is that cultural heterogeneity vitiates an international society and therefore an international political system, that when ways of life differ so greatly there is no common ground upon which a worldwide orderly, peaceful behavior can be developed. The prerequisite for an effective global political system, the argument concludes, is the creation of a world culture. Until this can be achieved, decisions made by governments of one culture area will, objectively, not fit the peoples of other culture areas. Subjectively, people will dislike and resist decisions made for them by "others" especially when the "others" are considered vastly "different." An argument on a more limited scale is that the growth of societies sufficiently integrated to assure with reasonable reliability orderly and nonviolent behavior will be greatly assisted if the members are culturally homogeneous.

If, in trying to assess the effect of cultural heterogeneity in a society, one accepts the relatively modest goal of a reasonably reliable orderly and peaceful behavior of the members, the evidence at first sight is inconclusive. Peoples with fairly different ways of life and subscribing to different sets of values have lived peacefully side by side for long periods of time. In contrast, peoples with great likenesses and similarities in their social characteristics, both "primitive" and "advanced," have warred against each other with great regularity. The evidence becomes even more confusing when the similarities or dissimilarities of members in successful alliances are examined. Quite obviously, no facile assumptions can be made regarding the effect of cultural differences. A more detailed analysis is required to reach reliable conclusions.

Culture may be defined as the totality of a group's behavior patterns in a man-made environment directed toward the attainment of chosen goals. The most basic goals men pursue are everywhere alike because basic human needs are everywhere alike. This likeness, on a high level of abstraction to be sure, diminishes the range of what appear to be fundamental cultural differences. It also raises the question why — if cultural homogeneity is conducive to social integration — it has not been more effective in producing

46

an orderly, peaceful world society. One answer, of course, is that cultural homogeneity is not, any more than heterogeneity, the only element in determining social integration. A more weighty answer is that this very general likeness is, quite evidently, not of a kind inducing people to harmonize their social behaviors toward order and peace.

For cultural factors to affect attitudes significantly, they must matter to people. Appeals throughout the ages for men to unite on the grounds of their likeness before God or their common humanity have been singularly unsuccessful. When attitudes rather than material interests are involved, people tend to relate to other people, people identify with other people, people join in peaceful groups because they discover special not general likenesses. Groups can provide identity to their members only if they can single themselves out and demonstrate their special character in comparison, and perhaps in competition, with other groups. Membership in the human race can provide no special psychic satisfactions to individuals and therefore fails to provide a bond for social cohesion and integration of social behavior. Two points emerge, both important for an evaluation of the relationship between the culture factor and the political system. The first is that to have an effect cultural similarities or dissimilarities must be on a sufficiently low level (not further definable) to matter to people. Whether, for instance, people eat with forks or chopsticks can probably potentially affect people's attitudes more than that all people eat; or how cigarettes are packaged in different countries is likely to codetermine more effectively whether one people is more "like" another than the fact that both smoke cigarettes. The second point is suggested by the first. Dissimilarities appear to be more influential than similarities, at least in the sense that similarities are no barrier to cooperation if that is wanted for other reasons, while dissimilarities create hesitancy and suspicions. These last two considerations lead to an examination of how cultural factors are related to politics and the political system once they are of a kind to matter to people at all. The question is posed in general terms because the problem is by no means unique to international politics.

An examination of the internal conditions of many nations again leads to inconclusive results. Many states containing the most diverse cultural groups nevertheless possess adequate political systems and orderly politics. The differences between a Bavarian peasant and an exporter in Hamburg, or between a Breton fisherman and a member of Paris's intellectual elite, are greater than those between a Minnesota and a Manitoba farmer. Yet

47

each of the first two have an effective, common political system; the last two do not. In India, Indonesia, and some other states, cultural differences are successfully used by interested parties to prevent the growth of an effective, common political system. In spite of having as closely related a culture as there is ever likely to be, Sweden and Norway decided in 1905 to abandon their common political system. For hundreds of years China was culturally a unit but lacked an adequate political system. Within states, those attempting to integrate the people into a single, unified polity make cultural diversity a matter of merit and pride. Cultural pluralism is praised — if only, perhaps, to make a virtue of necessity, but demonstrating that it can be done! Those belonging to an irredenta will do the opposite, of course, thereby justifying their wish to separate from the state.

This historical experience indicates that cultural differences need not interfere with political cooperation or sentiments of solidarity. It also indicates the reverse. Either alternative has been successful at times. In the first alternative the appeal is to tolerance, fascination with different ways of life, and similar favorable predispositions. In the second alternative the appeal is to the inclination of considering one's own culture superior, to fears of a threat from foreign cultures, and to similar negative predispositions. There appears to be no inevitability in the quality of the cultural factor determining what its effect upon a polity and politics will be. Instead, the psychological effect of cultural differences appears to depend upon the context in which they exist and above all upon the deliberate manipulation of the effect.

A similar conclusion must be reached from the evidence supplied by international relations. The historical record is clear that cultural differences have been used mainly to create antipathies in support of hostile policies or to strengthen the internal cohesion of a state against outsiders. When political cooperation and peaceful relations between some states were considered essential (e.g., during the lifetime of an alliance), the practice has usually been to suppress references to differences and to emphasize the "likeness" and cultural similarities of their peoples.[12] A striking example of this practice was provided in the United States during World War II. In order to arouse sympathetic feelings for the allied Soviet Union and Australia, pictures of overflowing churches in the Soviet Union or of diesel engines pulling trains in Australia were shown — implying how similar both countries were to the United States. The opposite was done in the case of Japan — until it was discovered that some of the differences making the Japanese so "unlike" the Americans (and therefore presumably inferior) were shared by the ally

China! A similar example, in a minor key, could be found in the United States again when it was discovered that one could play table tennis with the Chinese Communists, which really made them quite human . . .

By now the use of culture and cultural differences between states has become a fine art to create either sympathy or antipathy, depending upon the needs of a given foreign policy. States have developed many fine gradations in their sponsorship or condemnation of cultural relations, ranging from permitting private organizations to establish them via the signing of cultural treaties to the complete prohibition of any contacts. Such practices show fairly conclusively that it is not so much the similarities and dissimilarities of cultures but the use that is made of them which is important.

They can be used to assist in making international politics orderly and peaceful or disorderly and violent. Those who argue for a world culture (whose character remains rather obscure) — if by this is meant the elimination of great differences — have the one point that it would eliminate the possibility of using cultural differences for hostile purposes. But the practicability of creating such a world culture is so questionable and the time needed to create it in any case so long, that in the meantime cultural homogeneity and heterogeneity will remain a useful tool in the workshop of politics. This usefulness is, however, diminishing because there are increasing limits upon the possibilities of manipulating the social psyche with the help of the culture factor.

One set of limits on manipulation is given by the size of cultural differences and the intensity of the interests in whose service the manipulation is undertaken. The cases of European union and of American participation in international organizations illustrate this situation. The peoples of Western Europe have many cultural similarities, yet remain culturally distinct. But this distinction, not extreme in any case, could easily be underemphasized in favor of a strong interest in creating common European institutions. The Coal and Steel Community achieved supranational features; its Court of Justice is directly accessible to private individuals; weighted voting is the accepted practice in its organs; and every opinion poll shows great sympathy for more integration and unification. While the extremists may be impatient with the slow growth of European union, in view of Europe's nationalist history the steps already taken are considerable. They demonstrate that cultural heterogeneity need not be a serious barrier to effective international arrangements for an orderly and peaceful society. Characteristically enough, Europeans showed themselves much more hesitant about extending their common institutions to a far wider range of peoples. During the discussions dealing with the association of African states with the Common Market, it became evident, unofficially, that the wide cultural differences and relatively low interest in having the Associated States as members had something to do with keeping them at arm's length.

The case of the United States concerned the creation of an international organization after World War II. "Peace planning" had become a fad. Many "internationalist" groups asked for the "surrender of sovereignty" to Western-dominated organizations or an Atlantic community. Their enthusiasm dropped precipitously in regard to similar organizations with Pacific and Asian peoples or any global organization in which Western peoples might be outvoted by non-Western peoples. In most instances the refusal to share sovereignty with Asians was rationalized in complicated voting formulas, based on educational level, participation in world trade, volume of international mail, or some such criterion, which always resulted in giving Western states an overwhelming vote in any potential organization, but some people frankly admitted that they did not want to be outvoted by people of such different cultures. In this case an attempt was made to establish a neat balance between the interest in having an international organization and the reluctance to accept the "teeming masses" of Asia as equals.

A second set of limits upon manipulating cultural factors for political purposes, or perhaps more correctly a growing difficulty of manipulation, lies in the vanishing substance of cultural differences or at least for the most part of those which are objectively fairly insignificant but which nevertheless many people seem to consider most relevant to making people "different." The "Coca-colonization" of the world and "supermarkets from Afghanistan to Zanzibar" may make the world a duller place to live in, but both developments are symbols of growing cultural uniformities. So is the fact, reported by UNESCO, that lately about forty thousand books are annually translated from their original into other languages, and of these about half are in literature, often a culture-bound subject. To the extent that modern technology is introduced into developing countries, the culture inevitably accompanying technology will also be introduced. The mass man of industrialized society will become the archetype of man everywhere. Increasing communication will make every man aware of the relativity of his own culture and thereby reduce the significance he tends to ascribe to differences. At every stage in the widening of his horizon — an increase in his contacts, a greater familiarity with other cultures — the validity of his own way of life and social standards become to him less and less absolute. This change he must admit, even if he refuses to adjust his norms. The point can be reached when his own culture breaks down altogether. The "search for identity" among the youths of so many countries demonstrates this process. This increasing homogeneity in the more superficial but most public aspects of culture diminishes the usefulness of the cultural factor as a political tool; at the least it can no longer easily be used to mobilize hatreds on the grounds that another people is "different."

Related to this decreasing importance of culture as an issue of concern to the functioning of the political system and international politics, is the rapid growth of an international political culture in which virtually all states share. In actuality, when states meet politically, the way of life of their respective citizens is usually at least once removed from affecting the subject matter that brought these states together. The bulk of international politics and the corresponding behavior are between states, abstracted collectivities, whose behavior already reflects a synthesized or homogenized version of the behavior of many of every state's citizens, their interests, and their cultural peculiarities. To express this point in more general terms: when states meet, they do so on such a relatively high level of abstraction, as compared to individuals meeting as representatives of different cultures, that contrasts of culture have become greatly softened. There is no more need for a world government to postulate a total world culture than, say, for an effective German government to have all Germans drink beer or eat potatoes. The deculturization of a state's international behavior is further enhanced by the uniformizing effect of the international political system: states adhere to the style, manner, and methods by now customary in the system to a very large extent. It is brought to an apex by the universal adoption of nationalism which gives uniformity not merely to the form but also to the substance of international politics, which is to say that as soon as a people becomes nationalist its interests, demands, and actions as far as the international society is concerned become potentially very much alike regardless of the character of its culture.

The existence of an international political culture is evident in several aspects of international politics. The similarity in the behavior of officials representing their states on the international scene, in the demands they present, in the solutions they suggest, is astonishing. They appear to have lost most of their "national character." Their citizens' way of life at home has very limited influence upon the stance of the delegates in international political affairs. The goals which states pursue and the means they use are very similar across the globe. They are little affected by the cultural differences otherwise separating Dutchmen from Japanese or Bavarian peasants from Hamburg exporters. There is an extensive uniformity among the elites who in international affairs more than in other affairs speak and act for their state. It is reminiscent of the "international culture" shared in earlier times by the aristocracy and the clergy. By any criterion of "national culture" speeches in international agencies are virtually indistinguishable in form, type of argument, and very often substance. This may not be too surprising in the case of the older states which, in their innumerable encounters, have by now adjusted to each other and created their own language. The behavior of their delegates has become so stereotyped that remains of "national character" (such as British "pragmatism," French "legalism," American "moralism," Chinese "inscrutability") are difficult to discover. The traces that can be found are mostly in rhetoric, rarely in substance.[13] But even the delegates of the youngest states have quickly fallen into the common patter and pattern. Their peoples at home would hardly comprehend, were they interested in doing so, the language or positions of their spokesmen. Some of them (for example, Nehru) can most effectively act as transmission belts between their national and the international culture.

Quite evidently there is growing an international style in an international culture. Governments use the general and cosmopolitan tried-and-established methods which over the years have proved successful in the prevailing international system in securing maximum benefits for at least some states. The changes occurring in international practices, politics, and the political system are hardly due to the impact of any particular national culture. On the contrary, they are mostly due to the impact of technological developments upon nationalist behavior which all states have chosen as their own. As far as the international scene is concerned, they further de-individualize national cultures which had already lost much of their individualism as a result of univeral nationalism. They are forcing the goals, means, and methods of states into a common mold, producing an international political culture to which particular national cultures are becoming increasingly irrelevant.

The large body of commonly accepted international law and its constant use in international debates is formal evidence of agreement on much social behavior whether the law is used as a norm, a means of communication, or, as Communist states claim, a political tool. The point is that its meaning is understood internationally. Similar agreement exists on formal means and methods of international intercourse and on the less formal rules of the international political practice. The initial revolt of many new states against the "Western"-influenced rules of politics has given way to their acceptance by virtually all states, with only some modest demands for changes in special situations remaining. The system has proved quite compatible with a great variety of national cultures — an indication that these cultures do not seem to be too relevant for the international goals states pursue or the methods they use. The international society has been able to socialize its members with remarkable rapidity and ease at least sufficiently to make communication possible in such matters as the formulation of demands, diplomatic practices, and even political tactics. The now-existing international political culture is shared by all states and produces conformable behavior. This conformity is of greater importance for the international political system than the question of whether it exists because of compatible national cultures (like those of the Western states) or in spite of incompatible cultures (like those of many Asian and African states). The existence is the important thing, because, first, it facilitates maintenance of social order. Second, it will gradually infiltrate into national cultures and codetermine assumptions underlying the behavior of all states on the international scene. Clashes of behavior may thereby be avoided which would otherwise result from a negative use of cultural differences.

Even the interactions of private individuals are affected by this political culture cutting across frontiers, in their roles both as private individuals and as nationals. In their private roles, as journalists, teachers, tourists, or merchants, they may form a cosmopolitan section of mankind with their counterparts abroad. Private organizations may be multinational. The interests they share may be devoid of national characteristics, or these internationalized interests may be translated by these individuals into the terms of their own culture. Insofar as this situation prevails, the roles these individuals play may assist in diminishing national cultural differences. They may be instrumental in slowly creating an acculturated international culture. But if they do all these things, they do so in an insignificant degree relative to the bulk of international relations and contacts. They may, at best, affect the climate in which these relations take place and their importance should not be exaggerated. They cannot escape the politicized nature of the international society.

The other role they play, the role as nationals, forces them into a behavior pattern supportive of their own states' behaviors. This role too has its effect upon the international culture, and it is a much more powerful effect. Citizens are everywhere very much alike as nationals of their country, identifying their interests not only with their private personal needs but also with the overpowering "national interests" of their countries. They remain subject to the political supervision of their state. The American government had no compunction in cutting down the Fulbright program to serve political needs, nor did the Soviet government hesitate to cancel a tour of the Bolshoi Ballet to express dislike of American policy in Western Asia. How far a merchant can pursue his international interests is very much subject to political control. That the meetings of citizens from different countries and the interlinking of their interests may reduce the possibility of exploiting cultural differences is hardly deniable. But their roles as private individuals are severely restrained by their roles as nationals. When the two are in conflict, there is no question as to which dominates.

There is another facet of international politics which makes the culture factor of secondary importance. There are few if any international political decisions involving the entire culture of a people. Indeed, never the entire culture of a state but only some, relatively few, of its features are really relevant to the international society. Where the entire culture may seem to be relevant, for instance, in how a people perceives a situation confronting it or how it may in general respond to a crisis, the culture becomes at most a factor in the environment of international politics with which politics has to reckon but about which it cannot do anything. In this sense, in other words, the culture is again irrelevant. The political system needs to be concerned mainly with that part of any national culture having to do with the maintenance of international social order or decisions on social policies. Only a part of every state's behavior is usually involved, with vast spheres of a people's existence of no relevance. Neither the social way of life of the public nor the private ways of the individual are of much importance to world politics — except mainly as objects of psychological warfare! Moreover, many different forms of behavior in pursuit of agreed goals are acceptable to the political system. Its main minimal condition is that the state's behavior must not cause social disorder. This leaves considerable leeway for the behavioral expression of different cultures. The situation is similar to the relation between states and the central government in a federal system where the states are granted or retain rights because their subject matter is of no particular concern to the center in fulfillment of its responsibilities for social order in the whole nation.

The range of behavior relevant to the political system will to a large

54

extent depend upon its jurisdiction, varying from a minimum if it has night-watchman functions to a maximum if it has social welfare functions. But the relevance of behavior to the political system does not at all mean that the behavior to be enforced must be conformable. It must merely not be disorderly, and that leaves a wide berth for the exercise of cultural diversity without endangering the efficiency of the political system. In the international society the situation is particularly favorable in this respect, because the larger the size of a society the relatively narrower need be the range of coordinated behavior.

The conclusion emerging from these considerations on the role of cultural factors in international politics is not very definite — or rather it is definite that culture can definitely play varied, contradictory roles because they are manipulable. Cultural homogeneity is likely not to present barriers to international orderly and peaceful cooperation and may even create favorable predispositions for it. Cultural differences can probably be exploited with fair ease to create antipathy between peoples. But since it would be impossible to find two cultures in which there are not some features which are alike and others which are unlike (on a high or low enough level of abstraction) manipulators can always find some cultural features to mobilize sympathy or antipathy depending upon their political needs. There is no inherent quality in cultural factors making them necessarily favorable or unfavorable to international politics.[14] They are extremely malleable, psychological factors. Positive or negative reactions to them are most likely learned, hence manipulable, reactions. Altogether, modern developments in communications especially make cultural factors increasingly irrelevant in any case. Growing similarities in ways of life across the globe make appeals to "differences" ever more difficult. Even in the absence of similarities growing awareness of the relativity of cultures and their values makes appeals to differences increasingly ineffective.[15] Moreover, all these effects are related to the general public which most rarely initiates foreign policies anyway and plays mainly the role, like the cultural factor itself, of a tool rather than a master of the foreign policy maker. International politics takes place mostly between states, that is to say, actively between spokesmen for their states who have already created an international political culture to which the various national cultures are, to be sure, an environmental factor, but not directly related.

In addition to the psychological effect conditioning sentiments and attitudes toward culturally different groups, cultural differences might also very concretely produce conflicts of interest. Every culture has a hierarchy of interests. A high interest in one state may be a low interest in another. Where international agreement is needed for their satisfaction, conflict situations may easily arise. While it is true that conflict may lead to social disorder, this is a potential, not a necessity. Conflict, as has been pointed out previously, is an integral part of every society. The solution of the problem is not elimination of conflict but the institutionalization of its peaceful settlement. The international society is weak on this count and the elimination of this weakness, not creating one global culture, is the only possible approach. After all, even within one, culturally homogeneous state, conflicts of interest abound, the more so the more developed and complex the national society is. They do not lead to continuous social disorder because the society has created institutions for their peaceful settlement. Moreover, it is highly questionable whether in most cases the interests over which states come into conflict are due to cultural differences. More likely states pursue like interests competing for scarce resources to satisfy them. The main point is that even when conflicts of interest may have their roots in cultural differences, their disturbing effect upon the social order need not be related to these differences, and the institutions for their peaceful settlement are not necessarily dependent upon cultural homogeneity (as will be shown later).[16]

The Role of Norms in the International Society

The absence of common moral norms also has often been blamed for the inadequacy of the international political system. One assumption has been that common norms, by virtue of their being common to mankind, would foster a community from which arbitrary violence would disappear. Common norms, like anything else people have in common, would be a contributing factor to creating a community characterized (by definition) by relatively peaceful cooperative behavior (provided, of course, that the norms call for such behavior). Such norms already exist. They are embedded in the preambles of many international organization charters and underlie many generally recognized principles of international law. They have contributed little to the creation of a peaceful community. The reason for their failure will be seen when a second assumption is examined.

This assumption is that moral norms determine public behavior. If the norms forebade the arbitrary use of violence, for instance, they could prevent the deterioration of conflicts into wars. Goals and interests incompatible with these norms would be adandoned. Orderly behavior would result.

56

The Nature of the International Society

Even a casual look at the history of international relations would show the limited effectiveness of moral norms. This may be due to the possibility that so far norms have not been held in common by states, or that the norms they shared allowed each state to act purely in its own selfish interest (in the manner of Stephen Decatur's "my country, right or wrong"). There would be no problem in such cases. Such divisive rules, making a virtue of chaos, would explain the inadequacy of the political system instead of contributing to the opposite. The problem is that nowadays all governments publicly assert their adherence to basic moral norms no different from those applying to all behavior, adding that the substance of these norms, as they apply to social order, is the same across the globe. If these allegations are accepted at face value, the precarious order of the international society raises the questions of how effective moral norms are in directing international behavior and, specifically, of why international behavior is so often inconsistent with recognized moral norms. The fundamental answer is, first, that many interests which states seek to fulfill in the international society are considered so compelling that the application of moral values becomes a secondary concern in international politics; and second, that politicization extends to morality: moral values are degraded into rationalizations or justifications of actions undertaken on amoral grounds. Moral values may therefore prevail when they are not in conflict with national interests or when these interests are judged insignificant enough to allow moral values to predominate. A government may occasionally also have a missionary or knight-errant complex which leads to the subordination of interests to moral values. In the normal course of events, moral values are weak guides to international behavior. This weakness of morality results from the nature of moral norms themselves as well as their relationship to national interests.

When statesmen are confronted by a situation demanding a decision, they understandably ask what needs to be done to preserve the state's interest. Only thereafter, if ever, do they ask what might be the moral thing to do. Decision-makers are not necessarily amoral or immoral. Like all men, they are subject to some general influence of moral values as part of their broader environmental influence. But this influence is very minor indeed compared to the influence exerted by the dictate of preserving the sovereign equality of their state as the highest social interest. All the available evidence indicates the ascendancy of national interests over morality in the actions of governments. One reason is the chronological advantage the interest has over the application of moral norms. The interest arises first. It is acute in the face

57

of some challenge and triggers the start of the whole decision-making machinery. Moral norms are there, always available, but become active only when behavior stimulated first by interests needs justification. When the interest is as powerful as the national interest, moral values can rarely do more than affect in some minor way the form in which the interest will be expressed and pursued. A statesman who would sacrifice what is defined as the national interest to moral values exposes himself to the accusation of treason. The second advantage of interests over moral values is that norms are qualifiers, not initiators or ends, of behavior (another reason for making the chronology invariable). A treaty is never signed to prove trustworthiness, nor a transaction undertaken to demonstrate honesty. This relationship between interests and moral values makes morality subservient to interest.

The nature of moral norms also puts them at a disadvantage in comparison with interests. Norms are necessarily stated in broad, general, universally valid terms because they have to cover a multitude of unforeseeable situations. Interests needing action tend to be specific. Norms must be interpreted to fit the given situation. They are, in other words, extremely flexible. Everyone is against sin, but not everyone agrees with everyone else on what sin is when it occurs. Governments almost inevitably interpret moral norms to serve the pursuit of national interests. Thus while norms may be held worldwide, their interpretation to fit national interests makes their universality in the abstract fairly irrelevant. The flexibility of moral systems (and therewith different meaning to different people) is further increased by the possibility of inconsistency between individual norms in application. For instance, being one's brother's keeper may not always be compatible morally with economic competition. A statesman wanting to justify a policy decision can thus find norms supporting one or the other of mutually exclusive behaviors. His choice of norms to justify what he wants to do is further broadened by the differing intensities with which moral norms are held. Some can be suppressed or circumvented more easily than others.

The great flexibility in the choice and application of moral norms compared with the strength, the relative inflexibility, and the specificity of national interests, gives interests a decisive advantage over moral norms. Norms, far from being determinants of international action, are more often its servants. The national interests decide which norms will be applied and how they will be applied. Moral values held in common by states have therefore no great consequence for the international society. They are overpowered by national interests and cannot guarantee common, cooperative behavior.

Common interests are more likely to do that. Instead of postulating common values for the improvement of international behavior, the emphasis should be on a community of interests. The values already accepted by most states in their abstract form will then be interpreted and applied alike by all those states sharing common interests. Moral norms may then perform their socially beneficial function — inasmuch as they may do so at all — for the international society and its political system. Until then they too can be used as tools by the policy maker, mostly to serve the propaganda in support of his policies.[17] Having been so used throughout most of history, they have helped citizens to trust in the superiority of their state.

The Weakness of the International Society

When the major features of the international society are examined for their impact upon the international political system, it will be found that they either aggravate the task of the system or are immaterial to it. In any case, they rarely facilitate the system's task. The uneven relationships between states, the tenuous bonds tying some together, and the occasional virtual absence of any meaningful relationship make the need for a capable and comprehensive political system unconvincing. States are willing to take the risks of an inadequate system rather than abandon their intense desire to maintain sovereign independence, however illusory in fact that may be. Repeated worldwide violent conflicts and the ever-present chance of an escalation of local into global wars notwithstanding, states continue to nourish the hope that they can excise themselves from the network of international relations and create their "areas of peace," isolate themselves, or contain others. The ranking system, based upon the great inequalities among states, contributes a major share to a sense of insecurity in the world society and thereby adds to the burden of the political system in keeping it in order. Dissatisfaction with the allotted rank leads to unilateral attempts by a state to improve it, and the subjectivity of ranking encourages unpredictable actions, frustrating the very purpose of the political system. The effects of cultural heterogeneity are manipulable so that, if handled properly, they could be helpful to the political system. Unfortunately, most of the time in history these differences have been manipulated to the detriment of the international society's welfare. There might have been some hope in the rise of an international culture which would have obviated the use of cultural differences for detrimental purposes. But the substance of the existing interna-

59

tional culture, such as international goals pursued by states, methods of communication, means used to fulfill interests or settle conflicts, while largely
alike among states is not in common! Their effect is mostly divisive, often
negating the basic task of the political system. One only has to consider
such items as the preservation of national sovereignty, subversion and penetration, or the use of violence to solve disputes to realize that international
agreement upon their legality or at least on their like practice by all states
leads to a defeat rather than a support of the political system's major tasks.
Similarly, agreement upon abstractly formulated moral norms is useless for
the purposes of the political system when their nature allows them, in practice, to be made subservient to the clashing national interests of states.

Any one of these features of the international society can be exploited
to weaken the international society in favor of national societies. They can
be found in many national societies too. But not only does the international
society possess them all so that in their combined effect they can exert a
most detrimental influence upon the political system, but compensating features, such as psychological support of the society and loyalty toward it
or dense functional interdependence, as can be found in national societies,
are at best only in their beginnings. Understandably, each state is attempting
to protect itself from the consequences, thereby contributing to a worsening
of the situation, of course. There is a premium upon the selfish pursuit
of national interests by any possible means. Arbitrary, extreme, and socially
dangerous behavior, exactly the behavior the political system is intended
to keep under control, becomes the characteristic and, under the circumstances, almost necessary international behavior. A vicious circle is initiated
making changes most difficult. A weak society prevents the formation of
an adequate political system which could keep the weakness from ruining
the society. Yet the lack of an adequate political system obliges states to
rely upon their own resources for self-preservation, thus perpetuating the
weakness of the international society.

The Lag in Political Organization

The international society leads a precarious existence. The threat of disorder,
even destruction, is ever present. The social nexus between the members
of the society — whether considered as states or as individuals — is still
weak. The functions tying mankind together are not as varied as they are
in the more developed national societies and their volume is frequently

thinner. There is moreover a hierarchy of values prevailing which places the national interest (however interpreted) ahead of most of these functions. States are willing to forgo these functions, breaking the social nexus they represent, for the more valued sake of individual national identity. Self-isolation or the containment of other states illustrates this willingness. The usefulness of these functional relationships in sustaining an international society is further affected by the politicization of that society. As a result, primarily nonpolitical functions (economic, religious, cultural) producing a pluralism in integrated national societies and fostering interdependence and solidarity, can do so only with difficulty at best in the international society. At worst they assume a political character and are made to serve the single dominant political purposes. Thus the members of the international society become divided and aligned according to only the one overpowering political interest. The order and peace-preserving consequences of pluralistic membership in a variety of subsystems other than the political, in which the members may cooperate and find common interests, are greatly weakened. Needless to emphasize, the absence of any common commitment to the overarching interest of the international society as a whole (to a common weal, in other words) makes the divisive hegemony of individual national interests complete. Force tends to become not the *ultima* but the *prima ratio*. It tends to become the single, major tool of power and, considering its poor management in the international society, threatens the very fabric of that society.

In searching for reasons which could explain the discrepancy between the growing network of international relations needing ordering and the inadequate nature of the international political system trying to supply this service, chronology emerges prominently. As new needs arise, men act to satisfy them. If the needs are of a kind — and modern needs usually are — requiring social action for their satisfaction, men will act accordingly. They will eventually institutionalize these actions. But the political organization needed to keep these actions orderly and to integrate them into the existing social system follows rather than anticipates their appearance. There is a second reason why the rise of political institutions tends to be delayed. Men are more certain and more agreed regarding their needs and the wish to satisfy them. They are much less agreed about how to regulate these needs and the actions to satisfy them! Much social disorder arises from a lag between the growth of social needs and the rise of new social groups, and the growth of political systems to order them. The very slow development of international organization, international law, organized diplomacy, systematic methods for the settlement of international disputes, routinized ways for international contacts, as well as the very costly trial-and-error manner in which all these things evolve, is evidence that the international society is no exception to the general experience most modern societies have had as they grew into adulthood. In brief, the international political system has not kept pace with the volume and types of international relations needing political ordering.

Fundamentally, the difficulty which created the gap between the advanced social relationships and the delayed political system ordering them continues to affect attempts at closing the gap in the future: people are accustomed to their existing social unit. Their willingness to adjust to new ways of behaving is limited. When the unit is the state, their commitment to it is not merely a matter of habit but of emotional attachment, deliberately fostered and manipulated. Since the modern state was born several hundred years ago, most social sentiments and a very large part of every individual's social being are based on it. The citizen's socialization process is related to his national society. The individual's direct or indirect involvement in international matters is of relatively recent date. Few people are aware of it. If they are, the involvement is evaluated from the standpoint of the national citizen. His historic and personal social experience turns around his state as the center. His perspective on social matters is conditioned by his state.[18] Where this is not yet the case, as in many new states of Asia and Africa, the leaders are desperately trying to create just that situation for their citizens. As the largest, most adequately organized social units in modern times, national societies have a powerful attraction. Where they exist, governments and their peoples are determined to maintain them. Where they do not, governments and elites are determined to form them. The pressure for change, i.e., for adequate political systems beyond national systems, must be very high indeed before it can occur. The prevailing international political system with all its shortcomings indicates that this pressure has nowhere been strong enough yet. Whatever progress has been made, for instance in Western Europe, has not yet led to a political organization transcending national orientations.

A weighty factor keeping national societies alive by supporting the material and psychic satisfactions of citizens, but also by providing a foundation for their social habits, is the territorial basis of states. Nomadic or clan states and states in non-European areas were based not on territory but on persons. In the West territory has become so important that it is an integral part of the definition of society and state. By now the idea has been universally accepted and prevails everywhere. Its powerful influence is demonstrated by the fact that nation builders are not satisfied until they have a territory they can call their own (e.g., the Czechs before 1918, the Zionists); and similarly that governments of new states, carved out of colonial empires, are willing to condemn all the results of imperialism but are unwilling to abandon an inch of the territory that imperialists incorporated into what later became the new states (e.g., most states of Asia and Africa).

The principle recommends itself, apparently, for a number of reasons. Territory is among the more visible elements of a national society, giving it greater reality and concrete continuity. It separates the society neatly and clearly from other societies, facilitating its identification and the citizen's identification with it. As "fatherland" or "homeland" it evokes the warmth and coziness of family experience. It may even vicariously satisfy pride of possession. These are appeals to the citizen's psyche which his membership in an expanded society covering the globe could not provide. Material, economic requirements can also be well satisfied by a territorially based society. Indeed, expanding economic needs led to the initial merger of smaller (feudal) societies and then to their maintenance and hardening. These needs were served very adequately for a long time. The bulk of the citizen's relationships was located within the national territory. His material needs were taken care of within national borders. When these became too narrow, the initial adjustment was not to expand or abandon them, but rather to supplement national territory by the conquest of colonies, thus keeping the territorial state idea intact. The end of the colonial era and the widening of needs far beyond national borders has still not put an end to the principle of the territorial state. In many states, especially the underdeveloped ones, needs are minimal; in others, such as the United States or the USSR, internal resources remain adequate to an extent sufficient to permit continuance of the territorial principle; or else the limitations imposed by territory can be overcome by trade, capital movements, foreign investment, and other means. The incentives to abandon the territorial principle for material, economic reasons are not strong enough to overcome the inertia of existing social systems, an inertia greatly fortified by the psychological satisfactions citizens obtain from membership in their state.

A most important practical consequence of the continuing territorially based state, and the mentality on which it rests and which in turn it reinforces, is that publics and governments everywhere act on the international scene or react to international events in the traditional manner. They behave most parochially, and the political system reflects this national outlook. A dramatic illustration is the failure of states to settle their major conflicts by any means other than confrontation. No matter how ''internationalist''-minded groups may claim to be (say the Second International or the Soviets and the Chinese Communists), when international danger threatens their internationalism evaporates. They take refuge in their own state. They have nowhere seriously suggested merging two hostile states in the hope of converting conflicting interests into common ones. Notwithstanding official and unofficial references to international interdependence, there is no readiness to draw the consequences fully, for instance by implementing prevailing de facto relationships with adequate organization and regulation. On the contrary, every effort is made to express in international organizations their subordination to the individual interests of their members. The paradox is that the very creation of these organizations is evidence of obvious needs, but that their creators lack the courage of their convictions. They fail to endow them with the capability of being politically effective. With some minor and exotic exceptions, international organizations have been granted authority only to deliberate and recommend, making them inadequate to fulfill even their limited purposes.[19]

Changes in the International Society

The very existence of international organizations, with all their inadequacies, is symbolic nevertheless of the changing nature of the international society. But the available evidence is that these changes will be gradual and reluctant rather than radical and enthusiastic.[20] These organizations, like most of the purposes of international politics, were not aiming at the common welfare of the international society. Instead, they were undertaken for the sake of saving or strengthening a state and its interests. This is true even if out of collective efforts there emerges some truly international by-product, such as a regional organization, a collective security system, or an international public union. All these arrangements amount to tinkering with the basic system without altering its fundamental features. Even if some states have integrated themselves into a new, larger political unit, they have merely succeeded in transferring the weakness of the international society to a different level, namely from the level of one state vis-à-vis another state to that of a new collectivity vis-à-vis another state or another collectivity. This may be progress, but it is not a metamorphosis. It is hardly even an improved international society. No fundamental change can take place until states cease to insist upon their identity and act accordingly, which is really to say until peoples change their dominant prevailing attitudes toward states and the international society. The progress can be found in the fact that though manifestly all these arrangements are made by states to strengthen their individual, sovereign existence, latently and paradoxically they may erode the very foundation on which this existence is constructed. For, generally speaking, when no state can survive as an entity without the contributions of another (be it as an ally, the lessor of a base, the supplier of a strategic material, or whatever) the substance of sovereign independence becomes very thin and the form alone is not likely to survive for very long.

The irresistible force behind the change, evidenced by the institutions and activities of a political system, is the fact that mankind has developed into a society. There was indeed a time when mankind had, sociologically speaking, the characteristic of a crowd, making it unsuitable for a political system. States or some of their citizens related intermittently or haphazardly. Conflicts or friendships were ad hoc situations, and often almost personal. Interactions almost never turned into interrelations. Under contemporary conditions, states are no longer terminal, separate, and independent social systems. Uncounted linkages exist between national and the international societies. A strict separation between the internal and external affairs of a state is impossible. Interactions between states are enduring, relationships are patterned, contacts are voluminous. Out of lasting mutualities between states and their regular and conventional contacts, an abundance of relationships arose and social issues developed requiring mechanisms for handling, regulating, and deciding them. The system of international relations by now supplies a solid base and creates a solid need for a political system, whether this system represents, technically, a society or not. Mankind has moved a long way from being a global conglomerate of human beings or human groups.

The youth of mankind as a society may be held responsible, however, for the lack of psychological support on the part of its members. Their sentimental investment and their loyalties remain totally absorbed by national societies. This weakens the cohesion of the international society. Functional interrelations are the main bonds tying the members together. It gives the international society its particular character and can explain many of its inadequacies. But the absence of psychological support in the presence of the objective prerequisites does not make mankind any less a society. Like all societies, the international has its political system. But it is a system that, in its inadequacies, reflects the lack of psychological backing and its subordination under national political systems. Symbolic of the second-class nature of the international political system is the absence of a central world government. The peoples of the world are unwilling to be dominated by or bring sacrifices to a society to which they are not loyal and to which they are not sentimentally attached. The primacy of "national interests," however meaningless the concept may be in concrete terms, indicates the hierarchy of their values and the desired supremacy of the national over the international society.

The political system shares the paradox of the international society, naturally. It is intended to function so that one state is prevented from destroying the identity of any other state. Yet it is also intended itself to guarantee the full sovereignty of every state. There is no contradiction in the abstract here, any more than there appears to be in the international society whose existence is supposedly guaranteed by the guaranteed survival of its individual members. The trouble is that concretely the safeguarding of one state's sovereignty may require curtailing the sovereignty of another (e.g., an aggressive) state, and therefore quite frequently leads to attempts by every state at least prophylactically to curtail the sovereignty of another state. A closer examination of the international political system — against the background of the international society in which it functions — will clarify this paradox and uncover some reasons for the system's inadequacy.

3 The Objective Nature of the International Political System

IN THE VALUE hierarchy of states the international society is subordinated to national societies. The structure of the international society and the manner of its processes are shaped accordingly. By making the national social order their highest value, most nationals everywhere imply a willingness to sacrifice the international order to the demands of the national social order. Of necessity the international political system is subordinated to national political systems. A collective government for the international society was thus out of the question a priori. It could not have any place in a society whose members retain the right to reject that society if the interests of their own national society are believed to require this action. The international political system must perfom in a society whose members integrate their behaviors toward maintenance of that society only for the higher purpose of maintaining their own, well-integrated national societies. The system exists to maintain the member states and not the international society itself. This assignment imposes a severe limitation upon the system's task of creating and maintaining social order. It is designed to function and perform only until a state decides that its own maintenance justifies the creation of international social disorder. This is in stark contrast to national political systems, whose design is always planned for enabling them to maintain the national society as an absolute priority.

This limitation upon the international political system is not mere theory; or perhaps better, it is not in the theory at all but rather in the practice. States frequently create disorder in the belief that their national interests require it. They use force arbitrarily. They break treaties. They interfere in each other's internal affairs. They act abnormally and unpredictably. But they do not as a rule plead guilty to such acts. The laws they subscribe to do not condone them. But the political system as at present established makes these acts possible in fact. By allowing themselves to create social disorder in the name of national interests and build the appropriate enabling system, states may violate international laws. But by doing so — and this is most important — they do not necessarily violate the ultimate end. Social order can be maintained only because and as long as national interests coincide in wanting it — not because there is a common weal by which the political system orients itself.

A social order which in pursuit of its own ends can be disturbed at any moment by the arbitrary decision of one of its beneficiaries will prevail in the international society as long as states insist upon deciding what action the maintenance of their own identity requires. A formal, common organ (a government) empowered to make authoritative decisions for all states for the overall social order cannot exist. The creation of such an organ has been foreclosed by the firm establishment of the principle of sovereignty. According to general and unexceptional agreement this principle dominates the relations between states. All international transactions — representing the substance and reality of the whole international system — are based upon the overriding principle of sovereignty.

Sovereignty: The Base of the International Political System

The concept of sovereignty is out of fashion with academicians. There are a number of reasons for this. With the breakdown of the relative inviolability of states due to modern technology, sovereignty has become meaningless, so the argument runs. Related to this is another argument. States are no longer self-contained as functioning political units. The sources of politics even within states are now largely located outside states, just as internal politics greatly affect international politics. The mutual penetration of states or their integration are no longer merely foreign policy devices — bad or good — but almost inevitable consequences of advanced technology. The linkages between the internal and external politics of states are such that the division aimed at by the principle of sovereignty becomes virtually impossible. There is, therefore, considerable cogency to the argument that sovereignty as a working concept does not reflect reality and would, if used, falsify the analysis of international politics. Yet another argument has been that the meaning of sovereignty is very vague as well as complex and that it contains so many logical and practical inconsistencies that it lacks utility as an analytical tool. But, as usual, statesmen don't listen to academicians. They stubbornly stick to the concept of sovereignty in their daily political activities, and so often do their peoples.[21] If any proof were needed of the concept's practical significance, it could, for instance, be found in the much quoted principle laid down in article two of the United Nations Charter that "the Organization is based on the principle of the sovereign equality of all its Members."

States continue to claim sovereignty because to them it means supreme authority over their behavior internally and externally. It means the right to refuse recognition of any authority of any kind above their own in any area of human endeavor. In setting goals and choosing means to reach them, in deciding international policy and executing it, sovereignty is held to grant each state freedom of action. No possibility of legitimate interference or restraints from without is acknowledged. Any existing limits upon these freedoms which a state admits are construed to be self-imposed limits voluntarily accepted in the exercise of sovereignty.

The absolutism of sovereignty is brought in line with reality to some minor extent through agreement upon some exceptions or inherent limitations. There is an internationally recognized assumption that certain vague principles and rules allegedly spring from the very existence of the international society binding all states. Such an assumption is not only indispensable for tempering totally arbitrary behavior by formally agreed prescription but is a logical prerequisite for the legality of sovereignty. The statute of the International Court expresses these rules as "the general principles of law recognized by civilized nations." In practice, states most often mention these restraints subjecting them to law in reference to the behavior of other states. Regarding their own behavior, they tend to emphasize those aspects of sovereignty giving them much freedom of action. However, it is a compliment to international law that these principles are referred to quite frequently by all states. Indeed, virtually all conflict situations are debated in the Security Council in terms of these principles and rules. It is also interesting that all states refer to them, regardless of ideological convictions. Disagreement exists not so much over what these principles are as over who is properly adhering to them.

The main operational consequences of sovereignty reflect well the philosophy of previous centuries that the major purpose of international principles and laws was to prevent states from impinging upon each other. The "impenetrability" of states was more a function of sovereignty than of their territorial base. Thus, no state can be bound against its will; no outside interference in a state's internal affairs is allowed; all states are equal before the law; every state is entitled to its territorial and political integrity. These norms preclude the existence of a formal, distinctly organized political system comparable to any existing within modern states. They reflect the wish of states to make their own political decisions, formulate international issues in their own light, and solve international problems by their own means. These norms would, in theory, effectively prevent one state from dictating the behavior of another. They would prevent any political system from making authoritative rules of behavior for any member of the international society. But they are also highly unrealistic in ignoring the role of power which, in fact, makes illusory much of the legal content of sovereignty. Although in the practice of international politics sovereignty is constantly being violated it has not entirely lost its political usefulness. The ideal of the state in splendid isolation, which it expresses, is by no means defunct. Many states hold to it, often in a version adapted to contemporary conditions, so that they find insistence upon sovereignty useful for this and also other reasons. But how long the idea of sovereignty may be kept operative is doubtful. Some modern developments (to be discussed later) tend to strengthen its usefulness, a larger number of others to undermine it.

The ideal of sovereignty made some sense at the time of its birth, some three hundred years ago in Europe. Sovereignty had few effects upon the citizen's welfare. Decisions by states affected mostly themselves. Protection of one state from another often served national purposes better than elaborate international arrangements, in view of limited interaction. The territorial base of the state was useful because neat boundaries coincided fairly well with the effective exercise of sovereignty and because it supplemented the separative function of sovereignty. In short, sovereignty was technically more feasible and its intent was more realizable. The state seemed to provide security and welfare and was worth maintaining.

Less favorable conditions in modern times have not disabused large and small states of the belief that they can still derive advantage from sovereignty. Powerful states can exploit it, contrary to its intent, by retaining undue influence in international politics and dominance over other states. Weaker states consider it a protection of their individuality and a hindrance to big states who would identify their own with the world's interests. They fought hard to introduce it into the United Nations and they continue to cherish it. Impotent to produce changes in the system, they hope sovereignty may protect them against changes produced by others. However, pressed by political-strategic needs, weaker states have been inclined more often than powerful states to have their affairs treated internationally.[22] These expedient uses of sovereignty were quite untroubled by theoretical debates over the meaning of sovereignty. It has always been interpreted by large and small states in favor of granting states the largest possible measure of autonomy over their affairs. In contrast to other aspects of international politics which often developed by drift and haphazard, sovereignty has always been dealt with internationally with great determination and deliberation.

The great ingenuity exhibited in the elaboration of sovereignty for the protection of a state's freedom of action is matched by the disingenuity in the management of its practical consequences. States are neither truly autonomous in fact; nor do they have effective ways of settling in an orderly and peaceful fashion conflicts necessarily resulting from decisions made and enforced by sovereign states. Very likely, the failure to solve either problem is due at least in part to the impossibility of a solution. A logical inconsistency inherent in sovereignty is that a state's sovereignty ends where another's begins, robbing both of the desired autonomy. But this inconsistency or, for that matter, any disagreeable consequences or side effects of sovereignty have never been of more than secondary concern to states. Their intense desire for independence, integrity, and equality is too satisfactorily expressed in the formulation and formal application of sovereignty.

The cavalier treatment that the consequences of sovereignty have received may best be explained as a result of historical experience. For when sovereignty was born, the difficulty of achieving its promise on the one hand and on the other the need for the systematic solution of conflicts arising from the autonomous decisions of states were not as apparent as they are today. Increasing communication, mutualities, interactions, and interdependencies among states have gradually forced a reinterpretation, though not yet an abandonment of sovereignty. Loth to surrender their autonomy and individuality, states have, over a period of time, tried in a variety of ways to retain sovereignty while making it compatible with modern needs. At first some states tried to isolate themselves in order to maintain their separate identity, a hopeless enterprise in the light of the forces at play in the modernizing world. A larger number of states became imperialistic in order to control those territories on whose resources they thought they depended. They maintained their sovereignty at the expense of the sovereignty of others. But conquest has become unfashionable and been exchanged for cheaper, subtler, and more covert forms of domination. It appeared therefore, with the ending of colonialism, that sovereign statehood was on its way in rather than out, as indeed it was if the number of existing states is counted. But the content of sovereignty is not any longer what it was when the principle was first applied. There is enough left to provide some of the psychic satisfactions from national identity, but not enough to keep it from being anachronistic and inapplicable to modern conditions. By changing the content and substance of sovereignty states safeguarded its survival, without totally destroying international social order.

Social Order and Sovereignty

The compromise that had to be achieved was between the intense desire for national independence and that for social order. Modern conditions dictate that either desire can be fulfilled only at some expense of the other. The consequence is that an adequate formal political system becomes impossible because its likely prerequisite is the surrender of sovereignty altogether. What has been achieved so far is an informal political system. It is based in part upon the survival of sovereignty, and in part also upon the erosion of its substance.

From a sociological perspective, national sovereignty was the expression of an ultimate social order. It was an order not derived from a higher, more universal social order of which it might have been a subunit. Now that mankind has grown into a society there is a higher, more universal social order into which national societies could be integrated and become subunits. But there is widespread sentimental resistance to such a development. Mankind finds itself in an undecided stage in which it has created a more universal order, but in which sovereign states still represent unintegrated suborders. Notwithstanding all the difficulties this unresolved dualism creates, the retention of the principle of sovereignty has also had some beneficial results. Sovereignty can be seen as a socially organizing principle. Its survival spared the international society sudden structural upheavals. It provided some steady focus of social stability in an otherwise fast-changing complex of relationships. It forced the dynamism of international politics into established molds, limiting thereby the disintegrating effect of innovations without totally preventing adjustments. It prevented the complete disruption of a decision-making process by enabling states to remain recognized as formulators and executors of collective wills.

The erosion of the substance of sovereignty came from the pressure growing out of modern developments to make concessions to "absolute independence." It was irresistible because there was no escape from coping more constructively with the growing complexities of reconciling the consequences of sovereignty. But it has not yet been strong enough to produce a formal political system symbolized by a central government. The inextricable entanglements of modern international relations make a narrowly conceived sovereignty illusory. Virtually every state is expected by its citizenry to provide satisfactions which it cannot produce within the traditional range of its sovereignty, and that includes the preservation of its own sovereignty! A degree of cooperation and solidarity among states is required which was never envisaged by the original interpreters of sovereignty. International entanglements have created a most unfavorable climate for sovereignty in the international society. The ideal of separate states is giving way to the ideal of cooperative states — even though selfishness rather than humanism may be the major motivation for the change. This change results from rational considerations whose empirical consummation remains hampered by emotional attachment to the concept of sovereignty. Only a liberalization has taken place through a redefinition of sovereignty to make it more compatible with ongoing world politics. States remain reluctant to act out even this moderated sovereignty whose essence remains anchored in international law, the Charter of the United Nations, and the constitutions of other international organizations. Yet as a protection against the internationalization of national affairs, sovereignty is becoming increasingly less effective. Its comprehensiveness has been eroded by two different processes, one deliberate and open, the other surreptitious and tacit.

The first process is the invention of methods for states to negotiate, settle their conflicts peacefully, fight their wars humanely, discuss their problems in time before they turn into violent conflicts. These methods are binding only for states which have accepted them as such. Even then the commitment cannot be enforced. Most are nevertheless being used with the result that the content of sovereignty is somewhat eroded. The scope of subject matter that international conferences and agencies are permitted to deal with (though not in an authoritative manner) has expanded tremendously. There is virtually no topic excluded from international treatment. For instance the discussion of values of national currencies has become commonplace. In the not very distant past this topic would have been internationally tabooed under the protection of ''noninterference'' in a nation's internal affairs. The same is true of full-employment policies, health measures, educational policies, the protection of human rights, and so on. While sovereignty remains formally the foundation for all international activity, it tends to be interpreted restrictively in favor of broadening the bailiwick of international discussion. Decisions by majority vote in various organs of the United Nations and other international organizations seem to go counter to the principle of sovereignty. To be sure, these decisions cannot be more than recommendations and each state can interpret them for itself. And a state can leave the organization if it is displeased with the decisions. And, finally, any state joins an organization voluntarily to begin with. But, with few exceptions, states have not left organizations. And they have subscribed to the principle of majority rule. So, all these provisos may save the formal character of sovereignty. But its effectiveness in protecting national interests from becoming the subject of international debate and concern, or in guaranteeing states the widest freedom of action is diminishing, if not legally at least politically.

All these methods developed by states for social order are voluntary. There is no formal sanction for disobedience. Yet they contribute to order in the international society that has prevailed over long periods of time. States are obviously ready for orderly behavior and anticipate orderly behavior by their fellow states. The society is not run on the law of the jungle, nor even on what Georg Jellinek called ''anarchic law.'' States are denying the society a formal political system, but they nevertheless act in the expectation that the tasks of a political system will be fulfilled. Their expectation, though based upon the effectiveness of voluntarism, is not unjustified. It has an experiential foundation. It also has a foundation in reason. For there are good grounds why states should want to behave in an orderly fashion and should therefore willingly use these methods for orderly intercourse.

Not likely to be found among these grounds is the one that governments have internalized some moral norms so that a collective conscience produces orderly behavior. (Individual statesmen may have.) Nor is there an incentive for orderly behavior in the form of an overall, intensely desired common goal, such as induces citizens to maintain their state. Rather the grounds for orderly behavior are likely to be found in selfishness, untamed by altruism or other charitable motivations. Men have a psychological preference for order over disorder, especially when the disorder involves war. They also have a materialistic preference for cheaper order over costlier disorder, especially when order can serve national interests reasonably well. Finally, the influences of the system may produce orderly behavior while the goal to be achieved by disorderly behavior may not be worth the effort of bucking the system. Involved in nearly every incentive toward voluntary orderly behavior is a calculation of costs and benefits. Whenever a choice of actions presents itself, statesmen make that calculation. Since it involves unmeasurable variables, the subjectivity of the calculation's outcome makes the resulting behavior unpredictable. Yet under the regime of sovereignty no other alternative is possible since each state evaluates its own choices and decides upon its own behavior. Thus voluntarism may, but also may not, contribute to social order. The international political system can do no more than provide methods to make a voluntary choice in favor of order most attractive.

The second, more pragmatic way in which sovereignty is being undermined has to do with the realities of state inequalities. States may have no choice of action at all. They may have to act under compulsion by other states. Or at best they may merely have a choice among reactions to the action of another state, with little or no opportunity for initiatives of their own. For such states the substance of sovereignty may be very thin indeed. Yet this is the situation which has led to the growth of the informal political system side by side with the more formal political arrangements. It has little to do with sovereignty and dominates rather than serves the formal system. More than that, there are outright incompatibilities between the officially accepted principles of the formal political system and the practices of the informal system. This informality makes recognition of the actually functioning political system difficult. It must be discovered by deduction from the political phenomena in the international society and the attitudes of peoples toward their state and the international society. What then emerges is that, to be sure, individual states alone or in groups make political decisions for the international society, as sovereignty prescribes. But they do not make these decisions only for themselves, they make them for other states as well — and that is not envisaged by the principle of sovereignty. The political decisions in a given case at a given moment are made by those states whose power enables them to make the decisions binding upon the international society. These states, thanks to their power, become the ultimate authority, which is the essence of sovereignty. A premium is placed upon the highest possible power potential for each state, causing everything to be scrutinized for its political value and adding to the politicization of the international society (referred to earlier). The specificity of the political system is further obscured by this diffusion of decision-making throughout the society. The most important political functions are performed by states whose identity is in principle unpredictable. This diffusion of decision-making and the scattering of political activities, combined with the politicization, gives the informal political system an undifferentiated nature.

An argument can be made that national political systems are also to some extent undifferentiated. The formal and the actual locus of authoritative decision-making do not always coincide. Formally, the government will always be the decision-maker and actor. Informally, the real political power may lie in some unofficial agency — a labor union, an employers' organization. But at least in states the formal decision-making power is normally visible and distinguishable and supported by a consensus, making it authoritative. In the international society, since such consensus is lacking and is replaced, at best, by acquiescence or plain surrender, the substance as well as the forms of decision-making are diffused. The principle of sovereignty notwithstanding, supreme authority is with those states able to make their decisions binding, and in extreme situations whether a decision is binding can be determined only by a trial of strength in a war. The psychologically and sociologically unsatisfactory nature of this arrangement lies in the possibility that any state can potentially make a political decision for all states (while under the regime of sovereignty no state can make any decision for any other); and that such a decision will be based on an individual state's judgment of its own interest, unrestrained by even the pretense of a common interest.

The crucial point in comparing the national and international situation regarding decision-making is that the formal structure of a political system is not the most important thing in discovering its nature. The inadequacy of the international political system is not due mainly to the circumvention of sovereignty and the diffusion of decision-making. Such diffusion can be found in very orderly so-called primitive societies. Making sovereignty real rather than formal would not solve the problem of inadequacy — indeed it would worsen the system. The decisive factor making the national system adequate and the international inadequate is the differing psychological underpinning of each, which cannot be affected simply by manipulating the structure of the systems. The national political structure rests upon consensus; the international political structure is largely devoid of consensus. Citizens are generally willing to accept decisions by their governments. States are generally unwilling to abide by decisions made by other states. The ability of states to make binding decisions is therefore doubtful and the system becomes inadequate, being impotent to produce reliably political decisions. When states obey decisions by other states, they do so either voluntarily when there is ad hoc agreement with a given decision, or out of prudence for fear of the consequences of disobedience. In either case, the authority of the decision rests on an insecure foundation.

The magnitude of the difference between political systems with similar structures but dissimilar psychological backgrounds can be demonstrated by comparing the international with so-called stateless primitive political systems. Such a comparison has been undertaken in the past because some aspects of these primitive systems are reminiscent of the indistinct character of the international political system. But what the two types of societies have in common is little more than political functions which can, of course, be found in every society. The important question is how they are performed. Otherwise, similarities remain on such a high level of abstraction as to have little analytical value. A comparison of the international society with that type of primitive society may indeed be helpful in recognizing the nature of the international political system. But this is so more because of the differences under the surface appearances than because of overt similarities.

The first significant dissimilarity is that the informal political structure in these primitive societies has not been consciously created, whereas the international society has deliberately structured itself. This difference discloses a wealth of clues to the psychological aspects backing the systems of the two types of societies. A second dissimilarity is that the reasons for the absence of a distinct, immediately visible political authority in both societies are totally different. In some primitive societies integration of behavior is so strong, rigidity of behavior patterns so great, and social goals so fixed that a central authority is superfluous. Maintenance of the social order through custom is adequate. The exact opposite is true of the international society. The "stateless" organization of the society is due to a lack of integration; behavior patterns are largely unpredictable; and social goals are in reality the individual goals of the society's members. A third and related dissimilarity is the relatively simple set of members' interests in the primitive societies and their great complexity as well as variability in the international society. Conflicts in the one society are therefore less frequent and more routinely settled than in the other. There is, fourth, a blatant difference between the two kinds of society in the success with which their political systems function. In most primitive societies order is remarkably well preserved. In the international society the opposite is truer. Finally, in these primitive societies an

77

undifferentiated political system goes hand in hand with the individual's lack of any specifically political consciousness. In the international society nationals have a very definite, usually negative conception of the international political system. Their loyalties are explicitly to their own national systems and pronouncedly hostile to the international political system in case of conflict.

This comparison indicates that similarities in tasks (e.g., maintaining social order) and in structures (e.g., diffusion of decision-making, coercive sanctions performed by individual members) do not necessarily mean similarities in the nature of the political systems. Details are of importance. Above all, psychological factors are crucial because they may give different meaning to objectively similar institutions and processes. Obviously, a political system based on the sovereignty of its members must have some different features from a system whose members are transferring the exercise of sovereignty to one common organ. One of these features is undoubtedly the intent with which objective elements of the political system are used (and that will be examined in the future chapter). But even the objective features will have their peculiarities. These will be examined now for the international political system: first, the actors in the political system; next the making of political decisions; and finally the political processes.

The Actors

The substance of a social system has here been said to be the network of interactions between the members of the international society. It was left open and dependent upon the context whether these members are states, governments, some other collectivity, or individuals. For practical political purposes it is important to know who specifically and potentially the physical actors can be. The statesman, wishing to influence the behavior of states, must know who is responsible for this behavior and what the reasons for the particular behavior are.[23] The statesman could hardly devise successful strategies and tactics if the actor were to be defined as "the state" in abstraction from its governing individuals and influencing citizens. Propaganda is likely to be the more successful the better it can be aimed at the various individuals who in their different roles create "the state's behavior." The possibility exists that the nature of any particular individual is relatively irrelevant in taking care of the most established, elementary needs of states, such as territorial or political integrity. When the existence of the state is at stake,

78

there is usually not much doubt about what a state will do in general. Besides, the nearer and greater a crisis the smaller the number of individuals involved in making decisions — often because there is little doubt about what is to be done and that it has to be done fast. But the more a state's interests move away from their most intense, obvious and customary elements, the more individuals become involved in the decision-making, the more unpredictable becomes the political decision and the manner of its execution — for the range of choices widens. The study of individuals as the physical actors and their idiosyncrasies increases in importance. There are few occasions when it is adequate for a statesman to deal with the state as an entity. One among them could be when the power potential of a state is to be assessed; another, when relationships between two states are to be examined. Yet another and very important one is when a national public's feelings are to be aroused against or for another national public. Dealing with states as personified entities with evil or good qualities can mobilize emotional responses more effectively than most other methods. But good politics requires as precise a knowledge as possible about who must be influenced and how this can best be done.

The requirement of knowing the identity of the physical actors in the political system is of equal importance for the student who wishes to analyze or understand the system and who may be interested in planning for its improvement. The reasons are essentially the same, though the student's purpose may differ greatly from that of the statesman.

The problem raised by this detailed specification of the "actor" is twofold. One part is the rather old question of the collectivity versus the individual. Can a collectivity act, have feelings, a conscience? Is a collectivity a reality or is it what Morris Cohen called a "communal ghost"? The other part relates to the question, asked more often recently, whether dealing with the state as actor remains adequate for an understanding of the international system in light of the growing importance of so many relations across frontiers between units other than states.

States have solved the problem in principle in favor of the state as a collective actor and as the only actor. They have done so at least on the formal official level, although in practice they do not always accept this solution. As a matter of convention and convenience, mainly for almost inevitable practical reasons, the international society considers as decisions and actions of states the decisions and actions by those authorized for them through the internal arrangements of the states. Persons acting on behalf of states are not considered subjects of international law nor personally accountable for what they have done in their official capacity. The population of a state is held responsible for the decisions and behavior of their officials, regardless of agreement or disagreement of any citizen with his officials. This logical result of the insistence upon a state's sovereignty and identity has been brought to its ultimate conclusion by excluding individuals altogether as subjects of international law (with very few exceptions) or as participants on their own behalf in international organizations. Relations between two citizens of different nationality are not subject to international law either. The complaint that the individual is the "forgotten man" in international society is justified. This was not always the case. In Grotius's day international law was rightly considered law for human beings. Grotius and some of his predecessors maintained that international law regulated both relations between states and between subjects of different states. Their point was that two individuals not subject to the same municipal law were subject in their relations to international law. This idea went out of fashion as a result of the absolutism of the state and has remained so with only minor changes to the present.

Individuals now can be only objects of law, and obligations can be imposed upon them. But with some exotic exceptions, they cannot claim rights directly under international law. States monopolize jurisdiction over individuals. Whatever rights are claimed for individuals as human beings on moral or humanitarian grounds, on legal grounds these rights are granted them only as citizens of their states. Similarly, the responsibility of individuals acting legitimately on behalf of their state is the state's and not their personal responsibility under international law. The idea that collective responsibility should be replaced by individual international responsibility, promoted by the Nuremberg and Tokyo war crimes trials, did not take root. In some international organizations a few interest groups are gaining official status as active participants. Individuals and private firms have direct access to the European Court of Justice. Such exceptions hardly undermine the general principle; they may not even indicate a trend.

But the solution chosen by states in their official relations does not solve, even for them, the problem of dealing effectively with those individuals, the physical actors, who represent their states. Individuals are always the ultimate movers of collective behavior. The dialectic relationships between individual and collectivity make it inevitable that the norms and decisions of a society can become effective only through individuals, while norms and decisions addressed to individuals will affect the collective behavior of the society. Individuals are always the carriers of "collective" action and ultimately the source of national behavior. An analysis can never be complete — for the purposes of either the statesman or the student — if it restricts itself to an examination of the collectivity. True, individual behavior cannot be understood without taking into consideration its social context. But it is equally true that collective behavior cannot be understood without paying close attention to the individuals composing the collectivity. The aggregate behavior of states never represents the behavior of any one of the individuals producing it. But the motivation for the aggregate behavior can only be discovered by tracing it back to the components of the aggregate. Because of the mutual influence of individuals within a collectivity, the determination regarding which individuals must be examined for understanding which collective action may be very difficult at times. The continuity and fluidity of these inter-influences does not in fact permit an absolute dividing line. The difference between a maker of a decision and an influencer of that decision-maker may be blurred, except in the persons involved (which is all the more reason to keep these individuals and their roles conceptually as separate as possible).

E. H. Carr has argued convincingly that there really is no problem. The hypothesis of a personified state, he says, with rights, duties, obligations, sentiments, morality, and so forth, is neither true nor false, since it does not claim to be reality. It is a mental concept aiding thought about international politics. As long as statesmen accept the hypothesis and states act upon it, the problem of the hypothesized state-person dissolves itself. For some purposes the assumption is adequate. For others it is not.

The problem does not have to be solved finally in order to understand the nature of the political system and international politics, or to practice world politics. The collectivity can be considered from a variety of standpoints, each helping to clarify different aspects of the political system and its operations. It is important, however, to recognize the limits of any one viewpoint and not to generalize from any one about aspects for which it would be inadequate. Considering the state or some other collectivity as an entity is a useful shorthand expression and tool. It designates the group in question and the behavior presumed to be that of the whole group. There are situations in international politics which can be explained and analyzed quite adequately without much need for further dissecting the collectivity into its components. Other situations cannot properly be understood without attention to individuals involved. When, especially, knowledge is needed about the sources of collective behavior, focusing on the collectivity would not produce it. Then men must be investigated.

The other part of the problem of defining the actors in the international political system is the question of who else, in addition to states, may be an actor. The question has recently come into prominence because the volume of transnational interactions between units other than states has grown sizably. The argument has been made that as long as individuals, alone or in groups, play a role in the international political process, even a remote and indirect role, they should be included as actors. Such an assumption would misrepresent reality as well as rob the concept of actor of analytical value. In the final analysis states are always involved in international politics. If they are not actors initiating the process, then they at least identify themselves with those who succeed in initiating the process (individuals, groups, international organizations). They make the actions of these entities their own. They assume responsibility for them. If they do not, there is no state action, there is no official political process, there is no commitment for national publics. Actions of the other "actors" remain without official effect and become part of the environment in which states act. To call every influencing group an actor would confuse those who influence states as actors with the actors themselves.

All these new "actors" in international relations — usually citizen groups in various states interacting with each other and thereby either directly or indirectly influencing governmental policies — are not direct, immediate political actors in the international system. They are, at most, representatives of states, for instance in international organizations; and they remain such representatives even when the organization is entitled to conclude treaties. Or they may be using states, when, for instance, they are powerful corporations; or they are used by states when, for instance, cultural institutions engage abroad in propaganda. In every case, these groups can do all these things only if states are willing to play their appropriate roles. These groups are part of the environment, like geography, resources, communications, with which states have to reckon in shaping their foreign policies. The activities of these groups are at least once removed from international political decisions. Their political relevance is in their presence and their behavior. Their wills and activities are ultimately pertinent and directly political only if they receive the imprimatur of states. Some groups (say powerful oil companies) may receive this imprimatur more readily than others, and there may be complaint about whose and what interests a state supports. But, first, states have always acted on behalf of sometimes special, sometimes general interests, mainly because there is little else to act on behalf of. And, second, because a lobby may be powerful does not make it for that reason a political actor — it still remains an influencer! People may be tools of states; organizations may be forums for action; or vice versa. But states, willingly or unwillingly, continue to be the final arbiters of political decisions and actions. They remain, for the time being, the only actors in international politics.

If the concept of actor is to remain meaningful, actors in the international political system can only be those units making in fact authoritative regulations for human behavior aiming at the creation and preservation of social order. In the present international system such units can only be states acting through their governments. All transnational activities by other units, whether they be international organizations, business corporations, humanitarian foundations, or revolutionary clubs, are permeated by the politicization characteristic of all international factors and therefore ultimately subject to direction and control by governments (even if they can manipulate that direction and control). The orientation of their actions is toward getting governments to make political decisions, not to make decisions themselves. They could not do so because they are outside the authority structure.

To call units other than states actors would be to overlook that well-established nations are, sociologically and empirically speaking, very specific types of social units differing from mankind as a society and differing very much from all other so-called actors. States are, first of all, social units sui generis. Their power potential differs in quality from that of any other "actor." Their location in the social and especially the authority structure of the international society is quite different from that of any other "actor." In the second place, and most important, the relationship of the mass of citizens to each other and to those of other states remains, for the time being, quite different from the relationship members of transnational groups have to each other or to their respective states. Usually, members of transnational groups are not internationalists in the sense of abandoning loyalty to their particular state. On the contrary, they often count on the existence and strength of their particular state, which they hope to use for their own purposes. Nothing would please most of them more than to have a strong state and be very influential in it. In short, the social nature of the state leads it to behave in a typical fashion as an actor. This qualifying behavior is not equaled by any other so-called international actor and has unique

83

consequences socially, legally, and in every other respect. To muddy the fairly clear concept of the state as actor by adding other types of actors when these have totally different qualities and are therefore quite incomparable, would unnecessarily obscure what clarity there is and aggravate — not facilitate at all — the problem of analysis.

The argument that the volume and significance of transnational relations have grown so much that some of those engaged in them have changed character from being influences upon foreign policies to becoming actors in international politics is to overlook the fact that even when the tail has grown so big that it wags the dog, the tail remains a tail. It also overlooks the fact that virtually all other factors forming a state's environment have grown in volume and significance. Populations have grown, communications have grown, and so have gross national products, weapons, literacy, supermarkets, and, apparently, even people. All of these changed factors are affecting international politics, but they remain for all that the same factors. To some extent these various growths even cancel each other out. If one is being singled out, presumably all should be. But instead of going through this complicated process and starting an attempt to understand international politics all over again from the beginning, it seems more economical to fit these changes into existing frameworks laboriously constructed, as long as they fit. No convincing case has yet been made that the introduction of new "actors" would facilitate an understanding of international politics.

Taking this position here is not to deny either the desirability of adding other actors to states in the international society or a discernible trend in that direction. But wishful analyzing of the international system will not overcome frustration over the slow demise of sovereignty or conjure up an international community when transnational relations may at best be the harbingers of one. For the time being the evidence is only that there has been an impressive increase in transnational relations; that international civil servants can trigger political processes; that many more private transnational organizations than in the past have more powerful influences on the foreign policies of states; and that all kinds of linkages between different governments and private groups in different states exist to serve political purposes (namely, for these groups to affect their government as the only "actor"). The evidence is also that the easy transmission of ideas, abstracted from their individual originators, can trigger political interaction between states. These developments may be promising for the arrival of a more peaceful world in the future. They have already affected the character of the international society in many respects. They did, indeed, originally turn mankind into a society. But the essential features of the international political system have not been affected. The authority structure, the diffusion of decision-making, and above all the mentality underlying the whole international system remain, for the time being, what they were in the past. That these developments will eventually produce fundamental changes is likely, but they lie in the future.

The difficulty of deciding who is acting and who is influencing in the international political system, whether a collectivity can act or whether only individuals, has been a contributing factor to the popularity of systems theory in the study of international politics. The popularity has been so great that there is an abundance of suggested types of systems, almost one for every historical situation — which is as useful as having no system at all! The difficult decision could be evaded if all international relations and politics were a system running on its own laws in which individuals could be reduced to cogs. But such an approach is not very helpful in disclosing causes of social action, motivation behind decisions, sentiments behind attitudes — in getting at the roots of states' behavior. It does, however, have its uses for other purposes of analysis. And it is therefore worthwhile to establish the strength and weakness of the systems theory approach beyond the general remarks made about it in the first chapter.

There are some objective and subjective, and very seductive, reasons for representing international relations as a social system. It permits "grand theory" paralleling the "grand" scope of international relations; it is sufficiently comprehensive to encompass the complexities of the international society; and it is flexible (or vague) enough to allow for the application of many methods of investigation. International relations as a system also appeals to those eager to comprehend the totality of global relations and to those fearing that to lose sight of the whole will becloud reality and skew one's perspective. They would argue, for instance, that knowing much about military strategy and little about international tensions can lead to catastrophe; that the application of piecemeal knowledge is a dangerous thing. If the system is conceived broadly enough, the unrealistic separation between national and international politics could be overcome. Instead of speaking of linkages, which is a very helpful stopgap concept and still evokes two separate entities, all existing social units would melt into one great system and be part of a whole. One could then deal with the politics of this enormous unit, and the interweaving and interconnections of its politics would become obvious. The present difficulty of understanding them in the light of the traditional conceptual separation of national and international politics would disappear.

The idea of international relations as a global system helps to avoid over-specialization which, if permitted to flourish, could push practical matters in the wrong direction or, if its subject is minuscule enough, push matters in no direction at all. In short, approaching the study of international relations as a system serves as a corrective in retaining perspective, in recognizing the limits of existing knowledge, and in placing every element in its proper place. These advantages are true if, as has been pointed out earlier, system is understood simply to mean the interrelation of parts forming a whole, a logical concept for ordering parts, and not a scheme for causative explanation. The decomposition of the system into its parts will then not be limited by some artificial boundaries drawn as a result of conceiving the system as some organic unit with preconceived "natural" laws by which it functions. It will then be possible to single out all its parts, including those who in some way act within the system according to their free will insofar as this is ever possible under any given set of circumstances. This possibility, how-ever, is largely denied if the concept of the system is applied as is done in general systems theory; that is to say, as a closed entity, having purposes and laws of its own which determine the functions and the functioning of the "actors." The whole system is treated as if it were operating like a gigantic automaton with everything geared primarily to the maintenance and stability of the system. This automaton relieves the analyst from dealing with the complexities of human nature. The basic problems of a social system are solved!

Yet since a social system is the totality of human actions in their interrelations and without such actions there is not any social system at all, the emphasis is on actions, not on their automatism, and therefore the emphasis is on men. General systems theory, by trying to assume that men act on the basis of the system's law rather than on laws allowing some freedom of decision and action, tends to misdirect the analysis of the international system in general and of its actors in particular. For instance, international systems, instead of being stable and maintaining themselves, are in fact characterized historically by constant change. The actors in the system have a built-in mechanism for the destruction rather than the maintenance of the system, in the form of war. And the reason they have the mechanism is that they want it. An international system can change itself into another type of system or ruin itself through causes constituting an integral part of it. Men as members of the system can change it, a possibility general systems theory can handle only most inadequately. Men turn the social system into something quite different from mechanical or natural systems — an automobile can never change itself into something else! Finally, general systems theory tends to treat states as equal "actors" when in fact states are in principle unequal as actors.

General systems theory — or any conception of a system resembling it — ignores the role of issues in international relations except those relating to the alleged primary goal of system maintenance or stability. In actuality in the value hierarchy of the international system, the issues aiming mostly at strengthening and maintaining national systems are primary, with those maintaining the international system being at best secondary. Men pursue a multiplicity of purposes and the nature of the system depends very largely on these purposes and not the other way around. Men act as a result of motivations, which systems theory tends to ignore. The measurement of the stream of mail between two countries, for instance, may be most interesting to the postmaster general but tells little to the analyst, who ought also to know why there is a stream of letters and what their content is, to reach significant conclusions. The system concept, to be useful, must take into account the fullness of man's true and complex nature. For in the final analysis in any social situation man is behind it all. He provides the common denominator of any and every social system. Concentration on man would provide the necessary link between all social systems or units, from the family up to the global society. The study of the various systems in reality then is the study of man in a variety of social situations and environments which all become one whole through man as their most essential part. If social phenomena are to be explained, the focus of the investigation of every social situation must ultimately be on man. This holds especially true for the actors in the system, for they are its very essence. To speak of states as actors as if this were reality will forever leave the analysis of state behavior incomplete. It could only explain a number of actions when little more than description or objective correlation between actions is required. Motivations can only be disclosed by concentrating upon those who make decisions and occasionally also upon those who are indirectly contributing to the decision or who are directly executing it.

To the student of the international system, treating states as actors as a reality could tell him much about how the system functions but little of why. Yet such knowledge is crucial for the development of theory as well as any strategy for changing the system. The many blueprints for an ideal international system resulted almost entirely from goodwill and idealism, with virtually none based upon a precise analysis of the reasons for the prevailing system's shortcomings. In view of the relative constancy of the environment in which states exist, the best strategy for producing systemic changes is likely to be through human beings. To do that, their specific role in the system must be known, and to speak of states as actors in any final sense will not do. One must assume that the stubborn survival of the present nation-state system has something to do with the people composing it. Making all these people pawns in some automatic, extrahuman system is contrary to all the obvious evidence. They are not likely to be omnipotent in changing the totality of the system at will, but the opposite is not likely to be any truer. Human will can produce change within the system and of the system. Therefore, it is important to investigate humans and their influence as actors. This is important not just for specific items but for a general understanding of the whole political system and for world politics. This does not obviate the need to maintain a distinction between men whose actions influence political decisions of states and men whose actions are the decisions of states. Nothing is gained for an understanding of international politics by assuming that all acting men on the globe are ''actors'' in the international political system. Yet this assumption would become inevitable if such a distinction were not made, because no proper line between some men (beyond those belonging to the government) and all men as ''actors'' could be drawn.

The Making of Political Decisions

In the international society the making of a political decision is usually called a state's foreign policy. It is a most significant component of the political system. It defines the needs and wants (the interests) of a state and the means by which they are to be pursued. In other words, how a state will behave in the international society and how it proposes to solve social policy issues or allocate values is the essence of foreign policy decisions. The formulation of these interests and the choice of the means in relation to the same activities of other states determine whether the political system will be able to maintain social order.

Terminological precision requires a distinction between two aspects of what is commonly called foreign policy. One is the formulation of foreign policy, which involves establishing the overall goals to be reached in the international society. Great Britain's desire to maintain a balance of power on the European Continent or the wish of the United States for an open door in China are overall goals. The other aspect is the execution of foreign policy, which is the day-by-day decisions involving the choice of means and their application to reach the goals. There is a twofold relationship between the formulation and execution of a foreign policy. One is a close interdependence between formulation and execution in the sense that neither can meaningfully exist alone. This points to the other relationship. Without a decision to implement the decision on goals, there is no foreign policy at all. A crucial part of any foreign policy is the state's determination to make it effective by enforcing its decisions. Without such a determination, "foreign policy" is a misnomer for something else, for instance a unilateral declaration or an appeal, such as a state's announcement that it expects all states to behave morally or that it hopes no state will attack a certain state.

From the standpoint of the international political system, the importance of a state's foreign policy lies in the fact that it means either permission by the state for other states to do or not to do something; or, more often, a demand by the state upon other states to do or not to do something. In either case, the state's decision means a certain behavior on the part of other states and that is a matter of priority for the political system. But in especial two aspects of the foreign policy formulation and execution process highlight the inadequacy of the political system. One is its manner of implementation. The other is its formlessness and unpredictability.

The manner in which foreign policy is executed contrasts sharply with that in national situations. Within states the governmental political decision normally signifies the end or at least a midpoint in the political process. Even in nondemocratic countries there is a measure of institutionalized participation at least by those most directly affected by the policy decision. Once the government has made an internal political decision, the power at its disposal makes the execution and enforcement so much a matter of routine that very often administrative and judicial activities are excluded conceptually from the realm of the political. In the international society the making of a foreign policy decision signifies in principle the beginning of the international political process (and often the end of the internal political process of reaching the foreign policy decision). The next and highly political step is then to command obedience for the decision. In the course of this endeavor, states may modify their decision, or other states may react with decisions of their own which start new political processes. But in any case the full force of conflicting interests becomes effective at this point. Demand and counter-demand confront states in almost unmitigated harshness. Adjustments of the policy decisions result from power struggles, conducted the more determinedly the higher the interests at stake. There is scant influence of the international society's common weal, little softening effect of pluralistic interests, and few moral inhibitions to restrain the employment of all available means in pursuit of national interests. The order-preserving qualities of the political system are under greatest stress.

In internal national situations this power play precedes, not follows, the making of a decision. Its fierceness is tamed by all the community influences available within socially integrated nations and, failing these, by the over-whelming power of the government. There are many inducements to the citizen to adjust, compromise, and consent, thereby reducing hostilities. His knowledge that his government will prevent pursuit of anyone's interests beyond orderly and peaceful behavior makes him accept limits upon his own interests as well. On the international scene such inducements are weak and a common agency to impose limits on any state's interests is absent. The announcement of a political decision by a government is therefore potentially always a cause of tension and, at worst, of war.

The unpredictability of the decision-making process refers both to who will make a decision and to when and how a decision will be made or by what means it will be executed. Within nations, political decisions are in principle made predictably by the government and generally speaking in a predictable manner. The citizen can therefore orient his behavior accordingly, and the task of the political system is thereby facilitated. In the international society, insistence upon sovereign independence leads to the informality of the decision-making process because no state willingly subjects itself to a regulation of its foreign policy execution. There is a rudimentary formal structure at best. There are very few agreed built-in, structural, external constraints on the execution of foreign policy and, a fortiori, on its formulation. Most factors external to the state, yet affecting its policy formulation, are parts of the environment which the state may or may not take into consideration. That, for instance, Cuba has a Communist regime or that there is a wall across Berlin is part of the environment in which United States foreign policy must be formulated.

The rules of international law, inasmuch as they are effective, refer mainly to structural features giving the state its quality as an actor and defining the organs or individuals entitled to act on its behalf. They address themselves to the recognition of states, the credentials of negotiators, the ratification of treaties, and similar matters of form. Even then, they do so in abstract terms, leaving it to the states themselves as an "internal affair" to establish conditions in fulfillment of these formal requirements. International law leaves it to each state, for instance, to define the ratification process: whether a parliament must agree, a cabinet, or only the head of state. International rules have virtually nothing to say about the formulation of foreign policy, since from the legal standpoint this is essentially an internal matter, only its execution being of major international concern. But on the execution too international law is only slightly more explicit. To some extent the procedure which states may use for obtaining obedience to their decisions, i.e., how they may or may not act, is subject to international law. In general, however, the making of political decisions in the international society and their execution is left in practice almost entirely to the whim of the maker of the decision, limited mainly by his capability of exploiting this freedom.

The whole process of foreign policy formulation and execution, with all its uncertainties and formlessness, is quite contrary to the conditions required for social order. The unpredictability of who will make a political decision for the international society, when it will be made, what it will be, how it will be enforced creates a sense of insecurity in the international society. All states are therefore taking precautions against unexpected and possibly arbitrary demands upon them. They are trying either to deter other states from formulating demands in the first place or to nullify them after they have been made. The usual and almost the only way in which they can do this is to try to be sufficiently powerful for any eventuality. This method, as will be shown during a discussion on power, creates even greater insecurity than the process of making political decisions. The cure is worse than the disease.

The hope has been expressed that the growing volume of communications between states may defuse some of the explosiveness of the diffused and arbitrary process of making decisions. States instead of deciding in splendid isolation and then trying to foist their decision upon an unwilling international society will, it is hoped, use the many channels of communication to explore the situation before decisions are made. By developing such new forms of discourse as "parliamentary," collective, and multilateral diplomacy, increasing the number of international organizations and conferences, evolving a larger international civil service, and multiplying private international interest groups, states should become better aware of each other's goals, common or conflicting interests, friendly or hostile sentiments, and withal the chances of solving their problems in orderly and peaceful ways. More interaction and better acquaintance will help in attuning their political decisions to each other. They may at least discover in good time the boundaries beyond which their behavior can lead to disorder and violence. Foreign policies might be based on clearer perceptions and fewer illusions. States have increasingly taken advantage of these developments, and the hopes for more coordinated foreign policy making are not unjustified.[24] Formal and informal negotiations, soundings, tests of public opinion in affected states, and other methods by states to learn about each other are widespread practices preceding the formulation of foreign policy. Yet the serious danger resulting from individual and largely noninstitutionalized decision-making and enforcement has not been totally banned. The basic principle remains intact that final political decisions are made and enforced by states according to their national interest, at great risk to the order of the international society.

This unilateral making of decisions by states for the international society has raised the problem of the decisions' universality — one of the criteria of their political nature. Any given decision may affect only two or a small circle of other states directly. Within states this problem does not arise because the government is always presumed to act for the common weal, even if it addresses itself to only a select group. Moreover, apart from this idealistic assumption, states are usually better integrated than the international society, so that what affects one part of the population is likely somehow to affect the whole population.

On either count, the international society differs from national societies. It has therefore been asserted that the world is politically not yet one but at best a collection of separate political systems based on territorial contiguity (regions), the density of communications, or some other criteria of direct relationships between some states. Similar ideas underlay the world plans of Nazi Germany or the Japanese Greater East Asia Co-Prosperity Sphere. Reality does not support this conception. The nature of contemporary international relationships is such that no region can be singled out and isolated. For a number of reasons virtually any even bilateral relationship has universal implications and significance, though, of course, some more so than others.

First, the major powers with their global interests are sensitive to events everywhere, so that small states must consider the possible global implications of their political decisions and actions, however limited in scope these may be. Second, partial or sectional actions become universal because bilateral or multilateral relationships are overlapping, interweaving, and intertwining, forming a network of international relationships. No two states have relations only between themselves. Each state in a bilateral relation has relations to a third state so that a circle of concern grows out even of sets of bilateral relationships — what Robert McIver called "social conjunction." Third, the Security Council and the secretary-general of the United Nations are charged with anticipating threats to the peace everywhere. Because any event can be the link in a chain of events leading to war and because peace may indeed be indivisible, causes of violence may arise from the behavior of states anywhere.[25] Therefore the behavior of states everywhere is scrutinized by the United Nations for the effect it may have on the behavior of other states. Finally, the ubiquity of power combined with the preoccupation of all states with their own power potential in relation to that of all other states makes every state alert to the power potential of other states. Power assures universality to all political decisions.

There is a paradox here. The absence of a goal in common among all states, of a central government, and of serious concern for the common welfare of the international society, instead of diminishing the universality of political decisions by individual states, may actually enhance it. Citizens within a state need not feel concerned about every political decision, secure in the knowledge that their interests are protected through their government. In the international society every state has to secure its interests against infringements by other states and must therefore take careful account of the political decisions made by others, whatever their objective, lest the state's interests may somehow become involved. The uncertainties of international decision-making gives each decision a greater universality than is the case in national political systems, quite independently of which state may be most directly affected and involved by the decision.

The Political Processes

In contrast to the formlessness of decision-making, political processes are more structured. The reason could be that these processes, rather than the decisions, most directly affect states. These processes are the acts undertaken by states to execute their political decisions. They represent the political interactions relating members of the international political system to each other. They are the stuff of world politics. But they are not always easily recognized. First, there is no central government in which customarily political processes could be concentrated. States might substitute for governments, but not all activities by states on the international scene are necessarily political. As spokesmen for their peoples in the international system, they also speak on behalf of their citizens on nonpolitical occasions. On the other hand, states can engage in political activities through the intermediary of private individuals. The role or nonrole of the state in any given situation is not necessarily evidence of a situation's political or nonpolitical character. Second, the enormous politicization of the international society makes any process potentially political. The substance of a process is not necessarily evidence of the process's political or nonpolitical character. What may in national societies be of nonpolitical content, say cultural activity, may very well become highly political on the international scene. The principle can be stated that when a process is relevant to the execution or preparation of a political decision, it is a political process. But to recognize this relevance in practice may be very difficult indeed. Just to be on the safe side, states therefore tend to assume that all processes involving governments are likely to be political until they are sure that this is not the case.

The inherently, directly, and undoubtedly political processes can be broadly categorized as diplomacy, propaganda, and pressure. All international political processes fall into one of these categories. Their political nature will be discussed later. The interest here is in their character as part of the political system. As political interactions they are always related to making past or future political decisions effective, regardless of what substantively they may relate to in any given case. And because making political decisions effective is virtually always a function of power, diplomacy, propaganda, and pressure are tools of power. They are the transmission belts through which one state applies its power upon another. This character creates a dilemma for the international society in organizing or managing these processes.

Under the aegis of sovereignty, the society cannot very well openly and officially admit power interactions as legitimate. States in sovereign equality can only interact on a strictly voluntary basis. The society is thus forced either to be unrealistic if it avoids regulating power interactions or else to be inconsistent with its most basic principle if it decides to be realistic and regulate them. In fact, it is both, as for instance when it declares most wars illegal but provides rules for the conduct of any war at the same time. This hypocrisy enables the society to overcome the difficulties it has created for itself. The political system provides regulations for interstate behavior in accordance with the principle of sovereignty, but simultaneously also for behavior not in accordance with that principle. The aim is to cover all eventualities in order to save as much of the principle as may be possible under a regime based upon that principle itself. Even so, the regulations are incomplete. They cover interactions legitimized by the principle of sovereignty more than they cover the probably equally voluminous interactions not in accordance with that principle. The situation is of course not totally different from that to be found within states. Only, as in so many other cases, the consequences are vitally different for they involve the very existence of the international society.

The formal aspects of diplomacy are dealt with extensively in international law, custom, and usage. Innumerable international organizations supply facilities for negotiation and other peaceful intercourse. Preambles of international charters and constitutions are filled with exhortations to use these facilities. They also suggest standards for political procedures and norms for political goals (as for instance in the Universal Declaration of Human Rights). They provide structures in which international transactions can take place. The results of diplomacy in the form of treaties and other agreements can be formalized in every detail by rules provided for this purpose. Occasionally, the international society even puts instruments at the disposal of states for the common implementation (but not for the common making) of political decisions. The role diplomacy plays in the political system is to raise and clarify social issues and problems, to modify conflicting interests, to transmit information of mutual concern to the parties. The diplomatic process provides incentives for the prevention of conflicts, for avoiding their escalation, or for settling them by offering both technical or methodological as well as substantive solutions. Many methods for the peaceful solution of conflicts, ranging from good offices to arbitration, contain aspects of diplomacy. They are one example of the formal possibilities the international political system possesses even within the narrow framework constructed by sovereignty of influencing, if not regulating, international political behavior. The reason why these possibilities must be called formal is, first, that they are indeed formalized and, second, that only in theory are they presumed to apply between equals. In practice, the voluntarism in diplomatic negotiations is extremely limited. The application of power, however illegitimate according to the formal system, is one of their inevitable aspects. This is true even when a government refrains from deliberately using its power potential. Its existence alone is enough to make it a part of all political considerations.

INTERNATIONAL POLITICS

In contrast to the extensively regulated and structured political processes of diplomacy (in the widest sense), those falling under the general heading of propaganda are almost totally unregulated. The whole field of psychological warfare, subversion, infiltration, propaganda (in the narrow sense) is covered broadly and vaguely by the general rule that states must respect each other's integrity and must not interfere in each other's internal affairs. The General Assembly of the United Nations has on various occasions condemned these activities with little effect. The political system would find it very difficult to regulate these activities other than by forbidding them outright. And forbidding them effectively would be unacceptable because propaganda is a tool of power even small states can afford and can use with some success. A political system cannot otherwise positively regulate activities designed to undermine the very principle of sovereignty upon which it is built: it cannot determine how a state may legitimately subvert another and it cannot tell a state what it may or may not do internally even if such internal activity (e.g., broadcasting) amounts to propaganda. An additional difficulty in regulating propaganda is its often intangible nature. In a totalitarian state, an objective, factual news broadcast may be propaganda. The line between information and propaganda is very difficult to draw, and so is the line between genuine economically justified aid and aid given for propagandistic purposes, between a true desire to exchange professionals to learn from them and a desire to indoctrinate them as visitors, and between many different kinds of cross-national activities. There are, of course, forms of propaganda whose nature and intent as "indirect aggression" is quite clear. But even in their case it may be true — as is certainly true of propaganda in general — that the role propaganda plays in the international political system cannot easily be ascertained. Nations engage in it, like advertisers, in the hope that it may help them reach their goals, but they can never be quite sure that it does. They cannot predict the effect of their propaganda upon its targets and the targets' effect upon their own country's foreign policy decisions.

The third category of political interactions, the exertion of pressure, is very detrimental to sovereignty, possibly to the point of making it illusory. Yet it has been carefully regulated and structured for a very long time. There are the rules of war. There are rules for the compulsory settlement of conflicts by means of pressure, such as reprisal, blockade, and intervention. There are rules for the prevention, control, and rejection of aggression or the threat of violence. This is a paradoxical enterprise. Its rationale is presumably that the use of pressure may be so detrimental to social order, yet

96

is so nearly inevitable, that ignoring it (and thereby permitting its unrestricted application) would be worse than regulating it. Besides, since the technical means of exerting pressure are always and inevitably present in some form, this fact alone has effects upon international politics. And, finally, pressure, including force, can have very useful social consequences. It is, in fact, one of the indispensable tools for maintaining social order in any society. The problem for all societies is not the elimination of pressure as a social instrument, but the regulation of its use in the service of social order. The difficulty of doing so successfully lies in the effectiveness of this instrument for those who possess the superior means of applying it. Many national societies have achieved a proper regulation. The international society has obviously not, because of the drive for state autonomy and the unique support it derives from national superiority in the use of pressure. The result of this failure is so dramatic that the inadequacy of the international political system is popularly considered to be synonymous with the inability of the system to manage physical pressure. While this popular understanding is all too well justified, it nevertheless not only overlooks the fact that there are other types of pressure than physical force and violence but fails to realize that the instrument of pressure can also contribute to the maintenance of order, for instance by raising the price of disorder! The solution to this dilemma lies in organizing the international use of pressure in such a manner that the cost of causing disorder will always and most assuredly be too high. Attempts in this direction have been made many times and in a great variety of forms: the neutralization of pressure through the organization of counterpressure (e.g., alliances, collective security); the abolition of pressure through the abolition of its means (e.g., disarmament); agreements not to use pressure (e.g., the Kellogg-Briand Pact of 1928).

Because military means were the most common means of pressure in the past, most of these regulations refer to it. With the rising importance of economic tools as instruments of politics, adjustments had to be made. By the creation of numerous organizations for the regulation of economic matters, from trade to currency values, the range of opportunities for conducting economic warfare has been narrowed. But these, like all other arrangements to inhibit the use of pressure methods, must remain inadequate as long as the inequality of states can find expression unhampered by an authority structure in the international society which could prevent its exploitation for pressuring states into unwanted behavior.

INTERNATIONAL POLITICS

The Inadequacy of the International Political System

All these rules, methods, and institutions for regularizing and regulating the international political processes are insufficient — not because they lack scope but because they are ineffective. They were created to make international behavior more predictable and regular. And there is no denying that they have somewhat ameliorated the basic weaknesses of the international political system. They have served as safety valves in times of tension and hostility. There is every likelihood, for instance, that the possibility of bringing an international conflict before the Security Council (and receiving praise for doing so) has enabled states to forgo a demonstration of their military prowess by going to war over it. They can prevent conflicts from escalating into violent confrontations. They may even contribute to a peaceful solution of conflicts or to the moderation of violent solutions. But the uncertainties making the international order so unreliable apply to these processes as well. They can be initiated — or not — by states whose identity is unpredictable and under conditions whose nature is undefinable. Arbitrariness, happenstance, and even accident remain likely possibilities in the initiating and ending of the processes, as well as in their formulation while they are in progress. There are no guarantees to permit states the secure expectation that they will be followed as suggested or prescribed.

These processes fail to produce the regularity, uniformity, and predictability which are the major ingredients of social order. Only the will of states can assure the use of these processes toward maintaining order, yet this same will can also produce the opposite. This is so because in contrast to the understanding among citizens that the whole shall prevail over the parts, the understanding among states is that the parts shall prevail over the whole. In the implementation of these understandings, the citizens have granted their government the necessary power, and states retain it in the international society. The organizational expression of the political system's inadequacy is this management of power by states individually. The international political system will continue to have its present form as long as states want to reap the benefits from their individual possession of power. The nature of power, the manner of its management, and the social consequences of both can supply a far-reaching explanation of the political system's objective features and their major contribution to the system's inadequacies.

4 The Role of Power

THE INSISTENCE of states upon their sovereignty makes quite clear why power is such a crucial factor in international politics. Without power sovereignty has no substance. The autonomy in deciding their own fate at which states are aiming makes the possession of power indispensable for its realization. Virtually without exception, the goals pursued by one state are never entirely acceptable by another, if they are not opposed outright. The deciding state therefore has to use power to have its goal accepted, while the antagonized states have to use power to frustrate these goals. Unless some political decision is based upon complete consensus, its binding force rests upon the power backing it.

There are many elements creating power and many means to apply it. They can range from charisma to guns, and from friendly persuasion to brutal coercion. But the use of power always has as its purpose to give binding force to a state's decision — either imposing a demand or opposing a demand. However morally damnable the use of power may be, if states have the sovereign right to make their own political decisions this right must include the use of power to make them binding. There is no other way of providing meaning to sovereignty as long as states must safeguard their own interests. And since it is unpredictable what the exercise of sovereignty may substantively require from time to time, states must possess a power potential for all eventualities.

This situation highlights the contradictory nature of the formal international political system with its foundation on sovereignty. It implies, on the one hand, that states are free to exercise and enforce their rights. But, on the other hand, it is also inevitable that such an exercise is bound to lead to

99

conflicts which can only be settled through the curtailment of such rights. Since no state has ever been known to abandon its own rights in any situation on a truly voluntary basis, the uniquely important role of power is an inherent part of the contemporary international political system. It is quite independent of the likes and dislikes of states; of the reasons why states seek power, whether as an end or as a means to many ends; and of the moral judgments that are made of it as "evil power politics." States have at best some influence upon the role power should be permitted to play in their affairs or upon its means and methods. They have no influence upon power playing a major role, since this is determined by the nature of the system states are maintaining in combination with the nature of power. The proper understanding of the role of power therefore requires an examination of its nature; the consequences of this nature for the international political system; and the result these consequences have for the behavior of states.

The Nature of Power

The essential nature of power can best be understood as an interaction between persons in which one side is able to affect the behavior of the other side in a desired manner. The interaction can be face to face or mediated. The channels of mediation can vary greatly. They are equivalent to the international processes: diplomacy, propaganda, and pressure. Their aim is always the same. One side aims at producing a certain behavior by the other side while the other side either behaves or does not behave as desired. In rare historical cases, direct mechanical control has been used to produce the desired behavior (e.g., abduction of a leader to change government personnel, or threats against the life of a diplomat in order to get him to sign a document). Almost always a crucial psychological element enters the power relationship. It serves as a transmission belt between the application of power and the resulting behavior. The person exercising power places the target person (or persons) into a psychological condition which results in the desired behavior. The psychological element is an indispensable link in the chain of power relationships. The key factor of power can thus be considered to be psychological. To illustrate from the realm of international politics: a state blockades another state in order to place the population in such a position that its government feels obliged to behave in the desired manner; a state creates prestige for itself so that it gains influence in the decision-making process of another state; a state assists another state in order to create a sense of obligation which can later be exploited. No matter how a power relationship is defined (e.g., as an exchange situation between two sides in which they bargain over advantages and disadvantages; as a coercive situation in which one side insists on unconditional surrender; as an attraction of one state for another) or what means are used in the application of power, psychology remains the key factor of power as far as its effectiveness is concerned.

For this reason, too, dealing with states as entities and abstracting them from individuals can only result in incomplete analyses. Those responsible for applying a state's power and those reacting to the application are vital factors in determining why states act as they do. There is a possibility of assuming that some of their behavior is based upon their cultural environment and some upon objective conditions of their state. It is possible also to trace some of their behavior to the nature of the international system. But the impact of these external elements has limits. It may result in the creation of general, but never specific, patterns of behavior. It cannot fully explain the actions of states. There is always some leeway for the influence of the personalities of those responsible for the state's behavior. Their perceptions, motivations, attitudes, emotions are unique and sufficiently influential to make specific state behavior unpredictable. This uncertainty created by the psychological aspects of power has a crucial effect upon the role power plays in international politics.

Power and the Political System

Several consequences of these psychological aspects of power for the international political system can be distinguished. The first is that a psychological process cannot be seen. The existence of a power relationship is not easily recognizable from the outside. Even those objectively involved (passively) in the relationship cannot always be sure that they are involved. Relationships between two states may be perceived by one as not involving power and by the other as involving attempts at influencing its own or the other state's behavior. When, for instance, the Netherlands gives aid to Indonesia, the Dutch government may simply wish to clear its people's conscience from guilt feelings about former colonialism. In Indonesia there may be a widespread suspicion of Dutch neocolonialism.

A second consequence is that power is not a quantity of anything.[26] It cannot be accumulated. A state cannot "have power" in the abstract. A state can only "have power" over another state, namely, when it is able

101

to make that state behave according to its own desire. This makes "having power" by a state a matter completely relative to the target state whose behavior is to be affected. Popular talk about a state being "powerful" means no more than an assumption that such a state can very likely influence the behavior of many other states. And it can only mean that such a state can produce sentiments, attitudes, motivations among key groups in those other states so that they will behave in a certain, desired manner. Power is not a zero sum matter. The increased ability of one state to influence other states is not necessarily achieved through the corresponding "amount" of disability by some other states. In fact, and this is a third consequence, two states can simultaneously "have power" over each other, for instance the United States over the Soviet Union in Cuba and the Soviet Union over the United States in East Berlin. This possibility exists because states have a variety of interests on any one of which they may agree or disagree but which in any case they can pursue individually and separately. The greater the number of these interests — which are tokens of influence — the better can the power relationships between two states be balanced and the less likely is a relationship of total hostility or total friendship between them. These kinds of situations can be found among all states of the world. There is no way of drawing up a balance sheet to arrive at some figure indicating "how much more powerful" sum total one state is over another. Such a balance sheet would in any case be unfeasible in view of the complex network of relationships cutting across the globe. Through multilateralism and overlapping and crosscutting, many states are exerting power upon each other directly (bilaterally) and indirectly (through multilateral relationships), with each situation affecting every other simultaneously and also serving as feedback for newly developing situations. A whole complex of action-reaction processes exists at all times and power play is involved in each of them. What may have begun as a reaction by one state to another becomes immediately itself action in regard to a third state, provoking the third state's reaction and so forth in an unending chain. The interminable maneuverings of the European states between 1870 and 1914, with their ever-changing alliance systems, group formations, and balancing acts are a good illustration.

The fourth consequence flowing from the nature of power is that in addition to the incalculability of the psychological factor many of the means are also incalculable, and many of the methods by which they are used are totally unpredictable in their effect. Among the imponderable means are morale, stamina, persuasion whose effects in active exertion of power or its passive endurance cannot be measured. The same method is not always equally effective. It can have different effects upon the psyche depending upon the situation or the relationship in which it is used; or depending upon the decision-making process in the target country and the individuals participating in it. Moreover, the means and the methods are culture-bound in their effectiveness. Effectiveness can change with the changing interests motivating men. If, for instance, economic growth becomes more important to men than national grandeur, military power may become a less important tool than an influential role in the world's currency system. (Switzerland may yet be a mighty nation!) These uncertainties make it impossible for a state in building up its power potential to know what its real magnitude is until it is actualized in a concrete situation. At best, some of the measurable factors (weapons, industrial output, size of population) make a partial calculation possible without however permitting any reliable forecast of what the behavior of the target might be. There always remains a large element of chance no matter how uneven the power potential between two states may appear to be, an element which is further increased by alliances or their break-up.

Power and the Inadequacy of the Political System

All these characteristics of power are most conducive to making the international political system inadequate to its task. There are several effects which have never been managed successfully by the system and which, in combination with sovereignty, probably cannot be managed properly. One of these is the undue importance power considerations assume in the international society. This, compared to other political systems, is a matter of degree, perhaps. But power is so pervasive that it colors the whole international society in all its aspects, which cannot be said of national or other societies. Another of these effects is the enhancement of uncertainty in the social order of the international society. To the unpredictability of decision-making is added the unpredictability of the effectiveness of the decision due both to the nature and to the dispersal of power in the international society. How are these deleterious effects produced?

First, the only certain way for a state to know whether it has power is to use its power potential. Success alone will tell which state was the "more powerful." No other means of telling this exist. If all power potentials could be measured, if for instance the outcome of a threat to use force by one state against another could be reliably predicted, wars could be fought by computers. Until such time, the practical test is the only sure method. For states believing themselves to be "more powerful," this represents a great temptation to push their interests to the point of testing their power against that of another state. The involvement in the Vietnam war proceeded upon the conviction in the American government that the defeat of the Communist forces would be a small matter for the "powerful" United States. In a national system the terminal point of a power conflict is normally located before the use of violence, because the state is reliably "more powerful." Any political contest is not likely to have the potential catastrophic consequences it possesses in the international system. While in national politics brinkmanship normally remains just that, in international politics it can develop into violent conflict.

Second, a deleterious effect results from the diffusion of decision-making and what this means for the role of power. The need for states to enforce their own decisions incites them to "maximize" power potentials. The greater the power potential is believed to be, the more secure does a state feel that it will be able to take care of its interests and enforce its political decisions, and the less does it have to count for survival on the voluntary incentives states may have to behave in an orderly and peaceful way.[27] But the problem is to know what maximizing power means when the power potential cannot be adequately measured and when any power potential is always relative to a particular state and its power potential. The maximum of the power potential is an unknown quantity. Ideally, it should be greater than that of any other state with which the state might potentially be in a relationship. Nowadays that can be every state, so that every state should try to possess the greatest power potential. Rationality and incapacity will prevent most states from striving to reach this position, but some are clearly trying. It should be obvious, even to them, that maximization becomes inevitably limitless as a condition and endless as a process.

Third, the combination between the nature of power and the diffusion of decision-making leads to the growth of a circular, self-contained process. The need for a state to develop its power potential as a means to some end becomes itself the end for developing a power potential. The simple reason is that the construction of a power potential creates conflicts of interest for whose solution power is needed and applied. The ultimate end for which a state may wish to acquire a power potential — maintaining social order, surviving, obtaining a share of the world's wealth — becomes quite irrelevant.

The Role of Power

The obvious answer to the frequent question whether states seek a power potential for its own sake or as a means to other ends is that they may do both. The further answer must be that since the search for a power potential requires a power potential every state must in any case seek to develop that potential. In this manner, the search for a power potential to solve possible future conflicts of interest may itself become the cause and substance of future conflict. Such a conflict over power in the abstract, regardless of its future uses, is possible because some instruments of power can be accumulated and stored, like money, to be used for future needs. The search for the means to exert influence creates the reason for that search. From the standpoint of the international political system there is no need to go further, especially no need to go into the motives behind the search for power potential. The activities in pursuit of a power potential are themselves the object of the political system's preoccupations. This is all the more true as the satisfaction of a state's particular interest in a given case does not end its continued search for a power potential. Motivation is of greater interest to the policy maker, the psychological strategist, or the propagandist who has to cope with specific aims of states.

The cold war may be taken as an illustration of the system's concerns with symptoms of behavior before it can devote itself to motivations. Much of the cold war has been a power struggle. The two major contestants had few concrete, immediate goals in conflict. Each was mainly concerned with expanding its sphere of influence, which is to say that each was primarily concerned with increasing its power potential in preparation for a moment when some of their concrete interests might be in conflict. When such a moment arrives and power is applied, it is as important for the state to succeed in taking care of the interest as it is to maintain credibility in its power potential. For this last reason a state having once committed power to the enforcement of a decision may go far beyond the original commitment not because the particular interest demands it, but because the rank of a powerful state demands it. "Escalation," such as that engineered by the United States in Vietnam, may be out of proportion to the actual interest involved but is triggered by the effort to prove a superior power potential. It is in the nature of power and its place within the international political system that the ends it is to serve are often less relevant than itself as an end. Every state's power potential augments the needs for a power potential.

Fourth, the absence of any effective restriction upon the use of tools of power and the need to maximize power potentials vastly expand the range of tools usable as power tools. In view of the vital importance of possessing a power potential sufficient to assure at least self-protection and survival, a state cannot forgo enlisting the assistance of anything which might enhance its influence with other states — and indeed the international political system does not in fact raise any barriers to such activity. Citizens within a state are relieved of these needs since no matter what they might enlist to increase their power potential they can never normally hope to match the overwhelming power potential of their state. And to preserve this ratio the political system does impose severe limitations upon the citizen's arsenal (e.g., no possession of firearms; no inciting to riot). Hence the pluralistic nature of national societies, representing a mixture of political and apolitical interests and activities, and the overly politicized nature of the international society.

Power and the Behavior of States

States have two ways to influence the political decisions and behavior of other states. Either they can create situations in which other states have no choice but to act in the desired manner, or they can try to affect the perceptions of a situation by the decision-makers in other states in the hope of producing the desired decisions. The underlying assumption behind this alternative is that the decision-makers have an area beyond systemic influences in which their choices are free and decisive. This area includes the basic decision on what demands a state will make upon others, how strongly it will push these demands or oppose those by others, and what tools will be used in the contest of power.

The question may well be asked why small or poor states participate in the competition for a power potential. They are obviously hopelessly outdistanced by many larger and richer states. Yet they all do, as, for instance, their military budgets show. Some of them even devote a disproportionate amount of their resources to this purpose.[28] These states tend to justify their extravagancies on several grounds. Power is a relative matter, they argue. Small states may command obedience from yet smaller states or, since power is not measurable, perhaps even from larger states on occasion. There may be a chance to pool power resources and act collectively. Or, even an estimated small power potential might bring concessions from "powerful" states under certain conditions. Not all political demands by a state are vital, for instance, and might be subject to compromise. The nuisance value of a small state gives it some veto value, dissuading a larger state from acting against the smaller state's interests. It often takes less power to prevent a result than positively to achieve one (as, for instance, during World War II, when the German general staff decided that an occupation of Switzerland would not be worth the cost). Or the favorable location of a state in the international political constellation of states (e.g., a nonaligned state being wooed by several competing states) [29] represents a power potential which could be increased by the state's additional means of power. Or, finally, some power potential may enable any state to benefit from a change in world politics which increases its freedom of action as a result of the inability or unwillingness of the "atomic powers" to use their super-strength. As will be shown, the very existence of the "super weapons" restored the value of the more traditional weapons as components of a power potential, providing a new incentive to all states to acquire them, and improving their possibilities in the international political system. Under the "atomic umbrella" of their respective protector states, small states can fight wars with each other secure in the knowledge that more-powerful outsiders will no longer interfere. The great paradox has arisen that the predominant concern of the major powers to prevent violence among themselves has enabled the smaller powers to use it in the settlement of their conflicts.

The enormous inequalities among states are a fact no government will overlook. The widespread and quite justified fear of imperialism, neo-imperialism, or some other variant of outside domination testifies to that concern. But many governments of states below the top of the hierarchy have argued that the most powerful states, being the major beneficiaries and therefore effective supporters of the prevailing political system, force these less-powerful states to exploit the situation as best they can, even vis-à-vis each other, and that this requires maintenance of some power potential, however limited. Included in this potential of the weak are the constraints upon the use of power built into any social system, hence the endeavor of the smaller states to improve the effectiveness of international organizations or at least to utilize them as much as possible for their own benefit.

All states, small and large alike, are subject to some extent to the dictates of the international system. Insofar as they cherish their existence, they will subscribe to the system but will also be subject to the need of building a power potential. This is the area in which they have no choice. Nor do they have a choice in weighing all matters from the standpoint of their relevance to the power potential — their own or that of other states. For this reason the politicization of the international society is not really a matter of choice

107

for states. The borderline between what is Caesar's and what is not, is not only difficult to draw, but virtually does not exist. Behavior as well as things are all subject to the scrutiny of states for their relationship to power potentials, and rightly so because they can all affect the psyche of men. The result of this scrutiny is an essentially subjective matter. The ostensible purpose of a state's actions or anything else may have little relevance to the evaluation in terms of power potential another state makes of them. Every state has its own standards by which it measures its freedom of action, absence of restraint, or ability to influence other states or be influenced by them. This is another reason why motivation behind a state's behavior is not necessarily relevant to other states. It may be only one item entering into the evaluation process of other states. There is good reason for this. Actions have latent results not intended or even foreseen by the acting state, yet affecting other states. Stockpiling raw materials for the production of peaceful consumer goods may from the standpoint of another state improve the stockpiling state's military capability. This is simply another aspect of the fact that virtually everything can be evaluated in terms of a power potential and is so evaluated in the international society.

The most extreme consequence of the comprehensiveness of the tools of power is that the very existence of a state is by itself a power factor. No state today can avoid this quality and any attempt to do so (by isolationism, nonalignment, etc.) is condemned to failure from the beginning. The role any one state may play as a power factor can vary greatly. Obviously a big, rich state is bound to play a different role from a small, poor state removed from major centers of global politics. It is also possible for a state to make much or little of its very existence. But the basic fact remains that the existence of the state makes it a power factor. That this can be a source of frustration is shown by the wish expressed by one of Burma's prime ministers for atomic scissors with which to cut his country off the Asian mainland and ship it to a remote place in the Pacific Ocean!

When everything can serve to increase the power potential of a state, the hesitancy of states to surrender control over anything becomes very understandable. They wish to grant as little influence, i.e., power, to an international agency as possible. They tend to interpret international agreements narrowly. They make concessions most reluctantly. They are most parsimonious in making political commitments and very cautious even in making concessions to functional arrangements because their political implications are not always clear. When, for instance, the World Postal Union was first created, France tried to obtain political advantages in return for her membership (but soon surrendered, of course, because nonmembership was a powerful sanction). Always concerned that anything surrendered or abandoned might diminish the power potential, states not only want to retain everything but wish, when finally forced to make concessions, to cede as little as possible and to make whatever they cede as specific and circumscribed as possible. Adding to their concern is the fact that what is customarily done may turn into a legal norm — and states do not gladly add to their legal obligations. Therefore, the more specific and unique, the less "political" the subject matter of an agreement is, the easier it is to reach agreement. For this reason it is impossible to reach formal agreement on a power struggle (such as that represented, for instance, by the cold war). The relative success of the public international unions (such as the Universal Postal Union) compared to the limited achievements of political agencies is witness to this behavior pattern.

The international political system finds itself once again in a vicious circle. The diffusion of decision-making leads to the politicization of the international society, including the universal usefulness of everything for the power potential. This universality makes states cautious about transferring resources, functions, or jurisdictions to a central international organ. The absence of such an organ, in turn, is responsible for the universality of the tools of power. Of all the things forming the power potential, states are least willing to transfer the means of physical violence. These remain among the most important and effective components of power potential and they are, of course, at the same time the greatest threat to the social order. So much is this the case that often physical strength is used synonymously with power.

Power and Strength

The overwhelming importance of physical violence as an instrument of power has produced the argument that the birth of atomic weapons and the surfeit of physical violence have altered the quality of power and therewith the nature of international politics. This argument may be valid in its assumption that atomic weapons will not be used and that the denial by a state to itself of an instrument of power is indeed an innovation. Not so cogent seems to be the conclusion that the role of power or the nature of international politics has changed to make either of these factors qualitatively different

109

from earlier times. Any significant change seems to be not so much toward innovation as toward the restoration of multipolarity which was typical of the international system during the past several centuries.

What precise effect the arrival of atomic weapons may have had upon international politics is difficult to evaluate, mainly because the conditions producing these weapons have simultaneously produced general technological and social changes. The major organizational arrangement relating to the new weaponry has been the banning of atmospheric nuclear tests, a nonproliferation treaty among some of the possessors of atomic capability, and the limitation of some strategic arms by the Soviet Union and the United States. Otherwise there have been no notable structural changes in international politics. There have, however, been some changes in the behavior of states leading to some redistribution of power potentials. This reallocation, paradoxically, has favored the smaller states more than the largest states. These changes can be seen in the behavior patterns of the United States and the Soviet Union toward each other as well as in the behavior patterns of these two nations toward the rest of the states.

The United States and the Soviet Union are clearly trying to avoid violent conflicts in their bilateral relations. Wars they might have fought in the past are replaced by a cold war — an extension of the area of nonviolent conflict. They have had either to abandon some purposes formerly achieved by war or to find alternative means for their achievement. The nature of atomic weaponry has made the traditional relationship of force to diplomacy very uncertain. Traditionally force and violence have been employed to assist diplomacy in pursuit of national goals, but when force includes self-destruction it becomes obviously useless. The problem of the United States and the Soviet Union is how to convert the new weapons into tools of politics. Since they are unlikely either to employ or to destroy these weapons, they must, in groping for a political equivalent to war, make their new weaponry politically harmless or useful. How long this need will continue is doubtful, because the technologization and automation of aggression and defense systems increasingly withdraw major military action from political control. Once any part of the deterrence system breaks down, or once the first shot has been fired, there is no time left for political decision, let alone political action. Even now the marginal utility of these modern weapons as a power tool is so low that the United States and the Soviet Union have aimed at excluding them from their arsenal of applied power by agreeing to deter each other from using them. This agreement has largely restored the possibility

110

of dealing with each other in the manner of the pre-atomic era (while at the same time maintaining their superiority by persuading other states not to develop their new weaponry!). A very significant difference from the pre-atomic era results however from the new weaponry. The agreement not to use the weapons rests upon self-enforcement and the absence of accidents. It also rests upon the effectiveness of deterrence, which is, once again, an unmeasurable psychological matter. Deterrence can work only if there is fear of the new weapons and a belief that the opponent would use them in an emergency. The uncertainty about whether the agreement will be kept and whether the psychological state exists has made both nations cautious about initiating any chain of events that might risk either a breakdown of the agreement or certainty about the nonexistence of the psychological state. The other states of the world have become minor beneficiaries of this new behavior.

Outside the bilateral relations between the United States and the Soviet Union, much of the traditional world political behavior continues. The large number of wars fought across the globe since 1945 indicates that the use of violence for the settlement of conflicts or the maintenance of hegemony has not been abandoned. Traditional institutions like satellite states, buffer zones, and spheres of influence remain primary foreign policy goals. An argument can be made very convincingly, for instance, that the so-called bipolarity in world politics and thereafter the tripolarity are replications of very traditional struggles for spheres of influence. Such political pursuits seem quite unaffected by the American or Soviet ability to destroy any state of the world from thousands of miles away. Even the use of war as a political tool continues. Atomic weaponry may have affected which wars are to be fought. It may, in particular, have led to the avoidance of direct confrontation between the Americans and the Soviets. Imperialist wars aiming at territorial conquest or obliteration of a state are very much out of fashion. The birth of atomic weapons has hastened a process which began much earlier when cheaper and internationally more acceptable (because more disguisable) means for dominating states were developed. Major physical threats to states have become either interventionist wars in which strong outsiders use internal factions for their own purposes or vicarious wars in which outsiders permit smaller states to make war upon each other or actually pit them against each other, often as pawns. In either case, outsiders have to rely on insiders, and they cannot or do not want to use their major power tools, thus enhancing relatively the material and political components of the small states' power potential. Their defensive power is increased. Their physical survival is virtually assured. The chance is improved that by their own efforts they can restrain the imperialist enterprises of the major nations. In physical terms the balance of power between the major nations is transferred, in effect, to their satellites and pawns, which thereby find their political maneuverability improved. The defiance by several small states (Cuba, North Vietnam, Czechoslovakia, Albania) of the United States and the Soviet Union, not to mention political activities among smaller states themselves and against each other, shows the enlargement of their freedom of action as compared to that of the major powers, which has diminished.

There are other developments balancing the growing formal physical strength of the "atomic powers" which help to explain their actual lessening control of the smaller states. First, the highly developed technology in the armory of the major powers makes them quite helpless under some conditions, so that their means can be circumvented, for instance, through guerrilla warfare or civil disobedience campaigns. Second, the same technology that adds to the strength of the rich states also enables the poorer states to engage in some not too costly new activities, such as radio propaganda, or to play more important roles in international communications. Third, the growth of vertical communication within states (e.g., the democratization of policy making) has extended into the international sphere (e.g., "world public opinion") and has broken down the traditional separation between internal and external policies. Revolutionary ideologies or charismatic leadership can originate in the smallest, weakest states and create upheavals in every part of the globe. The expectations governments had to raise in their publics (often hypocritically) in order to obtain the necessary mass support for their policies are now cutting across frontiers and cannot easily be disappointed without risk to the governments themselves. The "war aims" announced during the two world wars, for instance, may not have been taken too seriously by those announcing them. They were effective, nevertheless, in arousing mass attitudes and mass demands, with the result that many of them became reality. This was true in regard to very specific institutions such as colonialism and racial equality, as well as to the whole climate in which international politics have to be conducted — for instance, an egalitarianism which has outmoded territorial imperialism and which makes the use of physical superiority more difficult than in the past. Finally, as economic goals increase in value everywhere and economic manipulations thereby gain a greatly enhanced importance as political tools, the importance of physical strength is relatively reduced. The American and Soviet ability to "overkill" mankind loses political effectiveness. The paradoxical function of the major instruments of destruction is mainly to prevent their use by their very existence. They make no impressive addition to the Soviet and American political power potential, while that of physically weaker but economically significant states grows.

These behavior patterns are symptomatic of the general phenomenon that enormously growing discrepancies in some components of power among states have not been accompanied by similar discrepancies in the controls some states have over others. In particular, physical strength as a tool of power is not as significant as it was formerly. In the relations between states with the greatest power potentials, this enforces recourse to nonviolent means. In other relations, the application of strength has to be modified, away from direct use in favor of vicarious use. Imperialist control has to be established and maintained by substitute means which are less crude and obvious (e.g., subtle economic domination, neocolonialism instead of colonialism) and which benefit the dominated at least to the extent that their physical integrity remains untouched. That this may also enhance political independence to some extent — especially in a slightly more liberalized international atmosphere — is evidenced by the break-up of colonial empires, the possibility of nonaligned postures, disengagement (more or less) from membership in blocs, effective caucusing in international organizations. Some of the new and weak states may not agree that their political independence is real until it is backed by substantial economic development. But they cannot deny that their formal political autonomy now enables them to agitate and work for substantive autonomy where formerly they were denied even this opportunity.

These changes in relative power potentials, caused largely by the uselessness of super-strength, prove, as was pointed out before, that the effectiveness of the components of the power potential (e.g., atomic weapons) is not just an inherent quality of these components. The effectiveness also depends upon the total context in which the components are used. The ends to be achieved, the character of the relationships between the states in question, the acute constellation of the international facts, the nature of the prevailing international culture, the internal situation of states — all are important codeterminants. These codeterminants were changed by the same innovations that changed modern weaponry, so that in interaction each helped sometimes to neutralize, sometimes to reinforce, the effect of the other. In sum, physical

113

strength as a component of power was diminished in effectiveness, leading to emphasis upon less radical means in the relations between states. At the same time, state behavior has become even less predictable because exactly those components of the power potential which were the most calculable have become less effective; and world politics has become more complex because a number of states previously too weak physically to count can now enter the scene as influential factors.

To the difficulties of measuring power or some of its components must then be added the variability in the efficiency of the components, for this depends upon many factors quite extraneous to the inherent qualities of the components themselves. The form of the power to be applied by a state will be quite unpredictable in view of all these uncertainties. Its choice is a very subjective matter. It depends upon the decision-maker's estimate of what instruments might be the most favorable under all the given circumstances in a situation. And the range of choice among all the instruments and their combinations is enormous. Power becomes the resultant of such a vast complex of variable and subjectively evaluated factors that knowledge of the important role power plays in international politics is not enough either to explain completely the international behavior of states in general or to predict a specific behavior in a given situation. Nor can power explain why states cherish sovereignty, though once they decided to cherish it the general role power must play in the international system becomes explainable. It then becomes clear also that the eternal concern of states with their power potential is one important, perhaps the most important, motivation of their international behavior. But this motivation is only a derivative of the previous question as to why states insist upon sovereignty, why the peoples of the world are prepared to pay such a horrendous price for it. Raising this question brings this analysis to its most crucial part.

Up to this point in the analysis, the inquiry has focused on how states behave. In investigating this aspect of international politics it turned out that within limits the political system, i.e., the political interaction patterns, imposes certain restraints upon its members, either obliging them to act or not to act in certain ways. The system itself can therefore also answer in part the question why people act in a certain way. But it can do so only in regard to behavior within the system itself. It can not adequately answer the question regarding the behavior that lies outside the system, that, so to speak, precedes the system and creates it and maintains it. Assuming that people have a large margin of choice regarding the kind of social system or political system they wish to establish (and such an assumption is made here) the fundamental question must be answered, if possible, why they have chosen the international political system that prevails, and why they keep maintaining or changing it? The answer will disclose the human foundation of the international political system and the roots of international politics.

5 The Subjective Foundation of the International Political System

THE NATURE OF the international political system is not accidental. It results from national wills. Its weaknesses are known and accepted as the price of sovereignty and its consequences. Not all members of the society suffer equally from these weaknesses, though they all acknowledge their existence. Those states at the greatest disadvantage — normally small and weak states — could be expected to be more opposed to the system than those who reap some benefits from it. But this is empirically not the case. On the contrary, many small states and especially the new ones often voice more support for a system of sovereign, independent states than some of the older, richer, and larger states. The states of South and Southeast Asia, for instance, find it much more difficult than do those of Western Europe to organize themselves into a regional combination, even though such a grouping does not necessarily involve any "surrender of sovereignty."

In the final analysis no state is prepared for such a surrender. In this respect the social behavior of all states is remarkably alike. Their main complaint usually is that the system is not effective enough to assure them their full share of sovereignty. Those weak states at whose expense the stronger states often benefit from the system have never yet asked for a change in the basic features of the system. They only wish to make them work more equitably, for instance by strengthening international organizations or other collective arrangements. They are likely to be quite aware that their insistence upon an international political system based on sovereignty and their demand for the fullest preservation of their own sovereign equality is a contradiction. But this awareness does not lead them to abandon either their insistence or their demand. The collectivized wills of states coincide on maintaining

116

the principle of sovereignty as the basic principle of the political system. They all willingly make the necessary sacrifices, indicating thereby that possessing sovereignty provides some powerful satisfaction to those who demand it. These satisfactions must ultimately be psychological, since all transactions in the international political system are human transactions. They are rooted in some human sentiments, attitudes, wills, predispositions — individual or collective. They are indicative, specifically, of a psychological commitment to a hierarchy of interests at whose apex stands the state. Indeed, all the behavior of states points to this crucial psychological dimension of the international political system. Every attitude poll confirms it when "national" indicators are juxtaposed with "international" indicators.[30] Every social and most individual decisions confirm it when a national interest is in conflict with an international interest.

The sentiments and attitudes backing the whole international system can easily enough be inferred from some of the system's institutions when these are not described, as is usually the case, as some self-contained mechanism independent of human beings, but when they are described as reflections of human wills. For instance, the lack of world government means the refusal to have political issues decided by others, or the wish to make them nationally. The use of force in settling disputes is the unwillingness to exclude this means from the arsenal of power tools. Playing a balance of power game may indicate readiness to sacrifice other states to the interest of one's own. Similarly, the existence of sovereignty results from the unwillingness of the world's peoples to abandon it. Put into social terms, and positively, the world's peoples insist upon a type of interrelations which can summarily be described as characteristic of sovereignty. These interrelations could be changed by the will of these peoples to become characteristic of something else. There appears to be no desire to do so, which is to say that the prevailing psychology produces the interrelations characterized as sovereignty. This psyche of peoples, meaning the sum total, synthesized emotional and rational activities of their citizens, is crucial in determining the nature of the international political system.

In reality no two individuals share the same psychology. It is also true that in every state the psychology of some people or groups does not support sovereignty. Strictly speaking, a collective psyche does not exist. But it is also part of reality that types of psychologies can be abstracted sufficiently to subsume under the abstraction the individual psyche of groups of people sufficiently large or influential so that the abstracted, collectivized psychology

117

becomes predominant in a society, yet remains specific enough to lead to certain types of social behavior. This is the situation in all states regarding the psychology producing the behavior patterns and cross-national relationships symbolized by sovereignty. The central element of this psyche, which types it, is the emotional component known as nationalism.

The Nationalist

A nationalist is a person whose sentiments are devoted to the state as his highest value. This may historically not always have been true. At different periods or different places nationalism served different purposes. It began as a liberation movement from the supervision of the state by the Church and switched to a liberation movement of the people from absolute monarchs. At times it helped maintain popular rights against attacks from the outside or by expanding them abroad. At other times it contributed to the maintenance of national traditional institutions, whatever their character. But whatever the particular aim, the state always was the primary tool for its achievement. And so, not surprisingly, the usefulness of the state made it a desirable end in its own right. Virtually simultaneously with the rise of nationalism, its major characteristic was emotionalism devoted to the maintenance of the state as the highest value.

The rise of nationalism shows that a nationalist is created, not born. His state makes him what he is in order to perpetuate itself. The only natural part in the creation of a nationalist is that every individual has human characteristics allowing him to become a nationalist. His emotional potential can be geared toward and actualized by the state — not any particular form of state, but any state. From the standpoint of the international political system, the important feature of nationalism is that it can most effectively mobilize social resources and efforts by emotional appeals which sustain the state's efforts to oppose any political influences from the outside while supporting the state's influence upon other states. For these ends the nationalist is willing to give his life. There are virtually no other social ends toward which sacrifices of such magnitude are made so (relatively) readily by such a large number of persons everywhere. The nationalist becomes by this quality the ultimate source and embodiment of the international political system and the key to understanding the nature and functioning of international politics.

The process of the nationalist's creation begins with the day of his birth.

118

The groundwork for making him a nationalist has been laid before nationhood and what that concept implies have any rational meaning for him.[31] The great variation in the traits, motivations, sentiments, and attitudes from individual to individual notwithstanding, the end product in the shape of a nationalist is remarkably alike across the globe. Nor does the diversity of cultural backgrounds make any noticeable difference. It has been claimed that Asian and African nationalisms are distinct from Western nationalism. What may be distinct are the demands Asians and Africans make of the international society. Naturally, the citizens of the "have" nations see no reason to ask for a greater share in the world's wealth, while many Asian and African citizens have excellent reason to do so. But the nationalism backing these demands, that is to say the sentiments relating to the rights and privileges of the states involved, are essentially the same. Nationalism lends itself equally well to the defense of a state's acquired high position and to a state's demand for a better position. Even the basic techniques for developing the individual into a nationalist and the gratifications held out to him as an inducement resemble each other across the globe, though their specific forms may occasionally assume the color of a particular culture. Where, as will be shown soon, in some of the newer states the techniques or gratifications are as yet inadequately available, the development of nationalists is difficult, much to the chagrin of the nation's nationalist leaders.

The uniformity of nationalist sentiments — their objects, their goals, their expressions, and above all the social behavior they produce or support — makes their genesis rather puzzling. Some very sophisticated attempts have been made to explain nationalism on psychological grounds, such as displaced aggression (instead of using one's own society as the object of aggression, one uses another society), or as the predispositions of a given personality structure, or as an expression of personal security or insecurity and a need for identity.[32] Other attempts aim at sociological explanations, such as social transmission of stereotypes from generation to generation, or the results of ingroup versus outgroup relationships. Most of these explanations sound quite convincing and it is likely that nationalism and the nationalist are resultants of a variety of such root causes and their combination. In the light of the basic similarity of nationalisms everywhere, there is no need to explain every one through national conditions. Indeed, the more that explanations of nationalism try to rely on particular cultures or their detailed aspects, or on particular social systems and very special customs, the weaker becomes their convincing power. The universality of the phenomenon would indicate that it has general roots so that discovering them would provide the most economical and useful explanation.[33]

But before this discovery can be attempted, a caveat must be introduced. Not every person behaving like a nationalist is necessarily a nationalist. He may be only a national. He is a citizen of his state acting in conformity with the behavior usually expected from a citizen toward other states and their citizens. To a very large extent his behavior coincides with that of the nationalist. What differentiates him is that he may not share the sentiments, or all of them, or their intensity, which motivate the nationalist. He acquiesces in, rather than enthusiastically supports, national behavior, or he may even occasionally oppose it. There are a number of reasons why the behavior typical of the nationalist has become typical of the citizen in general. There is, first of all, history. During the creation of modern states, the behavior to sustain them had to be made very explicit. The citizens' reason and sentiments were enlisted in its support, and this process is quite visible now in the new states of Asia and Africa. Once the states were formed and their existence was taken for granted, nationalist emotions could be reserved for moments of crisis, as they now are in well-established states. At those moments, special strains, tensions, sacrifices among the citizenry may weaken loyalty to the country. The required supportive behavior may not be forthcoming. Then the emotional support of the state needs special reinforcement. Nationalist conditioning aims at supplying it. Nationalist conditioning does not aim primarily to keep behavior constantly on a high emotional pitch. It aims rather to form a predisposition in the citizen to react in a nationalist manner when a challenge to the state's existence arises. In this way nationalism can be considered as one of the tools of power in the state's arsenal, to be mobilized for internal or external purposes in times of need (and to be kept in good repair while in storage). Thus, behavior supportive of the state has become historically established, without necessarily at all times being based upon acutely effective emotions.

A second reason for the predominance of nationalist behavior is the missionary quality of the nationalist. His strong feelings and enthusiasm impose his pattern of behavior upon his whole national society. To behave like a nationalist is the accepted way of behaving. Social pressure has so far always and everywhere been in favor of the nationalist. A deviator is immediately on the defensive.

A third reason has to do with the interests of those, the nationals, who may not share the nationalists' emotions but who behave like them nevertheless. They do so because their own positions and conditions are intimately tied up with the existence of the state. This may be so because their (privileged) class interest depends upon the existence of their state, because their livelihood (officials!) is related to the state and nationalism facilitates their tasks, or because their economic survival depends upon their state. At any rate their interests demand the maintenance of the state. They support it, not necessarily with their own intense emotional investment, but tolerating and occasionally furthering that of others. To conclude from this that most nationalist behavior is imposed by a (cynical) minority, that given free choice there would be very few nationalists, is to flout history. Indeed there are some striking examples of cases where an elite favored internationalism but was obliged to adopt a nationalist stance for themselves and their peoples: the peace of Brest-Litovsk, Stalin's formulation of Socialism in one country, the strategy of the Third International, the tactic of the United Front, Liu Shao-chi's "proletarian patriotism," and the behavior of many European socialist parties which nationalized mostly themselves. The point here is not to deny that some nationalist behavior may be imposed, but to clarify that much of it is solidly founded in the psyche of vast sections of many peoples.

The significance of the coexistence of the national with the nationalist is twofold. First, the emotional foundation of a state may not be as firm as it appears to be from an examination of the visible social behavior of the citizenry. Second (as will be seen), the elements going into the creation of the nationalist are neither immutable nor eternal. They are subject to change, mainly as a result of changing conditions in the environment of the state. The influence of the national is to facilitate or even hasten these changes. Therefore, even though the nation-state system carries the imprint of its nationalist foundation, it may be more a "survival" than is commonly believed. Emotional attachments to it may become fragile. The form no longer fully corresponds to the substance. The system may be amenable to manipulation if a determined effort to alter it is undertaken.

The Making of the Nationalist: Habit Formation

Three elements can be discovered in the development of the nationalist, distinctive enough to serve as categories for analysis. They are the nationalist's habits, rationality, and emotions. All three play a role definable with some accuracy. The effect of their interplay, however, and their individual and collective impact upon the making of the nationalist cannot as yet be measured.

Living in a social environment produces a habitual behavior. The systemic influence upon behavior is the strongest here. Habitual behavior is an important part of the individual's integration into his society and essential to the existence of any society. Social coexistence is largely built upon habitual forms of behavior supporting the regularities and expectations vital for the perpetuation of the society. The habit-forming qualities of social behavior and the social-behavior-forming qualities of habit reinforce each other. Both are indispensable for predictability, hence for social order.

Nations in their formative stage, and thereafter to maintain themselves, create the kinds of habits familiar as national behavior in order to overcome internal parochialism or regional loyalties, and in order to achieve identity among other external societies. When sentiments are added to this behavior, it becomes nationalist behavior. Once nationalist behavior patterns are set for the individual at an early age, citizenship with its benefits and duties, nationality and the relationships it requires with nationals of other states, become much of the time unquestioned, if not enthusiastically sustained, parts of modern social existence. The rites, symbols, pressures, rewards, punishments, and paraphernalia employed in this socialization process vary in detail from country to country. But they serve the same purpose everywhere, and quite successfully.

The habitual nationalist pattern of social behavior is predominant in old and new states. The state is built on habit, contended Sir Henry Maine. Harold Laski asserted that social order rests on the ''inert acceptance of orders obeyed without scrutiny.'' Like most other social units, the state must rely for its existence on the habits of its citizens. If they behave in accordance with custom and traditional practice, the coherence of the national society is assured. There is no need to recreate the requisite behavior from case to case as the need arises. The society renews itself from day to day, from generation to generation. The social behavior becomes routine. It runs on its own motion. The tendency is to embody all habits and customs into enforceable norms, some of a moral kind, others — mainly those considered crucial for the society's survival — of a legal kind. Indeed, the validity of moral and legal norms lies in the final analysis not in the sanctions behind them but in obedience to them by their addressees. Moral rules as well as customary law originate from habitual behavior and turn it into prescribed behavior. Deviation from social norms usually brings disadvantages, criticism, ostracism, even punishment, but especially so when it relates to nationalist

122

behavior. The sanctions are strong (a traitor to his country is shot) because the need for conformist behavior is great if the much-wanted state is to survive. The overall result is a hardening of nationalist behavior patterns, and therein lies a risk to the society.

There is a danger to the society unless the habitual behavior pattern is flexible enough to allow for change, rigid enough to prevent chaos and insecurity. Failure to adapt to new conditions offsets the benefits of habitual behavior by the cost of resisting innovation. On the other hand, when habitual behavior can no longer produce the expected results, anxiety may initially harden resistance to innovation even more. The wish to avoid the effort of acquiring new ways of thinking and behaving gives rise to the pretense that everything can remain as it was and can be handled in the traditional manner. A lag occurs between man's new environment and his ability to cope with it. Such a lag exists between contemporary international relations and the prevailing international politics. Quite obviously an international political behavior inspired by the nationalist assumption of strict separation of states cannot cope with international relations now producing a society whose members function in close interaction and coordination during times of friendship as well as hostility.

Nevertheless, changes are taking place in the habitual behavior of the nationalist. It has become obvious to even the most ardent nationalist that realization of his interests — even his nationalist interests, such as the sovereign survival of his state — requires behavior patterns of himself and his state which only a few decades ago would have been decried as traitorous. He now either tolerates them or actively supports them. The environmental and systemic factors, as well as the personal needs of the citizen which originally gave rise to existing habits, are continually changing, mostly in the direction of "internationalization." Inevitably, the habits will change with them. The basic forms of nationalist behavior are continuing, as are the practices molding them. But new forms are arising next to them, in coexistence, or even replacing some of them. And the content of these forms is changing as well. The overall appearance of international relations is assuming new shapes. It is, for instance, no longer surprising to see the United Nations flag wave next to the flag of the United States. Or, American membership in international organizations is taken for granted by a new generation whose predecessor fought it bitterly and often successfully.[34] Or, citizens no longer respond uncritically to demands for sacrifices in the name of the national interest (there was opposition to the British government's conduct of war against Egypt in 1956 and the American government's conduct of war in Vietnam in the 1960s). "National" heroes are no longer necessarily citizens of the nation (Che Guevara!).

The specific sources of these changes in habitual behavior patterns, in social customs, are not easily traceable. Obviously, modern technology is an important one of them. It is fundamental, and positively creates new behavior patterns. Some other sources are discernible, making changes in habitual behavior patterns at least less onerous. One of these is located within national societies. What has often been regretted as the "de-individualization" of human existence or the breakdown of a community spirit under the impact of modern life, makes the modern, large-scale state less realistic as the unit of identity for the average citizen. To put it briefly: the "homeland" bears increasingly little resemblance to the warmth and cosiness of a "home." The citizen finds it easier, to say the least, to identify with other units than the state so that resistance to changes in habits presently geared to the state as a psychological need will be weakened.

This internal change plays directly into the hands of a change stimulated by new international developments. The social distance between an individual and his national society in comparison with that between the individual and the international society is not as great as it was during an era of low social mobility and minor interaction between states. To the international elites of the past, mainly the aristocracy and the clergy, can now be added merchants, students, teachers, tourists, civil servants, technical experts, airlines personnel, and the like. International behavior certainly has a very long road to travel before the gap between international relations and international politics is closed. It may never reach the end of the road. But it is moving along, even if at a snail's pace. Habit remains a strong component of the national's and the nationalist's behavior. The socialization process remains geared to the state in its basic aspects. But as it becomes increasingly dysfunctional to the needs of the national society it undergoes processes of adjustment. These may proceed more slowly than the needs demand. And in many new states some forms of nationalist behavior are only just being introduced simultaneously with attempts to make the citizenry aware of their statehood and its international obligations. Nevertheless, new patterns of habitual behavior are growing. The traditional nationalist tends to become, increasingly, a museum piece.

Subjective Foundation of the Political System

The Making of the Nationalist: Interest Satisfaction

The rational, cognitive part of the national's behavior is not ever-present in his mind. He is likely to be acutely aware of it at times of personal or national crisis. But the importance of the state will occur to him at other times as well. At one time or another two main considerations are likely to occupy him. Both affect his personal life and both are related to the linkage between national and international affairs. One is the required adjustment of his personal behavior to the changing ways in which states decide social issues and policies or maintain social order. These decisions, even down to relatively narrow local levels, can no longer be made by states without regard for the international society. Many of them, directly or indirectly, have international implications. The other consideration is how the citizen can adjust his personal behavior to the needs of a world in which social coexistence on any level often raises global rather than merely national problems. Their solution requires the mediation of his state and, most of the time, in the manner of government assistance. In either case, there is interaction between the nationalist's behavior and the nature of international politics. It produces changes in the national and international political systems which have roots in the behavior of the national and are of concern to him.

The foundation of the nationalist's considerations in adjusting his personal behavior to changes in the national and international society are his own personal interests and, maybe, his moral values. One of the reasons why the citizen is loyal to his state is that to be a citizen is profitable. Whatever sacrifices are made for the state are compensated by contributions to the citizen's welfare. These vary with the nature of the state. They may range from a guarantee of physical security, in the nightwatchman state, to all the material satisfactions provided by the most highly developed welfare state, including the protection a state may grant to a citizen's foreign interests. The importance of these satisfactions is shown by the fact that the struggle for political control turns, in the final analysis, on the struggle to dispense and receive benefits. Even conflicts over ideologies, seemingly remote from material advantages, are mostly related to the distribution of benefits. In states with high standards of living, normally only debates over ideologies concerning the allotment of material values (capitalism, socialism, communism) become concrete public issues. Ideologies emphasizing immaterial values (religion, morality) tend to be relegated to the sphere of "private affairs."

125

They are adduced to help in controversies turning primarily on other issues. When there is plenty to go around, debate over whether there is a God rarely proves to be socially disruptive, while only the distribution of the wealth really matters in social policies. In poor states debates may seemingly rage around immaterial things like religious beliefs and language. Upon closer examination, however, the very important implications of these matters for the material well-being of the protagonists become quite evident. In India, for instance, the conflict over making Hindi the official language is really a conflict over government jobs, since only those who speak Hindi could obtain such jobs if there were to be an official language. In the whole Asian and African world, national material development is the predominant social issue (the much-vaunted Asian "spiritualism" notwithstanding). Without exception Asian leaders are convinced that improvement in standards of living is the key to nation-building. Communist states have to give priority to the production of consumer goods. In the wealthiest states "national goals" no longer refer to national prestige or territorial conquests but to the abolition of poverty and advances in mental health. A reading of the history of nationalism will quickly resolve any doubt about material welfare as a most significant element in the nationalist's behavior.[35] It shows that from its beginnings, both in the Western and Eastern worlds, strengthening the state's economy, either for purposes of power or to enhance the well-being of some or all citizens, was one of the major motivations first in creating the state and then in maintaining it. Economic considerations always represent an essential part of the national interest for whose sake the citizen may be asked to sacrifice his life.

For several centuries there was no discrepancy between the existence of the state in separation from others and the economic welfare of the citizenry. As long as the internal resources of the state could adequately satisfy the personal material requirements of the citizens (or that group of them in control of the society), nationalism and the material benefits to be derived from the state were mutually supportive. This situation remained intact at least for the dominant Western states even after the satisfaction of material wants required resources located outside the state. For at that point colonialism became a practical possibility and the required amount of foreign trade was fairly small. With territorial colonialism no longer a possibility, only the richest states with considerable flexibility in choosing their foreign suppliers, or at relatively small sacrifice able to do without any, can still satisfy a large proportion of their citizens' material needs with their own resources.

Subjective Foundation of the Political System

For all the others, once the material demands of the citizenry reached their present extent and quality, voluminous and enduring interactions between states became necessary. The need is so obvious that rationally the argument for a change in traditional behavior patterns is conclusive. International communication is clearly no longer the luxury it once was. The marriage between sovereignty and self-sufficiency no longer fits either the conditions of modern times or the irreversible expectations of many national publics. Even neocolonialism, so called, does not save the most resourceful nations from the need for close communication when, for example, material needs relate to the preservation of the biosphere.

The efforts of some twentieth-century romanticists to keep their states aloof from the stream of international relations, in isolation, or within a separate "area of peace," were condemned to failure. The pressure (more or less strong depending upon the attributes of any given state) of new external, environmental conditions has produced the widespread recognition that the satisfaction of material interests requires international interaction. A change in traditional behavior, attitudes, and sentiments has followed — not everywhere and not always in the same manner, but altogether sufficiently to affect the practice of international politics. Neither the national nor the nationalist are any more quite what they were. Not surprisingly, the impact of the rational dimension of nationalist behavior has been more effective than the other two. Material needs make themselves felt with relative speed, and there is usually a ready willingness to do what is necessary to satisfy them. When rewards are obvious and immediate, adjustments of rational behavior can be achieved more quickly than changes in sentiments underlying behavior. These variations in the speed with which the sources of nationalist behavior can be adjusted to new environmental demands may help to explain the mixture between modernity and tradition in the contemporary international behavior of states.

The empirical evidence for the inroads made by rational considerations upon traditional nationalist behavior can be seen best in the growth of international organizations. The Western European example is especially impressive. For centuries, appeals for a united Europe, from Dante in the fourteenth century to those in the twentieth, have remained without effect. But when the Western European coal and steel interests decided that unification was mandatory for economic survival, a united Europe was on the road to reality. Similarly, in Asia and Africa, where political nationalism and traditional political hostilities remain too strong to allow for effective regional organiza-

127

tion, the only causes that can now bring Asians and Africans at least to the conference table are economic, and the only organizations relating to the region that function are those involving the participation of outsiders who have benefits to distribute. Lesser adjustments in approaches to world order, to nonmaterial interests and to humanistic or intellectual endeavors, are perhaps more subtle but still evidence of a rational conviction that there is very little left in this world for which a parochial perspective remains adequate. Finally, all states are readier to "surrender sovereignty" in economic than in political matters, the reason being that, first, economic matters are more noticeably related to material needs; second, felt material needs are less subject to emotional, sentimental influences; and third, there is as yet insufficient awareness of economics becoming a primary political tool.

Summarizing, it might be said that rational considerations, especially when they relate to the satisfaction of material interests, are a significant component in producing nationalist behavior. This was historically true and justified because, and as long as, states provided these satisfactions. It is also likely to be true that the satisfactions a state provides are one of the attractions of being its citizen. The welfare state is therefore more likely to retain the citizen's support even when other attractions weaken than a state providing little more than security. By the same token, as material satisfactions from the state diminish, the citizen's support of his state may be expected to diminish. The history of emigration will support this argument.[36] It can therefore safely be assumed that just as material interests help in creating the nationalist's behavior, so can they be instrumental in changing it. Indeed, of the three major dimensions in the nationalist's behavior, the rational, material dimension appears to be the most sensitive to environmental changes and the first to provoke changes in the behavior. That it has in fact produced such changes is evidenced by the history of international organization and the internationalization of many human endeavors. At times, such behavioral adjustment can be agonizing for the nationalist if it is conscious, and he may for a while resist it. But there seems to be a case here where the environment and its effect on the individual's interests do enforce a change in behavior in the long run. To sugar the pill for the nationalist, the new behavior has sometimes been rationalized in traditional, especially emotional nationalistic terms. Cooperation with foreign states, for instance, has been explained as a measure to preserve more effectively the state's own sovereignty. Well it might. But the overall result objectively is nevertheless that rationally recognized conditions are leading to an "internationalist" behavior deviating more and more from the behavior traditionally associated with "nationalist." The development of the new behavior will be slow. Habits and sentimentally based behavior are not changed easily or radically. Moreover, since politics is the part of international relations most deeply submerged in nationalist emotions, emotionalism will defend the international political system as the last outpost against attacks from a new rationally based internationalism.

The Making of the Nationalist: Emotional Satisfaction

The emotional dimension of the nationalist's behavior is nationalism. It is composed of a cluster of sentiments having the state as their most valued referent. The image of the ideal state, the nature of the sentiments and their differing intensities, may vary from person to person. But the state is always the object of their solicitude. The uniqueness of nationalism lies in the comprehensiveness of the psychic energies invested; in the intensity and single-mindedness with which these energies are applied and utilized; and in the vast compass of national purposes for which these energies can be marshaled. There is no problem in explaining why national societies foster nationalism. There really is no great problem, either, in explaining why nationalism has such a strong hold over nationalists. It can be traced to the many psychic satisfactions it provides and to the thoroughness with which it is instilled in the citizen.

The personality attributes of the individual determine which particular satisfactions are attractive to him and in what mix. Nationalism can serve as an outlet for constructive social sentiments: social cooperation, civic-mindedness, mutual aid. It can flatter the ego and help in overcoming personal frustrations: it provides vicarious enjoyment in the greatness of one's state and identification with the eminence of national heroes. It can justify a double standard of morality and a relaxation from social restraints: the derogation and belittling of foreigners and other states is not only permitted but may be meritorious. It can permit relief for pugnacious drives: the outside enemy must be attacked. It can be the means for establishing the individual's identity and developing his sense of security.

There need not always be a direct and one-to-one relationship between the nationalist's emotional needs and the satisfactions he derives from nationalism. His support of the nation's power drive does not always mean a personal power drive. His participation in war does not always mean an expression of personal aggressiveness. On the contrary, participation in such national activities often requires self-denial and a surrender of personality to the point of death rather than an increase in personal power or the satisfaction of pugnacity. The nationalist may quite possibly support such activities because he desires to submerge or humiliate himself or for a variety of other motives. It may be difficult to see in any individual case just what motivates the nationalist. But it is easy to see that he obtains some psychic satisfactions.

Obviously, the personality attributes, the psychic needs making nationalism possible, are an inherent part of the individual. Nationalism, however, is man-made. The emotional involvement of the citizen in his state is deliberately produced. Since the state is not "natural," nationalism cannot be "natural." Natural may be the individual's personally experienced, face-to-face group membership. In it he learns what it means to love or to hate, to feel security and solidarity, and to have all the other sensations which he later transfers to larger groups. But beyond the range of his face-to-face group his emotions toward the larger group, his national society, are a manipulated phenomenon. With the factors familiar to him from his immediate experience serving as symbols ("father," "home," "neighborhood," "mutual aid," etc.) his emotions are transferred to a theoretically limitless group of people.

In modern times the state is the largest such group to which the individual's emotions apply. There were times when the group was smaller and there may be times when it will be larger. With proper manipulation, whatever the size of the group and at present in regard to the state, it becomes the most highly valued; more highly valued than the group in which the individual first experienced the reality of his emotions. It is possible also, by proper manipulation, to evoke the sentiments and emotions of nationalism toward a nation which is not yet a state and possesses essentially only its cultural aspects. This was the case with the Czechs during World War I, with Zionists, and with all those people feeling a sense of belonging together as a result of common characteristics, such as language, ethnic origin, traditions, culture, but still lacking political organization and territory. The opposite can be the case as well, in the sense that there may be formally a state but its people lack a sense of nationhood. This is true of many new states in Asia and Africa where many leaders, already inspired by nationalist sentiments, are trying to pass their inspiration on to their people as a prerequisite for successful nation-building.

The machinery for making nationals and nationalists is remarkably identical in all states, regardless of their culture. The specific forms, the details, may vary. The techniques are the same, presumably because the general goal is the same. There are only so many techniques by which the relevant psychic aspects of human nature can be enlisted in reaching these goals. The color of the flag may change from country to country, but the flag is being waved everywhere. The head of state may be an emperor, king, or president, but he is venerated everywhere as the "father" of the country. The object of national pride may differ, but national pride is aroused everywhere. The end product is always the national or the nationalist, supremely loyal to his state in its sovereign existence: exclusive, unique, cherished above all else, and always right. The efficiency of this machinery is proven by the universality and strength of nationalism as well the behavioral homage paid to it even by those who do not possess nationalist sentiments. With some exceptions of extreme activity (e.g., berating other nations, wearing the flag on one's lapel), the general behavior typical for the nationalist is the generally accepted behavior for all citizens. Nationalism has been able to impose its behavior pattern upon the citizenry to such an extent that the nationalist and the national can be distinguished more readily by their sentiments than by their actions.

As in the case of the other two components (habit and interest) major changes in the environment have led nationalists to adjust their sentiments (rather than their environment). But this adjustment is slow and quite uneven across the globe, where large sections are only just developing nationalism rather than modifying it. Its evidence can be found in a social behavior emphasizing cooperative rather than separative behavior among states. It can be found also in individual behavior: clergymen pray for peace rather than for victory; many publics prefer a pluralistic rather than their own national culture; individuals choose international figures as heroes, or accept foreign rather than their own societies as models.

There are a number of reasons for this change in sentiments, and they all point to an erosion of the conditions originally producing and supporting nationalist sentiments. Much interaction among states and the narrowing range of problems solvable with national means make it difficult to claim national eminence, exclusiveness, and superiority. When the very maintenance of sovereign independence requires the assistance of other states, it becomes difficult to look down upon them. Second, a division of labor now goes far beyond national societies. It has penetrated deeply into the international society. There are too many linkages between national and international affairs to make any claim of "splendid isolation" credible. Where in the past func-

131

tional relationships brought nationals together and represented some of the social cement, they now do the same thing, albeit in smaller measure as yet, for the international society. The nexus between citizens within nations is weakening (relative to the past smaller national societies), while that between nationals of many states is growing. It is a functional nexus, which destroys some of the uniqueness that formerly tied citizens together on a more emotional basis and set them very distinctly apart from foreign nationals.

Related to this changing basis of relationships is a third reason, briefly mentioned earlier. Under the impact of growing functional interaction among states and of dissolving emotional bonds among citizens, the state simply does not any longer offer the outlet it formerly did for the citizen's sentiments, nor stimulate or incite them. In many instances the state fails to provide the individual with an identity. Its aggressiveness is neither unquestionably accepted any longer nor offers an outlet for individual drives. Growing acquaintance with other cultures diminishes pride in the exclusive excellence of one's own. The thinning substance of national loyalties weakens nationalist sentiments. The material value of the state to the individual is reduced, while that of the international society increases. The national's loyalties, perceptions, predispositions are no longer so overwhelmingly and exclusively conditioned by membership in his state as was once the case. To the extent that the direction of his sentiments (toward the state) was influenced by the qualities the state possessed and that some of these qualities are now transferred to the international society, it is reasonable to assume that as a minimum the sentiments toward the state will be weakened, and that perhaps their direction will follow the transfer of those qualities, that is to say in the direction of internationalism (although it cannot be excluded that some needs formerly satisfied by the state, such as identity, might be satisfied by altogether different objects, such as a deliberate withdrawal into traditional or new primary groups — rock festivals, sit-ins, etc.).

The Consequences of Changing Nationalist Behavior

The main ingredients making up the national and the nationalist — habit, rationality, and sentiments — are all subject to changing content. Though the hardy survival of states, the birth of new states, and the continuing fundamental principles of the international system may indicate the opposite, the realities of international existence have clearly begun to erode the customary behavior of the national and the confident loyalty of the nationalist.

Changes have not yet reached the core of sentiments and behavior, but they have begun to nibble at the edges. They have not yet converted habits, rational considerations, or sentiments into a positive support for One World. But they have begun to undermine the method of maintaining one state at the expense of other states (making, for instance, territorial colonialism unthinkable). Changes have made the practice of international cooperation, even for national survival, commonplace, even if this may be truer of older than newer states, and even if in times of crisis peoples and states may revert to traditional, most nationalistic behavior. The development, in other words, is not even. There are advances and retreats. But the factors provoking changes will not disappear again mainly because people cherish them. They promise too many comforts even to the nationalist to resist them. The prospect of two cars in the garage is a most powerful incentive!

What the long-range effect of the changes will be is difficult to predict. Historically the general direction of developments is clear: it has been from smaller to ever-larger political social units. But increasing internationalism is no assurance that the One World is inevitably coming. In the first place, functional interdependence between related interest groups and their close cooperation is one thing, while the merger of whole national societies into a new larger political unit is quite another. In the second place, the objective and subjective conditions preceding mergers of smaller into larger political units in the past were usually quite different from those now prevailing in regard to national societies. There is not even certainty that regional supranational entities will arise. In the Western European Community there are, so far, a number of specialized international units resulting from the merger of smaller national entities. A political unit called Western Europe is still far away. Lord Home's dictum that Great Britain's national identity might be better preserved by the surrender of "some" sovereignty, or President de Gaulle's *Europe des Patries* could be either a station on the road to a merger of states or the end of the road.[37]

The changes man himself is producing in his environment will be a challenge to the habits, rationality, and sentiments forming national and international behavior patterns. As these patterns change in response, so must the international political system change, which they support and which, in turn, is intended to order them. But man-made changes are subject to the influence of man. If he insists upon preserving his traditional national or nationalistic behavior patterns, he could do something about his self-created challenges to them. There is no evidence that he ever was seriously determined to

133

do something about them. If the problem were only to predict whether man will preserve his nationalism in traditional form or whether he will permit new developments to modify it to the point, eventually, of metamorphosis, the solution would not be too difficult in the light of historical experience.

The problem is made much more complex by the fact that there are different challenges to traditional nationalist behavior, and their effects pull in different, partly opposite directions. This curious consequence is due, subjectively, to the different speeds (or none at all!) with which any of the three components of the nationalist's behavior may change; to the different intensities with which each component may affect the nationalist's total behavior pattern; and to the result of the interactions between these two factors. The objective cause of this consequence is due to the nature of environmental changes, especially to the fact that not all of them necessarily lead to greater internationalization of national affairs, but may, on the contrary, lead to the opposite result. An added complication is that the challenges to traditional nationalist behavior, though present everywhere, may produce different reactions from state to state, with very mixed results for the international society as a whole. An examination of some of the more prominent challenges to nationalism can illustrate the possible contradictory consequences for international politics.

The growing volume of international interaction has been mentioned as leading toward internationalized behavior patterns. It must now be pointed out that it could also have the effect of reinforcing behavior in support of sovereignty. More international activity requires more governmental decisions. Agreements on social issues and policies now representing international concerns can best be reached by governments and translated by them into national law and policy, at least until an international government arises. By satisfying an increasing measure of social and individual needs, the state becomes increasingly valuable to the citizen. He is interested in maintaining it. The strengthening of sovereignty thus can be the direct consequence of the growing effectiveness of international organizations in rendering service. Another example is that the growth of the welfare state and the tendency to plan for it are conducive to emphasizing national jurisdiction. Successful planning requires control over as many factors relevant to the plan as possible. Such control is the better assured the more a government can make itself independent of factors outside the state. A state may therefore seek to gain control over factors outside the state — and in an age of interdependence there may be very many — creating international friction rather than cooperation. On these grounds, for instance, the socialists of Western Europe were initially more reluctant than any one else (except the Communists) about European union. A third and related example refers to great inequalities in national capabilities. Some states aim at social goals which are sheer utopia for other states. Controversy will arise over the distribution and price of scarce resources. A solution will be difficult because what is a luxury to one party is likely to be considered a necessity by the other. Governments will be called upon, as they have traditionally been, to help out, and what began as an issue of international interdependence and potential cooperation ends as another conflict between states.

A fourth example of how the internationalization of problems can lead to separation rather than cooperation has to do with the highly politicized nature of the international society. The more interests or social policies that become internationalized, the more opportunities for conflict arise. This is all the more true because the internationalization of interest means, under the present system, their politicization rather than a contribution to pluralism off the political level. The multiplication of internationalized interests and their politicization places a great burden upon an already inadequate political system.

All these immediate effects of changes in the international environment upon the citizens and their states in the direction of preserving, if not strengthening, national behavior should be balanced against the possible longer-range effects upon behavior changes toward a more adequate political system. It remains doubtful whether the final result will satisfy those who are hoping for the growth of an international community rooted in the future interdependence of states, refinements in the international division of labor, improved effectiveness of international organizations, and closer communication between states and their citizens. Present trends indicate the development of functional pluralism rather than sentimental bonds. But there can be no doubt that the realities of national and international life are forcing changes in behavior patterns supportive of a more adequate political system which may be based not on an international community but on an international social system making social order and peaceful behavior at least more reliable.

The spearhead of this development will be practical reasoning, already the foundation for many changes in international behavior toward a more ''internationalist'' pattern. The most convincing example can be seen in the mutation of nationalism and nationalist interpretations of international institutions in the European Common Market.[38] European leaders find political

135

nationalism quite compatible with transnational economic and other institutions. Their support of international institutions, even some including international decision-making, was paralleled by unchanged, traditional nationalist ideas, beliefs, and behavior. This pragmatic approach shows, in addition to the strength of expectations of material benefits, the possibility of a changing content of nationalism. In particular, it shows that the aggressive, divisive qualities of nationalism are not an inevitable, inherent part of nationalism; that is, that the divisive nature of nationalism (not a characteristic of early nationalism anyway) may be no more than a historical phase which can be overcome by a changing environment. However, the habits and sentiments supporting nationalism will need more time for adjustment. They are mainly responsible for the lag between the realities of the international situation and the adjustments to them of the human psyche. The abolition of states is not going to take place in the foreseeable future. Changes in the role they are playing may not be too far away. There is no assurance and no more than a likelihood that an expanding international interaction will produce a social psyche everywhere supportive of the political system which future international relations need. In the meantime, until a greater unity among the habits, cognition, and sentiments among national publics produces an international behavior better designed to safeguard the international society, the prevailing contradictions will be clearly evident in the behavior of states.

The Contradictory Behavior of States

The need for increasing cooperation is realized everywhere amid the universal yearning for sovereignty. While the two are not altogether mutually exclusive, they are both mutually limiting and in their psychological roots somewhat incongruous. Their greater harmonization is gradually resulting from the need to satisfy national wants through international action. But until that process is completed, contradictory actions by states will remain typical and change will be sporadic and uneven because its underlying psychic conditions — habits, sentiments, and reasoning by peoples and their leaders — change at different speeds. These contradictions are most evident in the tenets of international charters, basic principles of law, and high-sounding appeals in preambles of treaties on the one hand. They refer to the kind of behavior states know would be necessary to make social order and peace more reliable. They can be found, on the other hand, in some of the concrete rights and obligations created by these very charters, laws, and treaties — not to mention official actions — which refer to that behavior states actually want to engage in, making the international political system inadequate.

Those tenets were expressly embodied in international instruments in the awareness that their effective application would take good care of peace and international order, would greatly improve the international society. Charters and constitutions of international organizations are preferred instruments to expound such tenets. They guarantee equality to nations large and small, they call for the abolition of violence, fair distribution of wealth, social justice everywhere, the expansion and balanced growth of international trade, the unrestricted movement of people, goods, and capital across the globe. Then there are the so-called general principles of law recognized by civilized nations. They ordain that treaties must be kept, that laws cannot be retroactive, that human rights must be protected, and so forth. And finally there are the preambles of treaties and official statements. They are not binding and usually verbalize pious hopes for better international relations. They are often hortatory in nature, suggestive rather than compelling. They express legal principles or general rules prescribing basic, overall behavior rather than concrete actions in fulfillment of finite goals. They typically suggest rationally arrived-at convictions about the behavior that would be needed if peace and order are to be preserved. These preambles and statements are not self-executing, they are not legal commitments. Implemental agreements would be needed to make them obligatory. But an examination of such agreements which are immediately binding will show that the rights and obligations they create very often belie the high-minded tenets.

The constitutions of international organizations, in their binding parts, commit all nations to the principle of sovereignty, which substantively is a denial of equality. In the Security Council the largest nations received permanent representation and veto rights. In many of the specialized agencies of the United Nations, the largest or wealthiest nations have special privileges, including greater voting rights. Since might makes right, the general principles of international law are often acted out in favor of the mighty, as demonstrated in the Nuremberg and Tokyo war crimes trials (though it should be pointed out that increasingly weaker states benefit from international law, as shown for instance in their expropriations of foreign property or the unilateral extension of their frontiers into the oceans). The legal obligation to desist from the use of violence in international conflicts is itself undermined by other rules of international law which, in anticipation of the breach of this obligation, regulate warfare. Bilateral treaties rarely contain any of the high-minded tenets in their binding clauses. They aim at specific, limited goals. The parties establish their respective obligations because they intend to fulfill them. These treaties represent a compromise or agreement on mutual interests whose realization both sides find favorable. They both have sufficient reason to act in the required manner so that there is no discrepancy between the rules of the treaty and the willingness to act in accordance with them.

There is, to be sure, nothing new in the contradiction between political constitutions and political practice. The "living law" does not always equal the letter or the spirit of the law. The novelty on the international scene is a reversal in the usual chronology. Usually, life refuses to be constrained by theoretical structures and moves ahead of formal law. Law tends to be conserving rather than innovative, tends to be left behind by living practice, and become a dead letter. This course of events is frequently reversed in the international experience. Charters, constitutions, preambles, and even legally binding principles ordain a system and behavior which, if they became reality, would make peace and social order more reliable. In fact, the "living law" and behavior of the international society remain far behind and are quite remote from these goals. The formal international organizations and institutions which nations have created reflect their rational awareness of a need for "internationalist" behavior, while actual state behavior expresses the remaining influence of conservative sentiments and, of course, the benefits some states derive from their great power potential. For this reason, international organizations are shaped to serve nationalism and internationalism at the same time (or to serve the schizophrenic behavior of states at the same time). They tend to have an idealistic touch, holding out the promise of a better future (in their preambles and perhaps in their very existence). In that respect they betray their usual origin in times of war when the suffering peoples of warring nations need a boost to their morale and inspiring "war aims." But they also maintain the fundamental principles of the traditional international political system by careful preservation of national sovereignty (in the binding clauses). In that respect, they betray the "realism" of their founding fathers.

The conclusion emerges that the concrete behavior of states in pursuit of their interests remains dominated by traditional habits and sentimental motivations. Their better knowledge of a different behavior needed to preserve peace more reliably so far finds expression mainly in some voluntary practices or fairly noncommittal general principles which may or may not be applied to specific actions, depending upon what the national interest at the particular moment is thought to require. The longer-range welfare of the international society and the possible national benefits to be derived from it tend to be ignored.

The failure to bring international behavior adequately into line with recognized needs is mainly a human failure. It cannot be blamed primarily on some objective factors beyond man's control. The behavior is not in principle unchangeable. It is historically conditioned and a resultant of human and humanly controllable conditions. It can be changed. There is an unwillingness to adjust, especially among the elites primarily responsible for international politics. Just as ultimately the foundation of the state is "the will" for it (Robert McIver) so must the social foundation of One World be the will for that. There is no such will, mainly because the urgency for a different political system is not admitted by the publics relevant to bring it about. The widespread distress over the inadequacies of the political system is outweighed by the advantages which it, apparently, offers to those responsible for maintaining it.

Among the elites in selected states there is contentment or at least complacency with a system that has served them well materially. Why should Americans, 6 percent of the world's population, feel constrained to abandon a system that has permitted them to use 40 to 60 percent of the world's annual production resources? Altruism has its limits! Such benefits are a strong temptation to believe that the system's weaknesses can be overcome by a determined effort to protect the nation from their consequences (e.g., by armaments, interventions abroad, etc.). In the many newer states of Asia and Africa, which hardly benefit from the system materially, the leadership obtains such enormous psychic satisfactions from heading a sovereign state that it too feels no great urge to abandon the system. The masses everywhere (if they are alert to the situation at all), and their leaders too, are so imbued with nationalism that major alterations in the emotional component of their behavior would have to take place before a decisive switch from nationalist to "internationalist" behavior could take place. It is this social psyche — the collectivized, synthesized psyche of a predominant section of every national public — which is mainly responsible for the character of national and international societies, for the nature of international politics, and for the inadequacies of the international political system. These publics are willing, when forced by circumstances, to make minor adjustments and to pay much lip service to needed changes and improvements, but always with the proviso that the fundamentals of the system be kept intact. The causes of the inadequately maintained peace and social order in the international society are thus to be found ultimately in the social psyche supporting this society.

National Communities and International Society

The social psyche prevailing among peoples across the globe creates a crucial difference between most national societies and the international society.* It is a subjective difference which can explain much of the adequacy of national and of the inadequacy of the international political systems. Citizens of a nation have a deep emotional investment in their national society. The society becomes a closely knit community and is valued as the highest social good. The international society is devoid of such an investment. It remains a loosely knit social unit and therefore a society (in the narrower sense of the word). The difference is not easily noticeable because it is rooted in the emotional foundations of the two social units. Objectively, their structures and function have great similarities. Both possess rationally and not affectively determined systems of coordination, organization, and interactions. The national society can exist (for instance, probably, India, Indonesia, Malaysia), possessing all the outward features of communities including a central government, yet lacking the emotional support of their populations in a degree sufficient to turn them into communities. When leaders in such states speak of "nation-building," what they most likely have in mind is the conversion of their national societies into national communities (turning states into nations!). On the other hand, the absence of a central government in the international society is not necessarily conclusive evidence of the absence of a community. There are large communities possessing neither a differentiated political system nor a unified central government. Communities as well as societies may either possess or lack central governments. Both have an organization for cooperation and conflict. Both are goal oriented. A crucial difference is, however, that in a community its own maintenance is always a high social goal.

The overt, rational, institutional features of the two types of society will not indicate what types of social units they are because the essence of the difference is internal to its members and lies in the spirit permeating all aspects of the two groups. As a matter of principle, a community and a

* The point has now been reached where discussion of *society* in the general, wide, and generic sense will be supplemented by consideration of two subtypes of the generic term: *society* in the narrower sense and *community* as defined in the next few pages of the text.

society (in the narrower sense) can be almost identical outwardly. But the quality of their performance differs, and so does the psychic satisfaction their members obtain from membership. For this reason, while both units have political systems, the community's system is far more adequate than the society's. The difference can easily be tested at times of crisis, which a community can more readily take in its stride than a society. Since the social psyche as the foundation of social units is so determinative of their specific character and their performance, especially that of their political systems, delving into more detail is revealing. A closer analysis will provide important clues to the inadequacy of the international political system and the international behavior of states.

The Character of a Community

The social psyche of a community indicates solidarity, oneness, togetherness, mutual responsibility. Typically, the member of the community is aware of his membership and conscious of benefits and sacrifices, especially those of a psychic nature. He identifies with a community more readily than with a society and, at any rate, such identification is more meaningful. When the community reaches the large size of a nation, the cohesion of the members is produced by the strong sentimental element of nationalism. Such a large-scale community is nevertheless derived from the individual's face-to-face experience in a small community. It is doubtful that a group as large as a nation could spontaneously elicit the sentiments or provide the psychic satisfactions of the citizen without his previous similar experiences in the family, school, or neighborhood. In any case, all nations rely on such experiences in socializing the citizen into his national role: father equals king, home equals country, the citizens are "brothers and sisters." The large-scale community becomes the generalized, abstracted personal experience transferred to it. The small-scale, individualized community becomes at the state level transmuted from a real objective entity into a spiritual reality. In the process of abstraction and transfer, the person-to-person relationships with their emotions become impersonal, but remain sentimental (i.e., nationalist). The relationships are now between the individual and his people as such, with "the people" personified in the real or alleged qualities of the nation. The individual's emotions are now invested in the collectivity. Fellow nationals are not cherished as persons in their individual, diverse qualities, but as an amorphous mass of fellow citizens with ascribed stereotyped "national" characteristics. The fulfillment of the individual's moral ends and social-psychological needs are derived from the community as a whole rather than from direct personal contacts or small-group membership. This does not mean, except possibly at times of great national events, that the individual citizen constantly experiences relations to his people as a whole. Rather, the community becomes real in the inspirational effects of smaller-group activities motivated by and directed toward the idea and unity of the nation, and occasional community-wide rites (the Fourth of July!)

The emotional bonds of a community can safeguard its existence for a while even in the absence of specific goals or in the presence of conflicting goals. To the member of the community, his emotional investment and its psychic returns make the perpetuation of the community itself a desirable goal. The community has an inherent value for the member, quite apart from other benefits that group membership provides.

The value of the society for its members is essentially instrumental. The association of the members is based mainly on utilitarian considerations and the pursuit of specific goals. Their basic nexus is functional interdependence. It is not supplemented by emotional ties. If, therefore, the society has achieved its goals or cannot achieve them, it ends, in principle, unless new goals or overlapping goals guarantee its continuity (as is the case in the international society).

Using a rather crude formula, a community might be defined as a society (performing all the functions of a society) plus emotional bonds (supplying unique psychic satisfactions). The two can share many forms. But "the spirit" of the community is unique, though imponderable. The sentiments of community can be inferred from behavior motivated by relevant emotions, such as willingness to make sacrifices for the common good, the ethnocentric elevation of the community above all others, pride of membership — all nonrational behavior never to be found in the international society.

The life of a family can illustrate some of these points differentiating a community and a society. As long as its members live together and the children are dependent, much of the family's importance is in the functions it performs for the children. When they become independent and the family members disperse, these goal achievements become irrelevant. Without emotional bonds, the existence of the family will end for all practical purposes. If the family is held together also by affective ties, if, in other words, it is a community, stresses and conflicts can be more readily absorbed while the members live together. Even thereafter, when there are no more functional

142

needs, the members will continue to identify themselves with the family, will derive psychic satisfactions, and in times of new need will quickly help each other again.

The behavioral consequences flowing from the community as compared to a society result primarily from the devotion of the members to the maintenance of their community and their dealing therefore with social issues in a manner which will not threaten the community's existence. The hierarchy of values in a nation, with the nation itself at the apex, and the general social organization shaped to realize these values, reflects the community spirit. The absence of sentimental bonds in the international society makes all transactions a matter of calculating profit and loss, with no loyalties to the society as such softening conflicts arising from the pursuit of clashing goals. The community does not alone depend for its cohesion upon specific purposes, specific institutions, specific internal subdivisions. It is an overall, comprehensive, emotionally supported unit and unity under whose umbrella political processes take place, social institutions exist, and social structures are maintained. The society lacks this umbrella. It exhausts itself in these processes, institutions, and structures. If any one of these becomes faulty, the whole society will immediately and directly suffer in the absence of that protective umbrella.

Society, Community, and the Political System

The adequacy of the political system is greatly affected by the community spirit. As "primitive" communities show, adequate political systems can exist even with decentralized and diffused decision-making when a community spirit prevails. Without that spirit such a political system becomes inadequate, as the international society demonstrates and as can also be seen in states torn by civil war. The effective, and not just the formal, centralized and differentiated political system known to orderly and relatively peaceful modern nations presupposes a community psyche. For its effectiveness rests largely on the cohesion and solidarity among the citizens. The community spirit provides the reality and substance of the national political forms. It more than any political organization enhances peacefulness and social order in the community. The reason is that that in a community, as compared to a society, the motivation of behavior differs, affecting both the quality and the kind of behavior. Considered as ideal types, the political system in a society relies on power relationships, whereas in the community it has additional reliance upon sympathetic relationships; the organization of the members often emphasizes hierarchy in a society but equality in a community; members act in a society in response to political pressure, which in a community is supplemented by loyalty to the nation; the politics of the society is command and obedience, which is mellowed in the community by voluntarism and altruism.

Community behavior involves great mutual trust and confidence among the members that for the sake of the community everyone will adhere to the rules of the game. The community spirit creates a predisposition for cooperative and peaceful behavior. Motivations and actions by members tend to be interpreted benevolently by fellow members — in contrast to the suspicions dominating the international society. The community sentiments affect the individual's perception of a situation and his decisions. They permeate all behavior and condition the actions undertaken to achieve lesser ends than the preservation of the community. The individual's desire to identify with his community, his nationalist urge to believe in the superiority of his nation, impel him to create a good community in which peace, order, brotherhood, cooperation, solidarity prevail. He expects that his nation will take in its stride the unending procession of goals to be achieved or problems to be solved without endangering its very existence. Arbitrary, destructive violence is therefore excluded *eo ipso*.

The extent to which the community psyche determines the adequacy and effectiveness of a political system becomes evident when it weakens (or is absent, as in the international society). At that moment the social order in the nation also tends to weaken, even without any changes in the environment. Tensions arise. Violence becomes a means for settling conflicts to the point of civil war. As the community spirit vanishes, the political system relies increasingly upon its coercive methods. Power and law rather than brotherhood and solidarity are emphasized. Quite rightly the rise of violence in many nations during the 1960s has been interpreted as the result of a declining sense of community. Authoritarian states make a special point of facilitating their dictatorial politics with at least the semblance of a national community. And the leaders of many new states are fearful lest loyalty to region, class, or caste may endanger the viability of the state.

The greatest benefit of the community psyche for the political system is that it creates a broad tolerance for conflict. The overriding concern to have a national community softens conflicts, limits the means used for their solution, and provides a basis for compromise. The task of the political system to control social conflicts and channel their results toward constructive social ends is facilitated greatly by the direction which the will for a community gives to social behavior. Under these community conditions, conflict is a potentially creative social force. In the international society, the potential endlessness of conflict escalation robs conflict of this constructive quality and more likely turns it into a force of sheer destruction.

The outward similarities between a society and a community, for instance in institutions, organization, structure, indicate that the community psyche and the political system can each have an existence of its own (but can influence each other in interaction). This relationship can explain the rise and decline of the community psyche, as well as the changing forms of national and international political systems in mutual independence. The hardy survival of "national sovereignty" is an illustration of the community psyche's influence upon the political system. The strength of political forms and their responsiveness to the environment, independent of social sentiments, are demonstrated by the growth of an "internationalist" behavior and a weakening of that a priori antagonism characteristic of former international relations. These relations have advanced to an antagonistic symbiosis. The antagonism survives in the unrestrained conduct of conflicts and the potential confrontations implied in much state behavior. The symbiosis has resulted from the inevitable coexistence of states and their unavoidable interactions. It is possible, and many idealists hope, that the prevailing nationalism will be unable to stunt the growth of forces making the nation-state obsolete. Just as larger and larger communities grew out of expanding interaction between formerly separated groups, so the increasing interaction between states could melt these into larger social units by generating a community psyche which could eventually encompass all mankind.

There is, however, also the opposite and more likely possibility that nations are the largest communities men can accept. The evident breakdown of existing national communities, the search for smaller new groupings upon which to lavish community sentiments and in which to find one's identity, may be indications that mankind will never be more than a society held together by functional interdependence.

There is no guarantee that functional interdependence over long distances, leading to sporadic contacts and consummated in largely indirect, mediated relationships between states, will create the loyalties of nationals, based upon daily encounters, clearly perceived needs, and massive contacts which formed the originally experienced (face-to-face) community. This will most certainly not happen when well-endowed states use functional relationships unequally for their benefit against poorer states. In any case the physical extension of a community has limits. Even the national community is not likely to be as strong as the "personal" (e.g., family) community. The chances of destructive conflicts increase and the elements "in common" decrease as the size of the social unit grows. Mutual personal involvements diminish. Bonds of mutual trust weaken. They have to be implemented by organizational structures assisting in the gratification of material personal expectations.

A final answer to the possible limits of a community's size could be given only if the sources of a community were known. Unfortunately, they are not. There is so far mainly speculation that certain or perhaps all the factors people have "in common" may lead to a community, or that they may only facilitate the rise of a community. The difficulty is that for every factor or collectivity of factors which seems to explain the existence of a given community, another community can be found in which they are not present (e.g., a common language is present in some, not in other communities; the same goes for religion, cultural or ethnic similarities, traditions, communication, etc.). Very likely also, as communities grow in size, many factors will have to be abstracted more and more to remain "in common." A point will be reached where the abstraction is so high that the commonness of the factor loses its effect. By the time the community comprises all mankind not only must the common factors be highly abstracted, but there is nothing left which could single out the group from other groups — yet this seems to be an important element in creating social cohesion and an essential prerequisite for the individual to use his group for identification.

For the development of an adequate international political system it is of the greatest importance whether mankind remains a loose society, becomes a community, or turns into a social unit in which the bonds of sentiment are replaced by an equivalent of similar cohesive force (perhaps a multitude of smaller, but overlapping communities and a dense network of functional dependencies). The elevation of the nation to be the national's highest social value, the community members' emotional devotion to the national group, and the minimal fear of mutual threat and violence produce a tolerance for conflict within nations which is the key element in the construction of a political system able to maintain peace and social order with reasonable reliability. This subjective foundation of a community is the single most important factor in making social controls on behavior effective, thereby setting limits to the destructive force of conflicts and helping significantly to solve the problem of the causes of war and the conditions of peace.

146

6 The Controls on International Behavior

THE ANALYSIS of the international political system and politics has so far concentrated on their tasks and purposes; on the nature of the society in which social order and peace is to be maintained; on the manner in which the political system is organized; on power as the force with which international politics operates; and on the predisposition of peoples everywhere to behave in certain ways on the national and international scene. It is now desirable to examine the specific controls on the behavior of states available to the political system in the pursuit of its tasks.

The Nature of Controls

Social controls are among the regulators of social behavior. They are virtually always effective through psychic and material rewards and punishments. Their aim is to reduce alternatives of behavior by exerting directing or restraining influence upon actions. They must be understood, in most instances, as a process affecting and guiding behavior rather than as a mechanism defining behavior. Their purpose makes them a form of applied power and largely a part of the political system. It also makes them conservative because their tendency, indeed their mission, is to fit behavior into the existing social system. They are, par excellence, the means to make behavior regular and predictable. They discourage behavior involving change, innovation, creativity, reform, and above all revolution. For however desirable such behavior may be in modern society, it threatens the established way of life the maintenance of which is the ideal goal of social controls. This preference of societies for conformable behavior causes difficulties for the effectiveness of social

147

controls. Too inflexible controls will be nullified by the dynamics of the society, yet too dynamic controls may permit deviant behavior beyond the society's limits of tolerance. The rapidity with which modern technology transforms modern societies, including the international, is clearly a major cause for the sense of insecurity prevailing everywhere. The international society is in a particularly unfavorable position because existing controls are weak to begin with and because the machinery to create new controls is greatly underdeveloped. One result is that states remain attached to outdated, largely negative controls, such as military threats, to obtain compliant behavior from other states when in fact the threatened measures could bring destruction to all concerned.

The dynamics of the society are only one form of pressure upon social controls. There are also very deliberate pressures by its own members. Those who benefit from the status quo will support controls maintaining that status. Those at a disadvantage will try to circumvent or change them. These differing interests in the controls came prominently into the open when the new states of Asia and Africa demanded changes in the international political system. They demanded, in particular, a "new international law" on the ground that the old law favored the older, richer states. They also demanded better representation in international agencies where some of the international social controls are manipulated. In general all states will aim at obtaining control of the controls. This ambition is, of course, what politics is all about!

The demands by newer states for the abolition or change of existing social controls is not unique to them. It is, rather, symptomatic of all states' unwillingness to have their sovereign independence curtailed by outside controls. By elevating sovereignty to the basic organizing principle of their society, states indicate their wish to institutionalize freedom of action unrestrained by outsiders. Their eternal quest for power indicates their determination to defend it. Their insistence upon sovereignty prevents the political system from imposing formal controls upon unwilling states. Their accumulation of a power potential is an attempt to frustrate even informal controls. How careful states are to hamper the rise of any controls is shown, for instance, by their close scrutiny of all international activities (e.g., cultural exchanges) lest they might affect future state action, or by explicitly refusing to recognize that certain activities might turn into informal limitations on freedom of action (e.g., de facto versus de jure recognition of governments or Article 59 in the Statute of the World Court, which specifically prevents decisions from becoming binding precedents for subsequent decisions).

The Controls on International Behavior

The dilemma for the political system is that controls become most vital when conflicts of interest arise, but that this is also the moment when sovereignty becomes most relevant for the protection of "national interests"! One unsatisfactory solution has been that states are assumed to accept controls voluntarily, in the name of and not contrary to their sovereignty. If they do, the controls were presumably unnecessary in the first place and they are then really more conveniences to facilitate communication. Another solution has been that controls are imposed informally by one state upon another, which makes them objectionable to the subjected state and poor regulators of behavior.

The reference to formal and informal controls raises the point of the categories of control that exist. There are mainly three. There are, first, what Emile Durkheim called the "natural" controls. These are inevitable restraints on behavior, independent of human wills, such as physical forces or physiological principles. States must accept them and can only try to circumvent, overcome, exploit them. At any rate, states must adapt themselves to them. They are part of the raw material with which international politics has to deal. There are, second, those social and especially political controls explicitly created and operated by men. They are always formalized and often institutionalized. Law, agreed procedures, and international organizations are examples. The dividing line between political and nonpolitical controls is blurred especially in the international society (and not too relevant in any case). The reason is twofold. The extreme politicization makes all controls, like most other things, political before they are allowed to become nonpolitical. And the lack of differentiation of the political from other subsystems of the international society makes the categorization of controls in any case difficult. The result is that virtually any restraint upon a state's behavior is quickly seized upon by states and converted into a political tool. This practice brings up the third type of controls.

All regular social interaction imposes limits upon behavior. Controls are implicit in human institutions whatever their ostensible purposes. Competition in a free-market economy, for instance, has primarily economic goals, yet it is at the same time a technique of social control. Education, even when directed at learning subject matter, contains at the same time control functions. Controls are embedded in most social activities, institutions, and structures for the reason that when a person is expected or trained or conditioned to do something in one way, he is expected, trained, or conditioned not to do it in another!

The effectiveness of social controls obviously depends to some extent upon what type they are. The natural controls are absolutely effective. From there on effectiveness depends upon the power of men to manipulate them. It seems for instance more difficult to escape from (and to change) the restraints resulting from customs, traditions, or social structures than to escape from (and undo) traffic laws. In principle, it seems that controls deliberately created by men (type two) tend to be less effective than those embedded in social institutions (type three). This likelihood is not surprising because formal laws and formal institutions are much of the time confirmations of behavior already adopted and approved informally in the practice of the society. The efficacy of manipulable controls upon the behavior of states, it becomes clear, depends to a great extent upon the nature of the differing controls in the context of the international society. The degrees of efficacy as dependent upon who is to be controlled, how the controls are created, and what controls are available will now be examined.

The Control of Foreign Policy Making

When states, i.e., collectivities, are the "actors," the problem arises who the target of the controls must be. Collectivities cannot be controlled as such. Those must be found who are responsible for provoking the action of the group and possibly those performing it. The focus must be on the decision-making process, the decision and its execution. In short, the focus must be on the foreign policy of a state in the broadest sense of that term. The targets of the controls must be the individuals relevant to the making and execution of the foreign policy. To find them is extraordinarily difficult. It is easier to point out why they cannot be discovered. In spite of very complete taxonomies categorizing types of foreign policies, very sophisticated schemes of decision-making, and many detailed analyses of foreign policy case studies, all analytical findings remain fairly gross. They have little predictive power. Even after the fact, they cannot answer with assurance how a given policy was formulated. Only in the rarest instances can they pinpoint who was most instrumental in producing the foreign policy — and even then they usually cannot explain why. Yet controls will be the more effective the more they can affect the individuals nearest to the making and execution of the policy. Controls influencing the masses are likely to be less impressive, at least in specific cases, then those influencing elites interested in foreign policy,[39] and these in turn will be less impressive than those influencing

150

the individuals directly participating in the shaping of the policy. The qualifier "likely" has to be used because the role of these various groups and individuals depends very much upon the political and social structure of each state and because the complexity of making foreign policy is such that even when the role is known the specific effect of these groups is not. In this context it should be remembered that, according to the International Press Institute's survey for 1972, four-fifths of the member states of the United Nations did not possess what could "genuinely be called freedom of information." In these states public opinion is even less relevant in the making of specific foreign policies than it is in the freer states.

Even when the making of foreign policy is considered in its more formal aspects as a process going on in a government agency designed for this purpose, it remains extremely complicated. The process calls for the participation in a variety of stages of different people acting in different circumstances and from different viewpoints. Different controls would be needed for maximum effectiveness at each stage in the genesis of the foreign policy. The usual picture of decision-making as a hierarchical process with the decision-maker at the apex is at best correct only in the most formal sense. Modern decision-making in states is a horizontal more than a vertical process. With the rarest exceptions, the final substantive decision is the synthesized product of many decisions by many individuals. The decision by an official formally inferior to the final decision-maker preliminary to the final decision (e.g., the decision not to pass on certain information, judged unimportant, to the president of the United States or the prime minister in Great Britain) may be as decisive in shaping the final outcome as any contribution by the highest decision-making official.

This situation highlights the obvious fact that the vast majority of decisions — at whatever level they are made — must be based upon subjective evaluations. There is no objective measure by which one among several alternatives could be selected as "the best." Short of eliminating a choice altogether, any control aiming, by its nature, at narrowing the choice will therefore always run the risk of remaining ineffective. For making a given choice unattractive to some decision-makers may make this choice more attractive to other decision-makers! Differing evaluations of possible decisions often originate in differing estimations of the problem at hand. Very likely two persons will perceive the same situation differently (and the controller may have a third perception!). They will have different perspectives on the problem. In extreme situations what is a problem to one person may not be one to another. Consequently the foreign policies the two persons will advocate may differ greatly so that what will be experienced as a control upon behavior by the first person may not be so experienced by the second (a treaty forbidding the use of atomic weapons will not be a control for the person never intending to use them).

The possibility of having different perceptions of problems will further increase the complexity of the decision-making process and its control by introducing different sets of individuals into it. Government agencies dealing with foreign affairs are usually subdivided according to geographic and substantive topics. Thus, a problem handled by the "Asia desk" may or may not attract the officials of the "Western European desk," depending upon how they see the problem at hand. The difficulty of knowing the many persons involved in making decisions or what their impact may be is compounded by the changing identity of the persons filling the role of participant in decision-making. There are the activities also of a multitude of minor officials who may never make important decisions but who may contribute collectively through many minor decisions to the final policy decision. There is no practical way to devise refined controls to influence these many categories of participants in the process of making foreign policy.

What is true of the individuals formally and officially engaged in the making of foreign policy becomes even truer of all the many people who in one form or another have some role to play in this process — be it positively as an interest group or as public opinion, or negatively as a public whose apathy denies support to a policy. What has been said of officials applies in part to all these groups as well: perceptions differ, problems are variously evaluated, groups do not have homogenized views, opinions are divided. In spite of voluminous research on the role of the public and elites in the making of foreign policy, very little indeed is known about what functions these groups actually perform. The unending chain of surveys about elite attitudes contributes little to the solution of this problem until it also becomes known what effects these attitudes may have upon final policy decisions. The same can be said of public opinion. Even when on rare occasions public opinion fairly solidly supports a particular view, evidence is plentiful to show that actual policy may deviate widely from that view. There is evidence only that the influence of public groups is minor, regardless of whether a society is "open" or "closed." [40] Controls designed to influence these groups are therefore relatively irrelevant, which has not reduced the enormous efforts expended everywhere to influence publics by propaganda.

The Controls on International Behavior

There is, finally, that group of individuals who influence a country's foreign policy without being citizens of that country. They enter as a result of the growing need for partly collectivizing internationally the making of foreign policy. The point has not yet been reached where a decision is made collectively. But in alliances, regional organizations, collective security systems, and similar institutionalized forms of cooperation, states consult and try to coordinate before arriving at their own final decisions. The linkages between internal and external politics are becoming so voluminous that foreign policy becomes an extension of internal policy and vice versa. As this happens, new individuals or groups are brought into the environment of the policy making process potentially greatly affecting the final outcome and becoming thereby targets of the political controls (as well as the controllers). The complications this development raises for the efficacy of these controls is obvious.

The participation of so many people, directly or indirectly, in the policy-making process makes any effective application of political controls upon state behavior extremely problematical. It is difficult enough to devise proper means for influencing human behavior. The difficulty is increased manifoldly when it is unknown whose behavior should be influenced. Modern technology has greatly increased this complexity by democratizing the policy-making process, broadening the material bases for reaching decisions, and multiplying alternatives for implementing them. There are so many ways to reach the same goals, so many substitutions possible among the means, and such a variety of people whose help can be enlisted that controls upon state behavior would have to be more versatile and refined than any now existing in order to be reliably effective. It is true that the same technology which has caused this complexity has also improved the possibility of controlling individual and collective behavior, but not to a sufficient degree. The maneuverability of states on the international scene has outdistanced the greater sophistication in social and political controls. Their effectiveness is becoming increasingly questionable as the introduction of larger numbers of people into the process of foreign policy making increases the unpredictability of its direction and results.

There are at least two factors alleviating somewhat the problem of knowing whom to control. The first is that in spite of internal-external linkages, of the interrelationships between foreign policies, and of the insolubility of national foreign policy problems by national decisions or actions alone, foreign policy remains nationally determined. The many elements going into the

153

policy-making process are in the end homogenized. The many influences impinging upon the process from its environment become a confluence eventually affecting those having to make the last decision. In the end all the data are perceived, evaluated, and interpreted in terms of the national interest. There are as yet only national policies, no international policies, for the international society. The final decision which becomes formally relevant to the international society when it appears there as a demand is a national decision made by the government. This narrows the focus. If controls cannot be effectively applied in the making of the foreign policy because there is no way of pinpointing all those having some influence, then there is at least that much clarification that the controls may still be applied with some effect to the national, official stages in the process — ultimately, if all else fails, to the highest officials.

The other factor facilitating the application of controls has to do not so much with whom to control as with the limited freedom of choice of any decision-maker (and representing therefore itself a control). There is a fundamental assumption of every foreign policy that it must maintain the state in sovereign independence. Certain behavioral consequences follow. They can be foretold, but only in terms of a very general approach. Predictably every state will devote itself to its own survival. It will seek to preserve territorial and administrative integrity, independence of action, mastery over internal communications, livelihood for its people, and a few other such minimal prerequisites for survival. Even if it were possible to agree on a catalogue of such essentials, it would be impossible to agree on the means to provide for them. Individual decision-makers thus still retain a freedom of choice. Controls will have to remain fairly general, and hence sacrifice along with specificity some effectiveness. But at least knowledge of the minimum requirements for state survival provides some basis for devising controls. Beyond this minimum, that is to say when states act to pursue less than vital interests, their behavior becomes even less predictable and the controls correspondingly less applicable.

One fundamental difficulty in formulating and applying political controls is that where foreign policy is not just accidental, individual judgments are crucial in every step of its making, not just of one but many individuals, and that the identity of some or all the individuals may be obscure. The same may be true in the making of internal national policies. The difference is that national publics wish to maintain their state. This enabled the creation of a central government with (usually) sufficient strength to control any behavior, regardless of its source or aims. The unpredictability of a citizen's behavior is balanced by the effective limits the state can set. Any uncertainty about who is to control whom and how is ended when the existence of the national society itself is at stake. At that point the political system has the capability of suppressing inimical behavior and enforcing the requisite social behavior. Knowledge of the state's capability is then a great inducement to the citizen to submit to lesser controls. The arrangement is simple, crude, and effective. Should all other controls fail, the state normally has an unfailing broad-spectrum, catchall control in the form of the central government's force. Even within states this control may fail, as civil wars show.[41] But there still remains a difference. Within states, such a failure is exceptional. The international society lacks not only such a catchall control commonly and collectively organized, it lacks altogether the complex set of political controls available to states.

States have been groping for a substitute which would help them overcome the difficulty of pinpointing whom to control in order to control the behavior of other states. They have found it in trying to influence the circumstances in which foreign policy makers must operate rather than in attempting to influence the makers themselves. If they can succeed in doing this, the individuality of the policy maker becomes quite irrelevant. So-called containment policies are a good illustration. If a state can be successfully isolated from the international society, who its foreign policy makers are becomes unimportant. Beleaguering a city-state in the Middle Ages is another illustration. Blockade yet another. Another closely related method is the threat of force and destruction. If the threatened state decides that it cannot resist violence successfully, it will have to surrender and, again, the individuality of the decision-makers becomes irrelevant. These methods have the added advantage of permitting the state that feels stronger than its enemy to exploit its superiority to the fullest and of securing success more probably than with almost any other control. It is not surprising, then, that the uncertain effectiveness of most controls and the difficulty of knowing the targets of the controls quickly tempts governments to rely on force as the control best designed to overcome both these difficulties.

Establishing the Controls

The difficulty of knowing whom to control is matched by the difficulty of introducing controls or making (latent) existing ones effective. The deliberate creation of rules, regulations, laws is part of the process. Another part is to use and make acceptable controls lying in the nature of things, but things men can influence (e.g., the behavioral controls implicit in either a market or a socialist economy). Behavioral controls are an integral part of human coexistence, but men have choices among the forms of coexistence and therewith some social controls. It is, for example, evident that anything, most importantly sentimental bonds, which fosters social relations and cohesion will strengthen social controls. When interests create interaction and interdependence, behavior interfering with the pursuit of the interests will be suppressed. One does not kill the goose that lays the golden egg. In addition to controls imposed upon a state by its internal conditions, there are external controls arising from the fact that all states are irrevocably involved in international relations. Their foreign policies must dovetail with those of some 150 others. This limits the freedom of action of even the most powerful states. Being a unit in the international system affects the behavior of states just as do their own characteristics. States act in a shared environment and must achieve goals through some form of interaction. There arise pressures of the situation, created by men to be sure, but which in turn determine to a considerable extent the options men have for their behavior. The system, in short, exerts inescapable but manipulable influences upon the actions of states. It does so through expressly formulated controls (e.g., laws), through instruments or organs serving control functions (e.g., centralized or diffused government, sacrifices for the general welfare), or through latent effects of institutions manifestly for other purposes (virtually all institutions calling for cooperation or mutual adjustment of some sort).

The interrelationships among all these elements of the society performing control functions will transmit the weakness of any one of them to all the others. They all share the burden of maintaining social order. The failure of one overburdens the others, occasionally to the point of breakdown. For this reason the introduction of specific and individual controls into a society (e.g., in the form of a law) as a piecemeal process is really exceptional, and the control so introduced is a fraction of the whole control system. The overall system of controls in a society — certainly as far as they are systemic — is an integral part of the growth of society in general. Eventually even individual controls, once introduced piecemeal, become a part of the control system that perpetuates itself from generation to generation. Similarly, the introduction of the individual to the controls must be a comprehensive and simultaneous process. He must be made to accept the limitations upon

156

his behavior, and in such a way that, as a minimum, he does not suffer constant frustration and thus be tempted to rebel against them. This problem is taken care of by the process of socialization, which applies equally to individuals becoming members of their national society and to individuals, groups, and states becoming members of the international society.

Conceivably, societies — states rarely among them — could be based essentially on command and punishment. In that case, socialization is hardly required to maintain social order. The international society has a good many characteristics of such societies. More often, and to some extent also in the case of the international society, command and punishment are supplementary to a more agreeable or at least acquiescent acceptance of social controls based on habits, convenience, rewards, self-interest, and similar motivations. Socialization is the mechanism by which these motivations are activated and the social controls are made effective. Ultimately, the existence and the strength of social controls can be traced back to the character of the socialization process. The assumption is therefore justified that the effectiveness of social controls in national societies and their relative ineffectiveness in the international society have something to do with the process by which individuals and groups are socialized as members of these societies.

Ideally, socialization produces behavior satisfying the individual's wishes while also satisfying the society's needs and expectations. It is a teaching and learning process in which through interaction the individual and his society adjust to each other's requirements. As the individual grows into his society, he learns to form a socially conditioned conception of his roles. He knows what is expected of him, what is forbidden or allowed. The rationale of the conditions upon his behavior is his survival in a surviving society. But since he is a member of many societies, both those smaller than his state and the larger international one, the question is, which surviving society? Since the rise of the nation-state the answer has been given loud and clear: the national society.

The individual is socialized as a national. The national society has obtained such an enormous influence upon all its subgroups that the state has become the overall determinant of the direction socialization takes. The state insures that the individual does not just become a narrow role player in a subgroup or just a human being in the international society. The state directs the socialization so that the individual will not sacrifice his state's welfare either to a subgroup of which he is a member or to any society wider than his state. This practice was illustrated by a group of psychiatrists who confirmed that they would keep all statements of their patients a professional secret, except if the patient revealed himself as a spy, in which case they would inform the F.B.I. This socialization as a national proceeds not merely negatively in subgroups; that is, socialization into subgroups not only does not interfere with socialization as a national, it very often assists positively in this socialization. And to the extent that subgroups so assist the nation they become transmission belts for the controls maintaining the national society. The national society monopolizes their services. The manner in which the primary group (family, neighborhood) or the small-group experience of the individual is exploited by the nation is exclusive. The transvaluation of the personal community experience for the benefit of the national community makes this experience for a still wider community unsuitable. The concepts fatherland, homeland, brotherhood of citizens, and so on specifically exclude other nations, set them apart.

The international society is remote from the individual. The small groups in which his socialization begins do virtually nothing to socialize him into the international society. Most individuals experience the international society, if ever, after they have become integrated into the national society, after they have learned and are enacting the behavior of the national. Their socialization into the international society, if there is such a process at present, is mostly a collective process mediated by the nation. It is an indirect and very likely biased process. The major and often only role into which the individual is socialized for the international society is as a national or nationalist. By comparison the significance of any other role, perhaps as a foreign trader, a tourist, or a student, pales. The state's monopoly over the individual's socialization severely limits any impact the international society might have upon the individual's behavior.[42] The idea of sovereignty is so dominant that technological and social changes are immediately related to their possible effect upon the state's power potential and autonomy. Indeed, the public's willingness to make sacrifices during times of war has often led to the greatest social and technological progress. The socialization process does not, of course, lead to identical behavior of all individuals. Its effect is uneven, with individual responsiveness varying greatly. But the homogenized result in conditioning the public — especially in behavior as nationals — will guarantee that there will always be support of the social controls chosen by states rather than by the international society. The chronological advantage the state has in getting at the individual first makes his international social relations an extension of his already firmly established national social relations. This sequence in developing the social nature of the national can help to explain the delay in behavioral adjustments which the new national and international conditions require, for the national socialization process is bound to have strongly conservative features. It will always tend to socialize individuals into existing known rather than into unknown future societies. Of social necessity the older generation transmits to the next generation the conditions of their society, makes the next generation aware of the prevailing constraints or alternatives of behavior, establishes and administers the rewards and punishments for behavior.

In many new states this situation is quite dramatically highlighted when very flexible and active individuals — often exposed outside their own society to other socialization processes — reject the contents of their society's traditional socialization process and wish to substitute a different, new content. The resulting tensions (the generation gap!) may be dissolved in favor of the traditional society or of the rebelling individuals. But the situation shows that change is possible and how it may come about. It is a lesson not only for national societies, but for the international society as well.

In the absence of the kind of upheavals many new states have gone through, the prevalent socialization processes everywhere, including now also the new states, remain directed toward turning the individual into a national. Their collective result is to give the national dominant behavioral characters, which resemble each other closely from state to state. The reason is that the processes everywhere aim at placing the state on the top of the citizen's hierarchy of social values. He is conditioned to solve any conflict among the various roles he plays or between one of his roles and that of another citizen in favor of the state. This is particularly true for his state's foreign policies, which he is expected to support as a patriotic duty, if necessary at the expense of his usual rights as an individual. Even in free societies criticism of foreign policy is looked at askance and at times of crisis condemned outright. Activist opposition and protest tend to be labeled traitorous (as for instance during Great Britain's war against Egypt in 1956 or America's war in Vietnam during the middle 1960s).

The characteristic result — if not also the aim — of the individual's socialization as a national is an utmost limitation of internal social controls upon the policy makers. The secrecy with which foreign affairs are handled in totalitarian states, the discretion often granted to governments in parliamentary regimes, the call for "bipartisan" foreign policies are all indicators of a practice to make the formulation of foreign policies as free from internal constraints as possible. It is reinforced by a notorious lack of interest among all national publics in their foreign affairs with the result that a nonexistent public opinion gives the government a free hand or that the public reacts after the fact without much hampering the government. The exceptions are represented mostly by stereotyped, sloganized general directions a public wants its policies to have, such as "splendid isolation" or "no entangling alliances," or to issues of a general nature and long duration, such as the recognition of the Communist government in China by the United States or whether Great Britain should join the European Economic Community. In general the socialization of the national means that a government can devise foreign policy quite freely within a rather broad framework constructed of the state's given capabilities and environment and of the citizenry's unrefined, if any, concepts about a desirable foreign policy.[43]

There is also a socialization process for states. But while nationals are, so to speak, socialized within the society from the individual up to the national society, this other socialization takes place from the outside in, from the international society down to the national societies. Here too interaction is the channel through which states are socialized. The means are contacts between members of the various states across their national boundaries. They can be private individuals, but they are in fact mostly officials: diplomats, international civil servants, foreign ministers. It is mainly through them that the creation and learning of the international society's social norms take place. The contacts can be on a bilateral or multilateral basis. They can be face to face or through symbols to which states react. International organizations are veritable schools for the training of diplomats. They are the most significant institutions in which the international socialization process occurs and in which mutual adjustments between the international society and its state units can be achieved. The process is continuous and mutual. Nevertheless, richer, older, more established states are more influential in setting the norms of behavior, just as the older generation tends to be within national societies. Age, wealth, prestige, high status are the attributes of leadership enabling their possessors to sway society and to direct the socialization processes. Many situations illustrate this condition.

A number of young, new states, for instance, entered the international society with preconceived, somewhat revolutionary concepts. Most of these states have quite quickly and tamely accepted the formal and informal controls established centuries ago and still conditioning the behavior of states. The idea of the European Economic Community has served as a precedent, often copied but never reached. Japanese nationalism has had a tremendous impact on all Asian states. The Western method of creating and manipulating nationalism has been followed everywhere. Colonists have decisively shaped much of the behavior of new states. European cultural traditions and Chinese cultural traditions have greatly influenced the Western and Eastern worlds. Sometimes examples are followed for prestige reasons, sometimes they recommend themselves for their reasonableness, sometimes they are enforced. In general, states learn quickly which behavior will bring rewards and which punishments. Historically and still today the older, most powerful, and usually Western nations possess most of the means of rewards and punishments and so their behavior and norms and controls remain precedent setting.

The socialization of states, as has been pointed out earlier, is in reality the socialization of individuals. For international politics this means that several generally identifiable groups of individuals must be considered who play different roles and for whom, therefore, different controls should be devised. There are the national citizens supporting foreign policies; special interest groups (lobbyists, journalists, idealists, etc.) seeking special influences upon the making of foreign policy; and the makers of decisions in the government agencies. The first two groups are fully socialized as nationals. Whatever support is expected of them for national foreign policies is likely to be forthcoming. They are not much exposed to the influences emanating from the international scene. International political controls are not likely to affect them directly or to any appreciable extent. This means that international controls, i.e., mainly controls coming from beyond the state, must be effective mostly for the makers of foreign policy decisions. They too are nationals. But they are socialized also into their role as decision-makers, and part of that socialization process takes place in the international society.

As a mediator between his national and the international society, the decision-maker is exposed in his role learning to influences from within and without his state. Both societies inform him what is permissible and what is not; what is expected of him; and what behavior will bring his state the greatest advantages. Like all socialization processes, the international socialization of the decision-maker brings him closer to other decision-makers in a pattern of behavior that they all share. There is a professionalism of decision-makers resulting from formal national and international norms as well as informal institutions and necessities. Decision-makers, especially on the highest echelons, often possess similar backgrounds, have like expectations of each other, conduct themselves in similar ways, use many identical sources of information, are accustomed to symbols peculiarly their own, and communicate frequently.[44] Their operational codes are largely the same, so that they all have similar understandings of the international controls applying to them.[45] There should, however, be no confusion of common professionalism and similar socialization with consensus and solidarity. On the contrary, the socialization of the decision-makers and diplomats conditions them to consider the national interest first and foremost, and to assume the worst of their foreign colleagues until these have proven themselves trustworthy!

The total result of the socialization processes, whether taking place on the national or the international scene, is therefore an emphasis upon social and political controls safeguarding the welfare of individual states rather than that of the international society. In particular, individuals, in whatever role, are primarily conditioned to be obedient to controls emanating from within their state or to support only those emanating from without which help in the survival of individual states. As the borderline between internal and external affairs of a state becomes blurred, as linkages increase, not only will controls geared more to the maintenance of an international social order impose themselves upon states, but the greater exposure of more people to the international society directly will also make the controls more acceptable. In the meantime, the controls prevailing in the international society are mainly those coming from within states, those inherent in the nature of things (mostly of the international society itself), and those depending upon the use of force. That they have some effect is shown by the measure of social order existing in the international society. That their effect is unreliable is due mainly to the arbitrary, unequal, and often intermittent nature of their application.

Kinds of Political Controls

The arbitrariness of political controls rests on the ability of powerful states to impose them upon weaker states while themselves escaping from them. The inequality exists because the same reward or punishment may have totally different results among highly unequal states. Under such circumstances the inherent potency of the controls becomes fairly irrelevant. And the importance of differentiating between different kinds of controls or of evaluating their relative effectiveness diminishes greatly when states can ignore controls altogether. No state can, however, ignore all controls. Its ability to be selective depends to a great extent upon a given situation. There is still some utility in examining the various kinds of controls and how they are supposed to be effective. For many of them are man-made and manipulable. The hope may therefore be permitted that their efficacy might be improved.

There are a variety of criteria according to which kinds of controls can be classified. There are institutionalized and noninstitutionalized controls. They can differ in regard to their methods, such as rewarding or punishing; or in regard to their appeal, such as positive incentive or negative deterrent. They can vary according to source, whether, for instance, they originate within or without the state. They can aim at man's motivation or at his action. A most important distinction is whether the controls are entirely dependent upon the will of man or whether they are in the nature of (political) things. Examples of this last category would be restraints upon behavior resulting from interaction and mutual dependence; from the established patterns in which states interrelate; from political habits and customs developed over centuries. These kinds of controls are only partially subject to human manipulation and they are continuously operative. Man's choice among them is limited and difficult. But while the choice is greater among the many kinds of controls constructed by men, the problem remains nevertheless which ones to apply. For whether or not they will achieve their ends depends upon largely unpredictable and inscrutable factors, all related to human nature. Among these factors are the nature of the specific controls, the specific persons and peoples relevant to the situation, and the specific circumstances of the situation. Those who must decide upon which controls to bring into play usually only know types of controls generally effective in classes of situations involving kinds of individuals. Yet the greatest effectiveness of the controls requires that decision-makers ought to know what specific controls should be applied in the specific circumstances. These details cannot be known with certainty. In the absence of an international agency applying some surely effective blanket control when all else fails, states tend to rely upon controls they themselves can enforce. The deciding factor thus once more becomes superiority in a contest of capabilities. To ensure victory in such a contest, each state then tries to gain control over the controls, either alone or in combination with friends and allies. Luckily for the social order in the international society, not all controls lend themselves to manipulation by just one state and some (e.g., rewards) are not resented as restraints upon behavior at all. The point here is that there are various ways in which state behavior can be guided and influenced — with some much more acceptable to states than others.

Those controls inherent in the nature of things are usually acquiesced in by states as being part of the environment. They can be situations in which states find themselves, situations that result from the cross-cutting of political processes without having been deliberately created. They can be social forces emerging from changes in the society that were not specifically produced as social controls (e.g., the modern cooperative versus the older separative international society — the state in isolation). Although the character of these controls could be changed by human will (systemic influences could be changed by a change of the system; restraints imposed by interaction could be eliminated by ceasing the interaction), this would at best be a long-range enterprise and is rarely undertaken deliberately. These controls may be effective because they are either taken for granted or accepted rationally as inevitable.

A second group of controls is intended to be effective through voluntary consensus. The binding force of moral and legal norms cannot itself rest upon some other moral or legal norms. It must ultimately rest on its voluntary acceptance by states when they joined the society of "civilized nations." Even this construction is not too useful because agreement on norms in general still makes possible disagreement on their meaning; because elevating fulfillment of national interests to the highest moral and legal priority nullifies in fact all other norms; and because the depersonalization of foreign policy making and international politics eliminates the controlling function of a conscience and the sense of responsibility. Above all, when submission to behavioral constraints is assumed to be voluntary, rejection of these restraints is relatively easy. In the end, whether states obey or ignore international laws, moral norms or recommendations, and majority decisions will depend very much upon how they estimate the outcome of their choice.

A third group of controls relies mainly on self-help to protect a state against arbitrary or unfavorable behavior by another state. Balance of power, collective security systems, alliances are part of this group. The basic idea of such arrangements is to assure a preponderance of strength should it come to a contest of capabilities. Their cheapest use would be as a deterrent, the most expensive as a guarantee of eventual victory. These arrangements are not primarily intended to prevent conflicts or settle them directly. Their manifest purpose is to avoid violence or, if they are applied aggressively, to obtain advantages. Their contribution to the nonviolent settlement of conflicts as a by-product consists in making the use of violence too costly. If that price can be raised sufficiently, conflict might be avoided altogether by suppressing a state's demand as hopeless.

164

The Controls on International Behavior

The fourth group of controls is primarily directed toward minimizing conflicts, regularizing their solution, and avoiding violence. From the standpoint of peace, they are more constructive than the previous group. International law, procedures adopted in international organizations, and the methods for the peaceful settlement of international conflicts belong in this group. Collectively, these controls are intended to encourage peaceful behavior among states; to offer alternatives to the forcible settlement of conflicts; to develop habits of adjustment and compromise; to keep channels of communication open; and to substitute community methods for confrontation methods in the pursuit of national interests. These controls relate to the symptoms of conflict rather than its causes. They attempt to avoid violent behavior rather than to create common interests which would tolerate conflicts and lead to their peaceful settlement. The international society remains characterized by an emphasis upon conflict rather than upon an increase in the social product made possible by collective action. Therefore the emphasis remains also on controls whose incentive is punitive more often than rewarding.

Only relatively recently has the growing functional interdependence among states become pronounced enough to become quite effective as a social control. In particular the economic interaction, or at least a sensitivity of states to each other, has developed into an important additional group of social controls. And it is a group which has at least the potential of rewarding peaceful behavior. The stakes in a conflict may not be worth disrupting the network of interests otherwise tying states together. Instead of threatening each other, states may make themselves most attractive to each other in order to produce the desired behavior. There is a positive incentive to accept the social controls. The purpose of many international organizations is to develop this incentive by producing a greater awareness of common interests and by stimulating the growth of such interests.

These various groups of controls do not exist in isolation from each other. They are often coeffective, either because they are simultaneously operative or because, in the case of some, the possibility of their application alone has some restraining effects. One obviously beneficial result of the interrelatedness of these controls is that the more effectively some controls discourage resort to arbitrarily used force or other disruptive means, the more will states be encouraged to develop the more peaceful and socially constructive controls. This possibility raises the broader question why these controls are effective at all, especially when they have a negative, punitive character.

165

INTERNATIONAL POLITICS

The Effectiveness of Social Controls

In pondering the potency of social controls, it is useful to recall that social controls are part of the mechanism a society has to make itself possible. Very likely, the more the members want their society, the greater the efficacy the controls are allowed to have. There is a relation between the members' commitment to their society and their willingness to submit themselves to the controls. This relationship is least evident where the controls are in the nature of things. For in that case, the choice is not whether or not to have controls. The choice is only about the nature of the things, e.g., the nature of the social system, of the interaction between states, of the organization of international communication. The relationship is most evident in regard to controls established and manipulated by men, mostly the deliberately created, institutionalized, formalized controls.

The efficacy of these controls depends fundamentally on the predisposition of their targets, much more so than upon any enforcement mechanism. Controls unsupported by an inner readiness to accept them can at best be effective only occasionally and not in a reliable fashion. They are likely to be, most of the time, forceful coercion because most other controls can be resisted or rejected too easily. The great importance of the subjective component of effective controls explains why the community spirit is such a powerful source of the controls' effectiveness. The following are a few of the results for controls when a community exists.

In a community, the conception of the common weal — minimally defined as the maintenace of the nation — permeates the ends the controls are to serve. The emotional commitment to the ends leads to acceptance of the controls. Quite possibly individual members of the national society act out of pure self-interest. But as long as they include the survival of the nation in their self-interest, the social and political controls receive their support. This element is missing in the international society, whose maintenance is not necessarily a part of national selfishness. A community, second, affects the hierarchy between power and law. The exercise of power being par excellence the application of political controls, law is par excellence the means to tame power. It is the control of the controls. The common weal of the community — by whomever defined — gives direction to the law as well as to the exercise of power. Both are imbued with the essence of the common social interests underlying the national community. Both represent the interpretation of these interests and their translation into directives for

166

behavior. Law and power are accepted in the name of the common interest. When there are no overriding common interests, as in the international society, but only individual, not collective stakes in the society, the relationship between law and power or the hierarchy among all the controls will be defined by purely individual, expedient national criteria. It will be enforced by the superior power of states, as suits their capabilities and purposes, often by force. This practice is a reflection of the purely functional nexus between states. Anything that serves the function will be done. There are no emotional bonds for whose sake the ultimate pursuit of political interests might be abandoned. If the function is considered valuable enough, the welfare of the society will be sacrificed. This cannot happen in a community where the group existence is the highest value. The usual principle that law legitimizes power is reversed in the international society.

In fact, the whole problem of legitimacy of the controls is unsolved in the international society — a third result of the absence of a community. When the sense of solidarity is lacking, a conviction arises that the political controls are illegitimate, hence unacceptable. With no agreement on the common good, there is no acknowledgment of obligation. For, usually, obligation implied in social controls becomes acceptable only when there is an understanding of common good and common interest which give the obligation moral justification and social rationale. In the long run, legal rules, political controls, or any other social controls based mainly on superior power, especially when exercised through force, do not become part of the normative order acceptable to those under the controls. For this reason rulers even in societies based mainly on brute force claim some legitimacy for their rule. The upshot of this is that international political controls, unless accepted voluntarily, become effective mainly when backed by irresistible power.

Since the benefits of a community do not accrue to the international society, the application or acceptance of political controls is determined by a state's capability to impose or reject them and by purely selfish considerations. Controls will be effective if a cost and benefit analysis demonstrates that it pays the state to submit to controls. In this manner the seeming contradiction between insisting upon sovereignty and tolerating controls upon behavior is partly dissolved. Controlled behavior can be beneficial for sovereign independence. But then the further question arises how such a balance sheet of costs and benefits can be drawn up.

The answer must be general because too many human choices are involved. Many subjective judgments enter into the calculation because many of the items entering into the account are imponderable. Prestige, good reputation, national unity, and similar factors are all involved in foreign policy considerations. After the calculation has shown what the balance might be, the decision will still have to be made whether that state has the capability of coping with it! In sum, it may be possible to say that controls will be effective when states find that it pays to heed them. But whether a state found in actuality that it would so pay can only be discovered after the decision was made!

Such complexity is not unique to the international society. It can be found in national societies. But in these the reliability of political controls is so much greater that the citizen's behavior becomes more easily predictable as being in line with the controls. The reason for this greater effectiveness, while largely based upon the existence of a community, in many cases goes beyond it. First and foremost, the smaller national societies are more fully developed. Most parts, sections, and subsystems perform well and thereby contribute to the adequate performance of every other. The latent quality of all these parts as social controls finds full expression. Second, the socialization process aims at the internalization of the social norms and the development of habits falling within the range of political controls. These norms and habits are specifically directed at the national society, not any smaller nor any larger unit. The socialization process is exclusive, favoring the national society to the detriment of any other social group. Finally, national societies are ongoing groups. Even new states are built upon previously existing societies of sorts. The task of the political controls is then mainly that of perpetuating and maintaining these societies, not of creating them. There is an existing agreement that there is a society, usually encompassing also its basic form. The controls thus implement a prevailing understanding among the members of the society, and this is a considerably easier assignment than to generate original agreement. On each of these counts the international society is at a disadvantage, which goes far in explaining the lesser efficacy of its political controls.

When the weakness of these political controls or their relatively limited number is considered, it becomes rather surprising how much regularity and even predictability there is in the behavior of states. The conclusion is inevitable that world politics takes place under fairly constraining conditions. The enormous number of ingredients going into the make-up of political controls — national attitudes, national interests, inherent systemic controls, given conditions of the environment, institutionalized restraints, personality influences, international interactions, to name only a few prominent ones — produce foreign policies of remarkable consistency. These policies possess permanent regularities and features in goals and methods surviving the most radical changes within states (thereby demonstrating a certain autonomy in foreign policy making in spite of voluminous internal-external linkages) and almost revolutionary (mostly technological) changes on the international scene. It is, for instance, quite easy to demonstrate the persistence of goals and methods, even in some detail, of Tsarist and Communist foreign policies in Russia, or of Manchu, Nationalist, and Communist policies in China. Governments, whether initiating foreign policies or reacting to those of other states, adhere to these consistencies in their own country's foreign policies and rely upon them in the policies of other states. Occasionally, these consistencies assume such symbolic importance (Monroe Doctrine, "no entangling alliances," "splendid isolation," "warm water ports," nonalignment) that they become virtually fixed points around which foreign policy has to be constructed.

Notwithstanding all these consistencies, too many uncertainties remain in the day-by-day formulation of foreign policy to make it sufficiently predictable for a reliable social order. Moreover, the frequent recourse to force as one of the means of foreign policy, though it may be predictable in some situations, is itself a contribution to social disorder. Nevertheless, even in the absence of the overall, catchall control by application of force to some states or in the fair certainty that it may not be used, the political controls of the international society produce some regularities in the behavior of states. That national egoism is likely to be the strongest basis for the effectiveness of these controls cannot please the moralist, nor even the pragmatist, because there is always the possibility that selfishness will dictate disregard of the controls. But the resulting modicum of social order should serve as a consolation and as an indicator that selfishness need not be totally detrimental to the international society as long as men everywhere prefer order to chaos. It is a confirmation also of the idea that the ends of the political system may partly be achieved by mutual adjustment (Charles Lindblom) or by tacit coordination (Thomas Schelling) even in the absence of a powerful central decision-making organ. These possibilities should, however, not be exaggerated. The excessive politicization of the international society provides very limited scope for such informal adjustments. In the overwhelming number of cases, any such arrangements can only be sanctioned by governments, who rarely act "informally" in international politics. Whatever may be found out about political controls, formal or informal, inherent in the nature of things or made by men, as long as the use of force by individual states remains one of them, the order and peace of the international society remains threatened. The most important question therefore remains to be answered, namely, what is the source and nature of international conflicts that can induce states to use violence to the point of war and possible self-destruction in their settlement.

7 International Conflicts and Their Settlement

CONFLICT as social behavior is as much an integral part of all social behavior as cooperation, competition, and other forms of behavior. But it represents a greater threat to the order of the society than other forms. For in a conflict, by definition, two or more states wish to be in command of something valued by each, of which only one can be in command. Each party is therefore trying to thwart the fulfillment of the other's wish. At least one of the parties is often eager and able to ignore controls upon its behavior and act in an asocial or antisocial manner in order to settle the conflict in its favor. The weakness of political controls in the international society seduces states into such behavior. It is mainly only a question of a state's will and capability whether it wants to engage in it.

Because in a conflict situation political controls become most obnoxious as well as most relevant, international conflicts are among the best tests of the political controls' efficacy. In the first place, a conflict situation imposes great stress upon the controls. To the extent that the conflict behavior remains within the bounds set by the controls, it confirms their strength. In the second place, to the extent that the conflict behavior makes a socially constructive rather than destructive contribution to the society, it testifies to the controls' flexibility — a most important quality in changing societies. Finally, if the controls can induce a settlement leading to new, improved social conditions, the conflict has demonstrated the creative qualities of the political controls.

These relationships between conflict, political controls, and settlement are in principle not unique to the international society. But the special character of the society gives these relationships some special aspects. In particular, the threat or use of force by individual states as a method for solving conflicts

171

is more frequent and prominent. Because a state can apply force arbitrarily and unilaterally, its destructive potential is greater and the social cost of settling the conflict can become enormous. Moreover, because in the international society the use of violence regularly provokes counterviolence, the more constructive methods of settling a conflict (e.g., negotiation leading to compromise) tend to be suppressed. The chance that a conflict may have socially creative effects is greatly diminished. The international socialization process fails in this respect too. It is the reverse of national socialization processes, where the aim is to inhibit the socially dysfunctional use of violence and to strengthen socially supportive methods of settling conflicts. The international political system provides for peaceful methods. But the uncertainty of their application causes national publics to expect war and states to have ready recourse to violence with impunity because the system decrees no consequences to obeying or disobeying norms of behavior. States are in practice free to choose among the methods for settling conflicts on the basis of utilitarian considerations. With no fear of a coercive authority above them — other than the opponent — and little restraint from internalized norms (a conscience), at least powerful states have options for settling their conflicts not available to citizens. They may successfully disregard political controls or exercise controls individually and arbitrarily, and they do.

If the political controls are to be effective in conflict situations, and if the methods for peaceful settlement are to be minimally helpful in preventing conflicts from becoming socially destructive — in brief, if violence as one likely form of social destructiveness is to be avoided, one among the conditions must be that a nonviolent settlement promises as much profit as any other.

To provide an incentive for using peaceful methods for the settlement of international conflicts is a difficult task for its designers. The political system disposes of few certain rewards or punishments. At times the assignment is impossible. For there can be interests in conflict important enough to each party so that they refuse to settle it in any manner other than a trial of strength: war. This extreme situation points up two problems in the relationship between conflicts and their settlement. One is that there may be interests involved which either by their nature or by choice of the parties do not lend themselves to a settlement. The other is that different kinds of interests in a conflict require different methods of settlement. In the consideration of international conflicts and of settling them in a manner most favorable to the maintenance of social order and peace, three aspects are of outstanding importance and will now be examined. The first is the

172

interests at stake in the conflict and how they affect the possibility of a settlement. The second is the range of available direct and indirect controls in their interrelationships (the total social control system) and how it may contribute to the peacefulness of social change as the source of most conflicts. The third is the methods specifically designed for the peaceful settlement of international conflicts and their potency.

The Stakes of the Conflict

The interest over which states get into conflict can be anything. This is owing to the limited supply of anything that men covet, including now fresh air. There are, however, differences in the possibility of settling such conflicts depending upon what specific interest is at stake. The nature of some interests is inherently such that they cannot be compromised, adjusted, divided between the parties. And one of the problems bedeviling the international society, as will be shown, is that states, in order to justify their conflict behavior, often pretend that a given interest involved in their conflict is of such nature. They then formulate their interest in all or nothing terms and, if they mean what they say and the interest is important enough to them, they will risk war to defend it.

Conflicts are insoluble because of the nature of the stakes when they are formulated in ideological terms; or more precisely when the conflict involves ideological systems. To the extent, for instance, that democracy or fascism, capitalism or socialism, have become missionary objectives of states and are incompatible, a conflict situation based on these ideologies cannot be settled. A nonsolution would be the only solution. Each state would have to desist from proselytizing; would have to exclude ideological preferences from political methods and goals. Many states have done this internally with some success when, for instance, religion becomes a citizen's "private affair." States could do the same and have in fact done so on many occasions. The strange ideological bedfellows in alliances or other cooperation throughout history show that states will ignore ideological differences when it pays them to do so. The prospect of immediate benefit from cooperation has often made states forgo long-range victory for their particular ideology. The "peaceful coexistence" of the Communist and capitalist worlds is merely a recent illustration of an ancient practice. This treatment of ideology by "realistic" statesmen illustrates the argument made earlier that in international politics ideologies are more often servants than originators of policies. States-

173

men may not perceive this as a matter of principle. They certainly act in accordance with it. Luckily so, for if international conflict were really to turn upon the victory of one ideology over an incompatible rival ideology, it would end either never or in the destruction of one of the protagonists!

Conflicts over vital national interests are a second category of those considered to be insoluble, although this is in fact not a matter of their inherent nature. To take an extreme case: when two states are in conflict over the issue of whether one of them should exist or not, the state to be abolished would certainly consider the conflict insoluble. In reality only this state's choice for existence makes the conflict insoluble, or even provokes the conflict in the first place. For all practical purposes, however, there are national interests which states do consider vital in the sense that they would not accept any compromise but would defend these interests to the bitter end. This determination is at the base of the struggle for power. The international political system makes a state's power the most important protector of its vital interests — its very existence foremost among them. In principle, no state can cease to develop its power potential. Inasmuch as this process causes conflicts, to abandon it would be tantamount to abandoning vital national interests. The most that can be expected is that details in the development of the power potential may be subject to compromise if they cause conflict.

The aggravating factor in the difficulty of solving conflicts arising from the struggle for power is that because of the politicization of the international society, the struggle for power permeates almost all international activities of states. It is virtually impossible to separate it out and isolate it. Statesmen are quick, first, to evaluate every conflict from the standpoint of their state's survival. Many issues in conflict, minor in themselves, assume an undue importance from that standpoint. They are always seen in a broader context and can rarely be solved on their own merits because the overall power struggle overshadows them. Statesmen are quick, second, also to evaluate everything from the standpoint of its contribution to the state's power potential. This means that everything can readily be related to the area of "vital interests." Obviously, under these circumstances the peaceful settlement of an international conflict always becomes a problem. The irony of the whole situation is — as was mentioned in discussing the nature of power — that the process of building up a power potential in order to protect vital interests becomes itself a vital interest and can generate insoluble conflict where there was none before. Quite correctly, for instance, one state may resent the development of a power potential by another because obviously the potential will be used in some future situation either to escape from political controls or to impose them upon other states. Even if the target against which the power is to be used is not yet identified, the experience has been that the building up of a power potential as such is a cause of tension among states, quite apart from the specific conflicts over details which may arise in the process. The factor of tension is therefore always related to the question of national survival and becomes highly relevant to the possibility or perhaps better the impossibility of settling conflicts without violence.

Tension is a special form of conflict. It is essentially a covert psychic discord, discoverable by deduction from overt behavior. No precise definition of tension can be given. It is possible, however, to say that this psychic state when found in international politics consists of a sense of anxiety about the relations between states. This sense is born from mankind's historic experience of enmity and strife. It is sustained by the fear of future threat and the expectation of violence. This anxiety is general, unrelated to any specific situation. It springs from a synthesis of past and anticipated dangerous situations. It is the social-psychological sediment precipitated from knowledge about centuries of hostile relationships as manifested mainly in an unending struggle for power. It is reinforced by evidence that in the growing complexity of international existence states which can afford to, tend to solve their problems by means of threats in the belief that this might be the easiest way out. And the greater that inequalities between states grow, the more does this means recommend itself to the states deeming themselves stronger. America's containment policy after World War II is a good illustration of this practice. Tension is a latent, psychologically based conflict from which few peoples can escape any more than they can escape from active or passive participation in the power struggle between states.

Any concrete, specific, and overt conflict can trigger the tension into an acute stage. Its unspecific and diffuse nature parallels the similar nature of the struggle for power. Both are interwoven as a mutual cause and effect relation: the struggle for power is a source as well as a result of international tension. Both color and permeate international relations. The ubiquity of both makes them a permanent feature of the prevailing international politics. There is no way of wiping out tensions rapidly short of wiping out social historic memories, together with the also historically based features of the contemporary international political system. These memories and the system interact, helping to perpetuate both, giving to each other their reasons for

175

existence. The memories drive people to take refuge in institutions which in earlier periods may have protected these peoples' interests: sovereignty, frontiers, buffer states, and the like. The institutions then produce animosities and violence forming the substance of these memories. In the future the gap between the realities of international politics and anachronistic attitudes rooted in past conditions is likely to narrow. Tensions generated in an earlier period will change in character or may disappear — when, e.g., violence between states is no longer a viable alternative or economic rewards rather than national grandeur become the aims of international activity. In the meantime, the psychology responsible for tensions remains a survival. The best that is likely to happen is a lessening of the intensity of prevailing tensions for certain periods when the pursuit of growing shared interests promotes rational conviction that violence is unrewarding, hence unlikely.

The behavior indicative of an underlying tension is characterized by suspicion and mistrust; by an inclination to interpret the opponent's actions in the worst possible manner; by anticipatory bellicose responses; and generally by negative, defensive postures. It is characterized by the story of two delegates in the United Nations building passing each other. One said, "Good morning," whereupon the other turned to a friend, saying, "Now, what could he have meant by that?" One serious consequence of tension is that it is likely to affect the perceptions of those responsible for making policy. Typical were instructions given to delegates of imperial Germany to international conferences in which they were warned never to accept any statement at face value, always to assume that a permanent conspiracy against German interest was afoot. In the mentality affected by tension, policy makers tend to see hostilities where none exist.[46]

Another serious consequence of tension is that a conflict over a concrete measurable (and soluble) issue (e.g., a piece of territory, the precise course of a borderline) may aggravate preexisting tension and serve as the confirmation of its reason for being. Or preexisting tension may turn an issue into a conflict which it might not have become otherwise. Open conflicts may thus be both symbols of existing tensions as well as conflicts in their own right, so that the immediate and apparent nature of the cause may not determine the importance or outcome of the conflict.

Amid prevailing tension every overt conflict over even a minor issue is endowed with the character and magnitude of a power conflict. A settlement of the concrete issue will not merely be difficult; it will scarcely affect the overall conflict situation which is the tension and which rages over the general power positions of the contestants. Disagreement between France and Great Britain over the ownership of some uninhabited islands in the English Channel was so insignificant in the absence of acute tension between the two countries that the issue was virtually unknown to the public. The ownership of some islands in the Ussuri River has the makings of a major conflict between the Soviet Union and China because of the prevailing tension.

Berlin after World War II provides another illustration. The city has become a symbol of the "East-West conflict." Neither the United States nor the Soviet Union has a major concrete interest in Berlin. Yet neither side would willingly cede an inch on any issue turning around Berlin. The smallest incident is handled with the greatest care as a possible cause of war. At the same time a settlement of the Berlin issue would presumably not basically affect the East-West conflict. Very likely, the chronology would be the other way around. A settlement of the East-West conflict would make the whole Berlin issue irrelevant as a direct conflict between the United States and the Soviet Union. But such a settlement, which would mean abolition of the power struggle between the two major nations, would require the abolition of the present international political system. Since this is not likely to happen in any foreseeable future, the two nations, like all others, will not willingly surrender any means they may possess for settling through their own efforts conflicts related to the struggle for power. Nor will they permit a settlement of such conflicts that requires any concession on their part unless superior power persuades them to do so. In this manner, the psychic state of tension creates the conditions which guarantee its own perpetuation. States have institutionalized this tension by dividing conflicts into those which they consider unrelated to their national survival and which they consider soluble, and those which touch upon their very existence and which they consider insoluble, such as the struggle for power. But states do not put this differentiation so crudely. The distinction is institutionalized in a more subtle manner, namely in the form of legal and political conflicts, sometimes more narrowly designated as justiciable and nonjusticiable conflicts.

The idea in separating these two groups of conflicts is that the latter kind do not lend themselves to settlement by legal or quasi-legal procedures, including arbitration. They are claimed to be soluble only by direct negotiation, or in any case only by direct methods relating the two contestants. The implication is that each contestant can apply all the means at his disposal, in short seek a political solution of the conflict. The distinction has been introduced into a number of treaties (e.g., the so-called Locarno Treaties of 1925). There has also been much sophisticated discussion among international lawyers turning on the question whether there can be "gaps" in the law. Is it possible that there are situations which the law did not foresee and to which it therefore does not apply, or is it true that what the law does not forbid is allowed?

Unending and inconclusive debate notwithstanding, the simple fact is that states make the distinction in order to escape the obligation to use established, generally agreed methods for the peaceful, orderly settlement of their disputes: When states feel that they can settle a dispute in their favor by using their own means they will declare it to be a "political" dispute. They may take this position regardless of what the legal situation is, possibly even if the law favors them. Much of the time they also take this position because they know what the law is and they are dissatisfied with it. They would not have any claim according to existing law. They do not challenge the interpretation of the law. They challenge the law that creates the unwanted situation. They desire a new legal situation, either because the prevailing situation has become unacceptable or because the facts have already changed but the law has failed to change with them.

From the standpoint of law this problem relates to its task of reconciling social order with the adjustment to new social conditions and needs. From the broader political and yet broader social standpoint, the problem is to make social change orderly and peaceful. This is the most fundamental and comprehensive problem of conflict solution because social change is the root of most social conflict. For the contradictory reactions of the society's members who are unequally affected by change produce conflict. The threat to orderly behavior from change occurs for mainly two reasons. The first is that change renders obsolete habits, customs, laws, and possibly whole cultures; in brief, it renders obsolete ways of life. And it does so — the second reason — in possibly surprising, abrupt fashion and with unforeseeable results. Change can be socially most unsettling. The solution of the problem cannot be to suppress change, because this is impossible. It can only be to organize the complex of change and its corollary conflict in a manner to advance the evolution of society.

A three-pronged attack becomes necessary. The first, already discussed, is the most basic: the most promising type of society for the gradualness of change and the peaceful settlement of conflicts is a community. The second attack, to be discussed next, is political. It relates to decisions on the preservation of orderly behavior, the distribution of material values, and the management of social issues. In other words, it relates to the development of procedures to make change orderly and its consequences peaceful. This enterprise involves the whole range of available social controls in their interrelationships; it involves the whole social control system. The third attack is legal, representing a specialized aspect of the control system. It is essential because in any but the most rigid, simple communal society the procedures for dealing with change must in part at least be established in explicit, distinguishable legal rules and channeled through machinery constructed for the execution of the laws.

Peaceful Change: The Politics

The political implications of social change are obvious. They lie, first, in the position of every member in the society. Change affects rights and duties, privileges and obligations, status and wealth. It affects states where they are most sensitive, in their power potential. Their attempts to deal with the consequences of change are most conflictful and always a potential danger to peace. They lie, second, in the process of change, regardless of its eventual outcome. Change in any society can be expected and sudden. In the absence of procedures to cope with it adequately and in the face of suspicions typical of international politics, the unpredictability of change makes it more dangerous to states than even its possible results. Stability in international relations is a value cherished more highly by most states than the status quo. Nations, for instance, often experience the threat and actuality of violence as less dangerous than the unpredictable and irregular occurrence of either. Quite realistically, because it is inevitable, change is not opposed as much as the irregularity and disorderliness of it. History is full of examples demonstrating that crises arise because of a highly uncertain direction of a state's behavior and that they recede as soon as the element of uncertainty vanishes, even though a situation, initially seemingly objectionable, continues to exist. A modus vivendi has been found and that seems to be a major concern to states. The Vietnam War presents a recent illustration. The United States and China had very tense relations over the expansion of American action until signals between the two nations made clear the limits to which each would go and beyond which neither would produce sudden or radical changes. Thereafter tensions not only disappeared but friendly relations were established in spite of the fact that American intervention in Vietnam continued.

In the international society, the erratic occurrence of change and the uncertainty of its consequences create tensions which are always harbingers of conflict. The international political system is a dual failure here because it provides only weak procedures for guaranteeing predictable and regular, i.e., stable, change and inadequate methods for preventing violence from resulting from change. The institutions of national societies, ultimately the catchall control of the government, normally prevent the deterioration of the conflict into violence. The citizens' knowledge that the terminal point of their conflicts is reached before violence can be used has a beneficial effect upon the growth of procedures for peaceful settlement of conflicts and stable change. Also, interests will not be developed which could only be fulfilled with the help of violence. For the same reason, some interests will not be pursued with undue intensity. Whole categories of interests will either be abandoned or not arise, reducing to that extent the conflict potential, while others will be adjusted to fit available methods for satisfying them. In this manner, national societies seek to contain the results of change within the limits of social order and peace. In the international society the deterrent of overwhelming strength as an inhibitor of interests leading to change and violent conflict is available mainly in the form of the chance that a state may be defeated in violent struggle.

The procedures for making change stable are most inadequately developed in the international society. The diffusion of political decision-making leaves the production of change primarily within the individual and unpredictable choice of states. The arrangements for stable change in states are almost nonexistent in the international society. There is no world public opinion. There are opinions, often divided, from individual states which other states may or may not heed and which, in any case, rarely lead to decisive majority votes. Legislative action is prevented by the principle of sovereign equality. Communication remains thinly or unevenly distributed across the globe. The formation of consensus is haphazard at best. Finally, the psychological satisfaction provided to the minority by a system which allows it to become a majority is absent. The minority position becomes intolerable and the state rebellious.

More informal political methods are not any more adequate. Indeed, their weakness is a cause of the formal methods' weakness. There is little pluralism. Historic memories keep alive outmoded interests or the means to satisfy them, thereby preventing a full appreciation of international interdependence and the full development of new means for the solution of conflicts growing out of real modern interests. Conflict situations are too little compensated for by cooperation for shared interests. The divisive effect of sovereign independence destroys the integrative effect of growing mutualities. Social institutions are prevented from integrating into a foundation for a growing community — instead, each is enlisted in the support of independent national units. If they represent a danger to sovereignty, their growth is often deliberately stymied. France's frustration of the Common Market's development into a supranational organization and the opposition of "patriotic " American societies to UNESCO are illustrations of national practices not limited to France or the United States. When tensions heighten among states, the international political system leads to a hardening of the contestants' respective positions, rarely to their softening, because the satisfaction of interests is too often a trial of strength. And such a trial includes potentially the use of violence for which somewhere along the line the public must be prepared. The mollifying knowledge that ultimately a neutral authority will decide on the conflict in the interest of all concerned is absent.

The international society, fully aware of the potential escalation of conflicts built into the system, has attempted to provide methods for peaceful change. Article 19 of the League of Nations Covenant specified that "the Assembly may from time to time advise the reconsideration by Members of the League of treaties which have become inapplicable and the consideration of international conditions whose continuance might endanger the peace of the world." Article 14 of the United Nations Charter declares that "the General Assembly may recommend measures for the peaceful adjustment of any situation, regardless of origin, which it deems likely to impair the general welfare or friendly relations among nations, including situations resulting from a violation of the provisions of the present Charter setting forth Purposes and Principles of the United Nations."

These clauses will save the international society from the accusation of ignoring change as the most general and basic source of conflict. They are, however, innocusus enough not to antagonize any member state and to allow each to do as it pleases. By proposing a clearly political solution, the problem of peaceful change is solved in favor of the strong, who hardly needed the support of international organizations in the first place. The suggested solution of any conflict resulting from change amounts to a contest of strength between the contestants — not a very dignified solution coming from a world organization for peace. Even so, these clauses were thought to be an improvement upon the *clausula rebus sic stantibus* of international law, according to which any one state could release itself from an obligation if it judged that essential conditions under which it had entered into the obligation had changed so much that it could not fairly be held to its obligation. In practice, the only improvement lies in the collective approval of the stronger state's action. There is, on the other hand, no point in being critical of the evasive regulation of change in the international society. The problem is insoluble by any one method — save the suppression of arbitrary violence by one state with a greater communally organized violence, made legitimate and overwhelming by international agreement. Such an achievement would require a type of society in which change would normally be peaceful anyway. In other words, making change peaceful is a matter depending upon the whole nature of the society. The international society is as yet far removed from possessing more than some of the requisite features in their early stage of evolution. Among them is the much vaunted interdependence based upon the functional needs of states.

Peaceful Change: Interdependence

Interdependence is mutual dependence. It tends to limit conflict between the interdependent parties. Functional interdependence refers, here, to the mutual need of one state for some complementary active or passive behavior by another for the satisfaction of an interest. As long as two or more states behave in such a manner, they are in a relationship of interdependence. The interests concerned must in some way be directly connected; otherwise instead of speaking of interdependence, one should speak of a variety of dependencies. Interdependence, for instance, exists when two states need mutual landing rights for their aircraft or when they have to cooperate in the control of a river whose waters both need for irrigation. Separate dependencies exist when one state needs the other's landing field, and the other needs the first's river control. Switzerland, for instance, is dependent upon the Netherlands for the harbor of Rotterdam and the Netherlands are dependent upon Switzerland not to pollute the Rhine. Both or more such situations can exist simultaneously: interdependence can be paralleled by dependence, conflict, cooperation, and other types of relationships. A key element in interdependence is the mutuality, whose existence is demonstrated when there is covariation in the case of any change in the relationship; i.e., when a change in the relationship affects one state, it similarly affects the other.

There is an alternative, broader conceptualization of interdependence, less balanced and symmetrically conceived. Interdependence between states may be said to exist when they are mutually dependent in the total set of relationships between them, when a change in any part of their relationships produces covarying effects upon both states. In this case the set of relationships tying states together is, so to speak, homogenized and considered one. This is not too farfetched a picture because states usually meet as homogeneous units, with all their contacts politicized and evaluated by the common criterion of their importance for each state's power potential. What may, under these circumstances, be a tight interdependent relationship between citizens in two states (e.g., in a trade relation) is not such at all from the standpoint of the general public. If one state can substitute for an interdependent relationship or can get along without it, while the other state cannot, the second state finds itself in a dependent rather than an interdependent relationship should the first choose a substitution. There is no longer a mutuality. The importance of this distinction, as will be shown at once, lies in the obviously varying political effect of the varying nature of the interdependence, especially whether it is a relatively inevitable or a voluntary one!

Only by ignoring this distinction could the widespread and often facile assumption be made that interdependence is favorable to peace and peaceful change because it reduces conflict, or at least prevents it from deteriorating into violence. States depending upon each other for the satisfaction of interests would not want to harm each other. The greater the number of interests involved in the mutuality and hence the stronger the interdependence, the costlier would be the use of violence. The gains of a possible victory in a violent contest must be held against the loss of the needed assistance. Such a calculation makes evident that the restraining effect of interdependence upon violence is limited by a profit and loss account. Interdependence would become a form of pluralism in which the use of force is diminished. In T. S. Eliot's words, nonviolent behavior can be expected when "everyone should be an ally of everyone in some respects, and an opponent in several others, and no one conflict, envy, or fear will predominate."

Such a favorable result is conceivable, but not automatic. The results of interdependence depend very much on many details. It is, for instance, very important between whom the interdependence exists in general: whether between specific, select states or all the states of the international society. If the interdependence is limited to a section of the membership, it could lead to factionalism rather than worldwide cooperation. In some respects the "North-South" division of the world illustrates this danger. While it is true that there is a rather imponderable sensitivity globally to happenings

183

anywhere and that ideas "know no frontiers," it is nevertheless also true that the spread of knowledge and in particular know-how and technical skills takes place much more among those states already relatively advanced, leaving the less developed states even farther behind. The results of interdependence are also affected differently depending upon how binding the mutuality is, what the nature of the interests is, whose interests are involved, what the national influence of the interested party may be, and the indirect effects of cooperative relationships upon other relationships.

If the interest involved is considered to affect the survival of the state, no other interest or amount of interests is likely to overbalance or even match the "national interest." If an aspect of the national interest is the object of interdependence, great sacrifices will be made for its maintenance. If national interests are in conflict, any interdependence founded upon other interests is likely to be sacrificed readily. The most that might be expected is that a large volume of interdependence may alter the hierarchy of interests, with the range of interests defined as "national" being narrowed and perhaps their importance being diminished.

If the interests represented in the interdependence are judged to have national importance, this may indeed have beneficial effects upon peaceful change. If they are merely those of a group of citizens, the effect would depend upon how well this group could convince the state to make their interests its own. Big, multinational corporations in several countries are notoriously successful in persuading states in this manner. However such corporations may exert their influence, whether by direct pressure upon governments, by governmental participation in their control (e.g., through a 51 percent partnership), or by the impact of their economic importance, this influence may diminish hostilities between the countries involved. Nationalist economic warfare between such countries could hurt the corporation interests and military warfare could destroy them. If large international labor unions were to succeed in their plans to create multinational labor organizations as a reaction to the growing power of the multinational corporations, they would add another transnational factor with potential benefit for peaceful change. However, the reality is that some multinational corporations are acting like neocolonialists and becoming symbols of neo-imperialism, so that their existence may increase rather than decrease tensions and conflict. And one branch of the international labor movement advocates as a strategy the strengthening of states to keep multinational corporations under control, which is also not very helpful in making change peaceful.

184

International Conflicts and Their Settlement

An indirect beneficial effect of interdependence upon peaceful change could be the unwillingness of people to fight each other for remote interests when over a period of time they have cooperated across national borders in pursuit of their more immediate interests. Habits, methods, and institutions may grow out of such cooperation which could transfer peaceful contacts into other relationships. Precedents established in one area might be followed in others. The sad fate of "internationals," the socialist among them, of the past when states entered into war is not necessarily an indication of what might happen to the new internationals of businessmen, scholars, hippies, civil servants, and the like. Their relationships are often built upon concrete interests or emotional ties which are more substantial and firmer foundations than mere ideological affinities.

The many qualifications to the possibly beneficial contribution of interdependence to peaceful change are indicative of the possibility also that interdependence may readily be sacrificed for higher values or that, where this may not be easily feasible, it could have disadvantageous effects.

In the absence of a spirit of community and the presence of a spirit of ethnocentrism, interdependence may be resented. It could be experienced as a limitation upon the highly cherished national freedom of maneuver. The less control states have over their conditions of existence, the greater is their worry (and rightly so) over their cherished sovereignty. An existing interdependence may be judged too unequal by one or the other side. Reciprocity, a basic principle of social relationships in general and especially so in relationships lacking the mellowing influence of community, may become blurred as the volume of relationships between two states increases. When a society reaches the size of mankind, the intermixture of relationships becomes immense. Mutualities become mediated or indirect; contributions and counter-contributions need not be any longer on a direct, bilateral basis. An increasingly refined division of labor makes an evaluation of reciprocity and mutuality extremely difficult. What remains is a vague awareness of interdependence between some states, but at the same time also a feeling by each party of being at a disadvantage. If such interdependence exists within a framework of fundamentally highly unequal parties (e.g., some interdependent relation between Mexico and the United States or between Belgium and Luxembourg) it may become a cause of annoyance, recrimination, and complaint. This vague awareness of interdependent relationships is well illustrated by the trade deficit of the United States, to which its people had not been accustomed for a long time and which the government therefore tried desperately to

185

balance out when the financial deficit was, in fact, more than made up by the dollar income from foreign American investments. The mistaken approach to this situation, as customarily to other similar ones, is to consider each bilateral relationship on its own merits instead of considering the totality of all relationships — a rather complicated enterprise, to be sure, in today's world of interacting states. What should count is the final balance, not each item in relation to every other item in the balance sheet.

There is a third possible disadvantageous effect of interdependence. Under the influence of nationalism and the dissociative climate of international politics, hostility in one area can quickly carry over into other areas of interstate contacts. Historically, this has been a typical chain of events — much more typical than the reverse process of cooperative activities carrying over into other areas. A fourth such effect could result from an unequal importance of the interdependence. One state may value it less than the other and therefore be less willing to make sacrifices for its sake. Or one state may have better opportunities to replace its partner by another, thereby turning the partner's interdependence into independence. But even if the mutual needs are equally great and neither partner has an alternative for satisfying them, inequality in their general power potential could greatly reduce the beneficial effect of the interdependence. At worst, the more powerful state could establish domination over the other — which is the fear of many weak states when they feel threatened by neocolonialism.[47] Quite clearly, any potential beneficial effect interdependence may have upon making change in the international society peaceful must be balanced against the possibility that the great inequality among states may make interdependence less compelling upon the behavior of powerful than of weak states.

All these considerations of the nature and effect of interdependence between states leave open the empirical question of the rise or decline of interdependence. The general assumption is that as a result of modern technology contacts between states have risen, needs have become more diversified, a division of labor has increased, and withal interdependence has grown. In absolute terms and considered over the long run of, say, a few hundred years the assumption is probably correct. But it is of doubtful validity in regard to certain types of interdependence between certain countries. In the richest countries, the size of their internal economy and their ability to supply their own needs have grown much faster than any interdependence with other countries, as for instance shown by trade volume. Also, their economic power, enormously greater than that of all the medium and smaller states combined, makes their interdependence highly voluntary and flexible while that of the weaker states is largely inevitable and therefore likely to turn into dependence much of the time.[48] The same situation prevails in regard to investments. In communications too the peak of interdependence is likely to have been passed. Long-range airplanes, ships and tankers of enormous capacity and capable of covering long distances, satellites, all make states much more independent of each other than they used to be when these means of communication were in their infancy. But these very same developments — e.g., the ability of a state to reach any other state without the intermediary of third states — have increased at least the sensitivity of states to each other and have made them in that sense and respect interdependent. In the political-strategic field, for instance, the existence of rockets, missiles, satellites, and the like has made states pay attention to each other which have otherwise few contacts and which would, in days past, have hardly known about each other. In a much less concrete, but nevertheless real, fashion such mutual sensitivity has also resulted among many, mostly developed states from economic interdependence. Even when such states have no voluminous economic relations, their domestic policies regarding employment, taxation, currency, and the like in one state usually have immediate repercussions in other states.

In summary, it may be said that unquestionable increases in contacts and interaction among states do not necessarily mean increases in interdependence. They may make some states more independent (especially the richest and most powerful among them), others more dependent. What interdependence there is may benefit peaceful change in the international society, but not necessarily so. Yet, presumably on the chance that interdependence will be beneficial or that it can be manipulated to some extent to become beneficial, the international society has been inclined to further the growth of mutual interests and functional cooperation among states. There is always the subsidiary hope that making states aware of their mutual needs, and providing methods and machinery for satisfying them, may in the end lead to a sufficiently dense network of interdependencies to make violent conflict unprofitable.

Peaceful Change: Functional Cooperation

The League of Nations and much more so the United Nations have been the formal evidence of the general trend toward increasing mutual functional relationships among states. Though the charters of international agencies tend to advance high-sounding principles and aims for the vast range of their operations (foremost among them the maintenance of peace), most of them are directly geared toward the creation of material improvements in the hope that an incidental result might be the strengthening of peace. But this hope has not been a strong motivating power behind the creation of these international organizations. Had it been, the organizations would have been given greater strength. Also, the contemporary regional organizations, existing or in the making, are deliberately created for economic reasons (e.g., the European Common Market), but often are not viable as economic means because political conflicts interfere (e.g., all the purely Asian regional organizations).

Whatever the strength of the hopes for peace behind the creation of international organizations, an incidental consequence of functional cooperation may well be a constraint upon international conflicts. Such cooperation may also be the break in a chain of events which leads from minor conflict to larger conflict to violence. The theory here is simply that a small conflict, settled at its inception, cannot become a large dangerous conflict and that it is easier to settle a minor than a major conflict. There is special cogency in these arguments when they relate to international politics. Quite apart from the absence of a powerful central government which could stop violent behavior of a state, the politicization of the international society can make even minor conflicts relevant to the power potential of a state. Conflicts always possess the dual quality of being conflicts in their own right and of being factors in the wider struggle for power. For this reason the settlement of the conflict on its own, inherent merits becomes so difficult. But there can be no doubt that the settlement of a conflict on its own merits would be highly desirable. It would then not be a contributor to larger conflicts rooted in power struggles and would not be worth a violent struggle regardless of its own merits.[49]

From this viewpoint the attempts to provide mechanisms for the handling or anticipation of minor conflicts in international organizations are most reasonable. Especially helpful are the methods of dealing through cooperation with conflicts at an early state in their development on grounds of their inherent nature (economic, social, cultural, etc.). There are two important reasons why early handling is advisable. One is that as international conflicts grow in importance, nowadays the masses must become involved to support their nation's position. At least the masses must be involved until the state of violence is reached, at which point the technicians take over, pulling levers and pushing buttons in some underground post. As long as the masses are involved, passions rather than reason tend to prevail. The restraining power of social controls weakens, either because they are forgotten or because norms inhibiting antisocial behavior by the individual somehow undergo a metamorphosis when they are applied to the state as a collectivity (right or wrong, my country!).[50] It is for instance difficult to imagine the public becoming passionately aroused in defense of the nation on the issue of the level of import tariffs on watches. But when for some reason this issue can be turned into a symbol for a power struggle with a competing nation or in a situation of tension, such an arousal is not merely conceivable but likely. This leads to the second reason why early handling of conflicts and restriction to their inherent primary nature is important. Those interested in the subject of the conflict may be able to satisfy their needs in a functional international organization created for just such a purpose. If the need cannot readily be taken care of — as is known from history — the interested parties may not merely lobby but endow their case with national importance in order to mobilize greater support for their case. The watchmakers will claim that maintaining their industry with protective tariffs is in the national interest so that their skills will be kept alive for the moment of national emergency when watchmakers have to produce instruments for making war. Erecting a tariff wall will lead to retaliation and thus a chain of events will have been initiated whose end may well be catastrophic. So there are two reasons why functional organizations can be useful: they may prevent popular passions from becoming involved, and they may obviate the need for interested parties to arouse popular passions.

No claim can be made, certainly not be proved, that the solution or nonsolution of these relatively minor and often isolated conflicts will be directly related to the growth of major power struggles. They may, however, have marginal significance and certainly in borderline situations, if enough of them can be settled, worse conflicts might be prevented. The accumulation and escalation of numerous economic and mental health problems in many states before World Wars I and II, none of which alone might have contributed importantly to the wars, probably contributed their share through their mass impact.

An additional immediate benefit of settling conflicts by expanding functional cooperation would be the improvement of a state's economy. In modern times it seems that the higher the level of well-being in a state the lower its inclination to fight wars with equally developed states. This may be so not because satisfied states are necessarily peaceful states. It may be so

189

because wealthy states own more destructive matériel, making war costlier; have much to lose in a violent struggle; and, above all, have more maneuverabilty to get what they want by peaceful means. As economic growth rather than national grandeur becomes the major social goal everywhere, cooperation is a more promising method than fighting. The Soviet Union's more peaceful approach to international affairs than the Communist Chinese' may be a contemporary illustration of this phenomenon.

If these favorable consequences of functional cooperation are indeed possible, even though not certain, the future holds some promise for the peaceful settlement of conflicts. For it is obvious that the longer-run effects of technological progress will enforce more international functional cooperation. The exploitation (or the dangers) of such technological possibilities as are provided, for instance, by weather control, development of ocean resources, space exploration, food distribution, information exchange, preservation of the biosphere, make international action necessary. There will be growing need for restraints upon activities and therefore for international regulations, for supervision and monitoring, for trading of data, not to mention for positive cooperation to benefit from new developments. Initially, there may be attempts by individual nations to control these matters, but their nature precludes control. As nations realize the futility of their attempts, they will surrender to the inevitable and cooperate — as they have always done (e.g., in the creation of postal services, control of disease, etc.). Once this stage has been reached, violent settlements of conflict become too costly and more peaceful settlements will be used.

These developments lie in the future. In the meantime, it is doubtful whether an increase in official organizations has been accompanied by a decrease of violent conflicts — perhaps there would have been more without it.[51] Unfortunately for the possible peace-keeping function of international organizations, the chance of diminishing the seriousness of international conflicts has not been fully exploited. The stimulation of functional relationships must rely upon the individual judgment of states. Organizations can only recommend them, demonstrate their usefulness, warn of dire consequences in neglecting them. They cannot force states to establish them. Similarly, because they lack authority to make decisions, the organizations cannot decisively interfere either prophylactically or therapeutically in international conflicts, even when they relate to relatively minor matters of mutual functional interest. Unless the functions themselves are considered important enough by states to ignore or diminish conflicts, there is no external force which could compel states to continue their cooperation. The same weakness and lack of authority afflicts the application of peaceful methods for the settlement of conflicts and the whole system of international law.

Peaceful Methods for Settling Conflicts

By general agreement, the United Nations has become the premier institution for the preservation of peace. It represents a comprehensive, largely formal and legal system for the settlement of international conflicts. Together with its specialized agencies and other organizations it aims, as an integrated whole, to achieve its task. The underlying idea is that nations shall be brought together to work out their destinies and settle their conflicts in peaceful cooperation. Sovereignty prevents the organizations from doing more than encourage and support cooperation. They cannot command or enforce. Yet, when cooperation fails and as the danger increases that it may be replaced by violence, the United Nations, and especially the Security Council, can change from making recommendations to making decisions, binding nations to act. But because the Security Council is nothing more than the collectivity of its individual state members, the exercise of the right still rests with individual states. Experience has proven to be highly unrealistic any assumption that states preparing to use violence or expecting to be violated will submit to the decision of other states, even if they are impartial outsiders. When the existence of a state is threatened, the passions of its people are aroused to their highest pitch.[52] States which have not allowed functional, so-called nonpolitical organizations to interfere authoritatively in even minor economic, cultural, or social matters are most certainly not going to allow any interference in critical matters of national existence.

In line with the chain-of-events theory (that big oak trees grow from little acorns) on which the arrangements of the United Nations are based, international agencies for the settlement of conflicts should possess authority to make binding decisions when conflicts are in an incipient stage; when they are specific, isolated, and minor; when they are not yet perceived, because usually they are not yet part of the vital national interests. This may require international action in "domestic affairs." But rejection of such intervention — in minor matters more than major matters — has forever prevented the proper definition of the beginning of conflict and aggression, the identification of the aggressor, and effective prophylactic as well as settlement action. Impeding conflicts from leading to violence has become increasingly difficult

191

as the complexity of modern technology makes the determination of aggression — its timing, its perpetration, its very nature — ever more uncertain. "Preventive retaliation" need not necessarily be the cynical disguise of aggression — under modern strategy and with modern techniques it may indeed be a measure of defense. On the other hand, the complicated nature of modern warfare certainly also facilitates the use of semantics to cover up guilt or an escape from obligations. When a state is not subject to internationally agreed norms regarding violent conflicts because it calls its war "an incident" (as the Japanese did in Manchuria in 1932) or gives it no name at all (as the Americans did in Vietnam in the 1960s and 1970s), semantic subterfuges can undo all methods for the peaceful settlement of international conflicts.

The ability of an international organization to be effective in preventing or settling violent international conflicts requires authority to act at the earliest possible moment. As it is, the United Nations has been granted permission to act only at that late moment in the escalation of international conflicts when the optimum point of being effective has been passed. That the United Nations has such permission at all indicates once again that the members of the international society agree on what would be needed to preserve peace. But leaving decisions to use this permission for authoritative action to individual states nullifies the practical results of this agreement. The arrangement is, at best, the expression of an ideal which the states had neither the courage nor the desire to approach.

There is no need, however, to write off international organizations as totally useless for settling international conflicts peacefully. While the formal, mainly legal, arrangements are not likely to be effective most of the time, the service these organizations can render in many informal ways — for instance, as safety valves or as warning signals in developing conflicts — is considerable. They have several influences toward the prevention of violence. They provide, first and foremost, a forum for discussion. There is no substitute matching the effectiveness of debate, negotiation, argumentation, or just plain talking for settling conflicts peacefully. Second, conducting a cold war in these organizations is preferable to conducting a hot war on the battle field. The opportunities for verbal aggression in these organizations can satisfy the urge for a show of military prowess. Third, addressing "the world" from a platform of an international organization can help individual leaders to rid themselves of their personal or national frustrations, preventing them thereby from choosing violent means to "put their states on the map." Fourth, international organizations have been used many times by states to save face when they wished to retire from the brink of war to which their own policies had led them. Finally, small or weak states can vent their grievances instead of building up tensions. They can even influence world politics at moments when the major nations are uncertain of their policies.[53]

In large part these results of activities in international organizations are produced by using the organizations as attention-getting devices. In this, but only in this sense, can the organizations be said to help in the formation of a world public opinion, by which can only be meant the formation of coinciding national public opinions. Yet because public opinion everywhere condemns the use of violence in international affairs, the publication of conflicts in these international forums may not only be a substitute for the use of violence but positively discourage the use of violence by individual states. The important point remains, however, that the influence exercised by these organizations is upon individual national decisions, not upon any common collective decision. It is still a national decision whether a conflict is to be settled peacefully or violently, and this is mainly a decision by the major nations.

Compared to the imponderable influence the existence of international organizations may have upon the avoidance of violence in conflict situations, the effect of methods specifically designed for this purpose — negotiation, good offices, mediation, inquiry, conciliation, arbitration, and judicial decision — is relatively more measurable. This is least true of diplomacy, which is, of course, used more than any other method, but whose success is not always clear. It is not easy to determine why states reach a settlement of their conflict in the course of negotiations. The cause may be the nature of the settlement, the persuasive power of a diplomat, the discovery of mutually satisfactory alternatives. Or it may be a condition in the environment surrounding the conflict situation, such as the comparative strengths of the parties or the significance of the conflict's objective. The important thing is that with the help of diplomacy all these factors can become effective and keep the conflict nonviolent. There is no other method possessing the comprehensiveness, flexibility, and refinement, or allowing for such imagination and creativity, as diplomacy. It is, in practice, not only inevitable but most useful as well.

The other methods are more measurable because it is clear when they are being used and what the outcome has been. On both these counts the contribution of these methods has been disappointing. Their failure can be explained in part by a historical process applying to them as well. The formalization of methods for the settlement of disputes (in all societies) usually precedes the formation of legislatures or the executive. The reason for this sequence is simple. Agreement can more readily be reached on the forms in which norms are to be interpreted and applied than on what the norms are to be and who is to execute them. Essentially, states have so far not gone beyond the first step in this sequence.

Another reason for the failure of methods for the peaceful settlement of international conflicts lies in the attitudes of states themselves and the nature of the society and the political system that results. In spite of a careful design of all these methods, states are reluctant to use them. Their reluctance increases in proportion to the finality of the result of the methods. Their willingness to submit themselves to any existing method depends rarely upon what method might be best suited to the nature of the conflict; rather it depends upon what method the state thinks will bring it the greatest benefit. While disputes over the nature or details of a method are rare, those over which method if any is applicable are frequent. Strong states, confident of their ability to take care of their interests, will favor methods nearest to direct confrontation between the disputants, such as bilateral negotiation. Weak states prefer the involvement of third parties, not to solve the conflicts but in the hope that their presence will somehow neutralize the preponderant strength of their powerful opponents.[54] An excellent example was the presentation of the Twenty-One Demands by Japan to China in 1915. They represented a serious threat to China's existence as an independent state. The Japanese insisted on keeping negotiations over them secret as a matter concerning only the two nations. The Chinese saw their only chance to save themselves in publicizing the demands, and they did so with considerable success. The relative enthusiasm of weak and small states for using international organizations in their international politics can be explained by this expectation that internationalization of their problems will produce a more favorable solution than direct dealing with powerful opponents; or, perhaps more correctly, since small states are little more willing than large states to have outsiders actually settle their problems for them, they expect that internationalization will create a climate in which their opponents will be more amenable to a compromise solution.[55]

The general principle in whatever use is made of these methods is that the popularity of a method diminishes to the extent that the settlement of the conflict is transferred to third parties and that the stakes in the conflict increase in importance. States, even small states, feel safer when they can keep control over the settlement of a conflict — though they rarely resent international support for their cause. The many commitments by states to submit their conflicts to settlement by peaceful methods have so many legal escape clauses that for all practical purposes these commitments do not exist. The situation illustrates, once again, the schizophrenia in the political behavior of states. Their recognition of the need for peaceful methods and their desire for order in the international society are surpassed by the awareness of the possible risks to sovereignty and the intense preference for individual national welfare. If a state believes itself to be stronger than the opponent, self-help is expected to bring greater benefits. Also, peaceful proceedings by third parties may introduce subjects either state may wish to withhold from international discussion. And there are vagaries in such proceedings to which neither contestant may wish to expose itself. Finally, the proceedings can be final and without appeal; and the results may be unenforceable to boot. A state will understandably hesitate to disclose a willingness to make concessions during the proceedings and a readiness for compromise when an opponent can at any time disavow its own position. These inadequacies, seemingly procedural, are in fact the expression of substantive concerns rooted in the general and more fundamental characteristics of the international society and the attitudes upon which it rests.

The expectation is quite unreasonable that states will submit important interests to the civilized procedures of peaceful settlement when international law itself gives them the choice to use their power for the enforcement of their claims. In the great majority of cases, the prevailing psyche will lead them to rely upon their own power if there is any prospect of success. They will be greatly encouraged to do so additionally by a belief — widespread among Communist and new states — that existing international organizations and legal systems protect essentially capitalist or imperialist interests. This suspicion is a specialized aspect of the much more widely distributed sense of uncertainty regarding the impartiality of the peaceful methods. The greatest appeal of these methods and their greatest usefulness would be in the ability to depoliticize and denationalize conflicts. In the existing international system, this is an almost impossible achievement for two reasons: one, the excessive politicization of the whole society disallows the exclusion of almost anything from political consideration; and two, in almost all the methods third states are inevitably involved in one form or another and there is no state isolated enough from world politics to function as an objective, disinterested arbiter or judge, equally credible and confidence-inspiring to the parties in conflict.[56]

The predominance of the national over international interests, which makes every third party appear suspect, also tends to create dissatisfaction in one or both parties to the conflict with the results of the methods. If the method is judicial (as in the case of the International Court of Justice), there can be no confidence in the interpretation or application of law when its very validity and content are in doubt. When the method is nonjudicial (as in the case of arbitration, and possibly also mediation and conciliation), it cannot be expected that states will agree on what is just when they cannot even agree on what is right. Only the unsatisfying consideration that to obtain partial satisfaction (in arbitration) is better than getting no satisfaction (when the case is lost on the battle field or in the courtroom) may induce states to submit to peaceful methods. Under such conditions, hostilities tend to remain alive.

Here, as in the case of the effectiveness of social controls in general, the absence of a community spirit or even of its preliminary requirement of a high interest in common is the basic cause for the failure of the methods for the peaceful settlement of conflicts. International law suffers from the same flaw, of course, and can therefore not be any more effective in settling conflicts peacefully — especially when the use of violence by individual states under existing law is possible. Under the regime of sovereignty there is no way of imposing laws or rules, their interpretation or enforcement. The binding force of legal rules and hence their successful application depends ultimately on the acceptance of those subject to them. If a law is obeyed not out of conviction of its validity but because it is imposed by force, there is no norm but only coercion. Conceivably, such a conviction may grow gradually, but the process is not very likely in the international society because it is not a community. For law expresses rather than creates a community. It reflects rather than controls power relationships. International law, being dependent upon individual states, is incapable of harnessing power. It is the servant and expression of power, not its control. It is further weakened because the high values it allegedly embodies do not correspond to the low values usually motivating states. Perhaps law anywhere is obeyed mostly because it serves the rational calculations and selfish interests of those subject to it. Even then, in national societies, selfishness is a constructive social force as long as citizens make their society a priority interest. The subordination of the international society to national societies diminishes the socially constructive consequences of national selfishness and weakens it as a pillar of international law.

This low rank of the international society in all national hierarchies of value has a much more detrimental effect upon the effectiveness of international law than the often-blamed cultural heterogeneity. Newer states of Asia and Africa admit frankly that nationalism and nationalist behavior are not subject to international law but rather its source. The moral force represented by nationalism, they argue, justifies overriding traditional law and creating new law. This, they claim correctly, is the way international law has always been made. These individual national sources of international law, it has been argued, make any supportive unity behind the law impossible; the resulting moral pluralism destroys any basis for the law's validity. This argument would be cogent only if each nation's nationalism represented different moral values. In reality, the moral values underlying any nationalism, new or old, Western or non-Western, are fundamentally the same. It is not any great discrepancies in abstract moral values relevant for the international society which make the application of international law difficult. It is the great variety in the interpretation of the norms (what is sin?) which makes so many incompatible behaviors possible.

Another, related explanation for the weakness of international law claims that abstract rules of law have altogether little meaning in Asian and African cultures, that their social order does not rest on a symbolically valued system or law or legal institutions. Because the normative order within these societies and that regulating relations between them is believed to be so different from Western concepts and traditions, there is a suspicion that any acceptance by Asian and African governments of Western-inspired laws, institutions, and organizations is a ruse to disguise their international behavior in accordance with their own traditional practices.

Several answers weaken this argument. First, the international behavior of Asian and African governments neither was nor is so fundamentally different in its intergroup relations from the behavior of comparable Western governments. They do not reject international law in principle. They reject specific rules that do not serve their purposes, in favor of more acceptable ones. If there are no acceptable ones, they tend to derive their claims from moral principles which, they hope, may turn into legal precepts. Such practice makes their positions seemingly political rather than legal, which in fact they often are not, and which, in any case, results more from disappointment with the substance of existing international law than from a culture lacking appreciation of law. Second, the constraining effect of international law on Western states is not as great as the argument seems to assume. Third,

197

in Asian and African states Westernized elites are in almost sole control of international politics. They seem to understand quite well how international politics function and, moreover, they are very adept in translating, when necessary, conditions and consequences of an international culture into cultural equivalents of their own. Fourth, cultural differences as they may relate to international law are mitigated by the normal experience that the relations between states are shaped much more by the inherent purpose of these relations than by the nature of relations prevailing within each state. If international law serves this purpose well, all states will find it acceptable. It then becomes possible to order the international relations of states through universally accepted laws which may be quite different from the internal laws of any one state. This remains true even if at times governments engage in international politics not so much for any purpose inherent in international politics but for purposes of internal politics (e.g., to create unity within the country or, for an individual leader, to strengthen his position through an international success). The reason is that if states want to relate to other states they must use the channels, including their rules, agreeable to all states. The Soviet Union, for instance, has quite willingly submitted to and often selfishly exploited democratic and parliamentary procedures in international organizations which it rejects and condemns for internal application. By the same token international laws aiming at individuals, such as human rights standards, which have no ostensible connection with relations between states will find a much less ready acceptance.

The point emerges that when states agree to live up to legal rules they may not feel any moral pressure to do so. They find it useful to do so, perhaps mainly because not to do so would lead other states to reciprocate in kind, with highly undesirable consequences for all concerned. They consider these rules useful means of communication. International law becomes an efficient technique of social interdependence (Theodor Geiger) with little bearing on the particular cultural preferences of any one state.

A reliable social order requires a hierarchical judicial order, whether expressed in a Western-type legal system or in an Asian or African type social group and ranking system. Such order is required not necessarily to guarantee justice (a strongly culture-bound concept) but to maintain right (a less culture-bound concept), and not necessarily to be applied exclusively but to be decisively present and available when other methods of keeping social order fail. The international system, however, strongly supports the expectation by states that on occasion their own welfare can best be achieved by their own individual means even if at the expense of the society's welfare. States therefore aim at reserving a wide freedom of action, which means rejecting social controls and all the methods for the peaceful settlement of conflicts. These controls and methods can begin to function effectively only after the nature of the international society has disabused states of the idea that taking care of their interests with their own means can be more beneficial than taking care of them with the means and methods of the society. In feudal and national societies, the settlement of conflicts through self-help and trial by combat proceeded until, gradually, the conviction grew that the interests of all concerned could be better fulfilled through the collective means and methods of an orderly society. Nothing better can be expected from the members of the international society, and there is just a faint hint that such a conviction is in fact beginning to grow.

8 War and Peace

THE ANALYSIS of international politics and the political system indicates why there is such a great temptation for states to use violence. The peoples of the world have no sentimental commitment to the international society. National interests dominate international interests. Consequently, from the standpoint of the international society's survival, power is poorly managed, social controls are inadequately developed, the tolerance for conflict is low, and needs are badly fulfilled. Self-help is of the essence for states to secure their welfare, and force is considered a useful means. War is an ever-present possibility. It is a curious feature of the international system to possess the built-in opportunity for self-denigration and even self-destruction. But states do not always succumb to the temptation the system offers them. Why wars take place is not at all clear, especially not when all states proclaim peace as a most desirable goal. Even more problematic is why a given war occurs between two given states at a given time. Statesmen and scholars alike have struggled with this question throughout man's history. Their search for an answer has usually been based upon the assumption that when there is war, something must be causing it. It could, however, be that there is something absent which permits wars to break out. Such an absent factor could never be discovered by focusing attention on the war situation. The search must be extended to include factors possibly safeguarding peace. The causes of war may then be found to lie in faulty conditions of peace!

The usefulness of this search requires at least the theoretical possibility that war can be avoided or controlled. If war is assumed to be natural, beyond the reach of men, to search for its causes would be fruitless for practical purposes. Fascist and National Socialist doctrines came close to this position when they argued that the state is an organic, living creature, destined to fight for survival. For men to try to influence war was merely a sign of decadence. Quite distinct from these doctrines, but nevertheless reminiscent of them in its assumption of determinism, is the argument that social (rather than individual) life is biologically based and perpetuates itself through evolution, apart from man's conscious direction. This argument differs from those doctrines in its admission that the biological laws themselves permit men to create an environment in which they have choices, can adapt, use their will to influence their destiny. Through genetic pre-programming, however, men will always behave in such a manner that the group survives and evolves. The group is not accepted as merely a mental concept. It is considered a biological phenomenon. The group, not just its individual members, has genetically conditioned preferences for survival, though this is expressed through evolution endowing the individual with incentives for preserving his and thereby his group's survival.

In contrast to the Fascist and National Socialist doctrines, this argument at least includes a role for human beings in the genesis of war. It thereby joins most other attempts to explain the existence of war. At least until a definitive answer can be provided to the question of war's origin, it seems essential to consider the possible influence of human choices on peace and war. But since these choices must always be made within the context of some social system, it becomes necessary to investigate first the social framework as a codeterminant of the range of choices available to men, and then second to examine man's psychology as another crucial determinant of man's choices.

The Influence of the Social System

The preceding examination of the international political system has already referred to conditions allowing war to take place, or even facilitating if not necessitating it. Even though social systems are created by men, as has been pointed out before, they begin over a period of time to assume an existence of their own. Its members have expectations and behavioral habits which cannot be easily overturned or ignored, certainly not in toto. "The system" constrains the individual's choice of action — whether he acts alone or in a group. But the individual can also change his behavior and thereby affect the system. Thus social behavior affects the system and is affected by the system in continuous interaction. Since the international system, i.e., the behavior pattern of the peoples of the world, makes war possible, the social system must be part of the explanation of war's existence. A social system cannot produce results independent of the wills of the system's past or present members. On the other hand, the members cannot act in entire independence of the system. In any case, however, reference is always to patterns of behavior by people, and if these patterns are regular and the individual behaviors of the members form a network of action in interdependence, there is a system. When something is being said about the system — for instance, that a dictatorship as a system is more conducive to war than a democracy — it really means that certain individuals and groups in a certain behaviorally defined constellation of relations toward each other are relevant in certain ways to war in one case; and that certain individuals and groups in a differently defined constellation of relations toward each other are relevant in other ways to war. It tells something about how wars may become possible through the system, but very little about why. Examination of the system alone could never provide a full explanation. It could only disclose, for instance, what choices of behavior are readily available. It could indicate how decision-makers, leaders, or a people may behave in the light of each other's behavior patterns or other involved decision-makers, leaders, or peoples. It could not be very helpful in finding out why a given choice was made. Quite possibly, for instance, the international system may provide better outlets for certain personality traits (e.g., aggressiveness) than another social system. But this is not the same as being a stimulant for aggression. Examination of the system cannot tell much about ultimate causes of violent state behavior because these are located in the individuals composing the system and making the choices.

The explanatory value of the system concept lies in its function as an intermediary and perhaps in disclosing the range of available choices. As an influence upon behavior and a channel for events, the system — being as much a description as a conditioner of behavior — is relevant to the total overall analysis of the connection between humans as likely originators of war and the existence of a war. But the examination of a system will not make a significant contribution to solving the preliminary problem of a causal relationship between human nature and war.

This conclusion is fairly obvious on the ground alone that wars have been typical of social behavior since time immemorial. They have taken place in every known social system, which is to say that all social systems somehow allowed for war, some more readily than others. Whether the differences between the "more or less" permissive systems are sufficiently significant to provide clues to the systemic causes of war and conditions of peace is doubtful but remains to be seen. The same is true in regard to the question whether the "more or less" depends upon the nature of the systems or primarily upon the mentality of people producing different systems. The inclination here is to assume that the reasons for the "more or less" peaceful nature of social systems depends more on the people than on the system.

An examination of the frequency of wars throughout history may show cyclical increases and decreases. But it shows no reliable correlation between wars and political processes, internal political systems, different international political systems, weapons systems, and many other environmental factors. Changes in any system may encourage or discourage the use of violence. But this, again, is not related to any particular system. Instead, it is related to the fact, already mentioned, that social change is always a cause of conflict and hence of potential violence. But this change, which occurs in every social system, is not the ultimate cause of the violence. That cause can be found in the interests and motivations of men who are affected by the change and who then determine whether there is to be violence or not. The initial and fundamental desire to use or not to use violence originates not in the system but in the psyche of men. The system's contribution to the final decision is mainly in enhancing or diminishing the likelihood of violence by trying to direct the social change and its consequences for the individual.

This understanding of a social system seems particularly apt for the international system. Its details have been more deliberately formed by men than is true of any other social system. States try to act most deliberately, leaving little to chance, the subconscious, or the habitual. Every aspect of the national social and the citizen's individual behavior has been carefully shaped, maintained, and supervised by the state for its international implications. Unanticipated results are fewer in number and more quickly brought under control than in any other social system. Precisely to avoid unforeseeable results states hesitate to commit themselves to general obligations. Even so, accidents are unavoidable but wars rarely fall into this category. When the international system provides for war by establishing rules for it — every type of international system does — it means that those constructing, maintaining, and supporting the system envisage war. In going to war those who do, act within the permissive framework. This framework encases the behavior typical for war and a public accepting war. At the same time, of course, the international system tries, first, to prevent the use of violence, then to minimize the evils

203

of violence, and finally to stop the use of violence. But it does so, as has been shown, with very inadequate means and, perhaps worst of all, it cannot prevent the profitability of war. Yet that wars may be profitable to those who win them may be one of their great incentives.

Insofar as national social systems may contribute to war, the same applies to them, *mutatis mutandis*. They too are man-made. They too experience violence, and very likely for the same reasons as international systems. Their contribution to international violence may take place most likely in two different ways.

One way would be due to the nature of the national system. Capitalism has often been blamed as the root of imperialism and war. If this accusation is true, it means that those in control of the social system have shaped and are using it to serve their particular interests through expansion and violence. The same goes for fascism, communism, or other systems prevailing in states that initiate war. None of these systems is "natural." None is inevitable or beyond human influence. If there is a demonstrable relationship between any system and war, the system could be changed.

Another way in which a national system might contribute to war is through its instability. Abrupt, disruptive social change, by upsetting the social order, could endanger internal peace and conduce to international violence. The creation of internal peace and unity through the provocation of conflict and war with an outside enemy has been a trick of governments throughout history. The promotion of one's own society at the expense of others has been a typical nationalist practice. But none of these conditions are sufficient to cause wars, because they do not always lead to war while states with systems not having these conditions also go to war. No reliable predictions can be made about the effect of internal conditions of a state and its peacefulness or war-mindedness. All attempts to establish statistical correlations between war and a country's social stability, or to discover historical evidence for such correlations, have remained inconclusive.[57]

A social system, without actively promoting war, could still be a cause of war passively, namely by attracting war-making states through, for instance, its weakness. The rapidly rising number of civil wars and coups d'état relative to the number of international wars since the end of the 1950s — mainly in developing countries — offers increasing opportunities for intervention by major nations. They will be taken advantage of especially when the state in question is situated in a politically important area.[58] Vietnam, Korea, Nigeria, Zambia, Western Asia are regions in which such interventions have led to wars. The reward for the winning interventionist nation consists of special privileges and concessions so that what looks like an "internal struggle" becomes for practical purposes the functional equivalent of old-fashioned war.

Since there have been wars under every national and international system known to man, it is unlikely that each particular system, by coincidence, provided different and particular reasons for the existence of war. It is most likely that the social character of man as the common denominator of all systems has most to do with the existence of war. Not any special feature of a given system but some general feature of all social systems is most likely to be the cause of war, with the special features exerting, at most, a stimulating or retarding influence. And those general features are most likely to be found in men who play decisive roles in every system. No system is so tight that it eliminates human choices. Even the existence of atomic weaponry has been unable to do this. It remains true that in the final analysis the cause of events in which human beings are the movers is in men. In searching for the causes of war and the conditions of peace, the most fruitful approach seems to be to concentrate initially on man, while never ignoring that he acts in a natural and a man-made environment.

Man's Traits as Causes of War

The number of man's traits held responsible as causes of war is almost unlimited. The temptation is all the greater as very often in psychological explanations of personal or social phenomena any trait can somehow be made to serve as an explanation. A man with an inferiority complex may become either a dictator or a mouse! There may be good reasons for these kinds of alternatives. To some extent human psychological traits are behaviorally neutral. The concrete behavior they may lead to depends upon available outlets offered by the environment, including the social system. It also depends upon the mix of traits. If the explanations of all psychologists are accepted as valid, the whole spectrum of human traits is covered as a cause of war. This is no explanation at all, for it is obvious that human beings have responsibility for human actions. Various authors therefore usually limit themselves to singling out certain traits or psychological factors as primarily responsible for the existence of war.

One group can be classified as destructive: aggressiveness,[59] hostility, rivalry, bias and prejudice, hatred, sadism, projection of national shortcomings upon the enemy. Another group relates to balancing or compensation, such as boredom in private life, thirst for adventure, social frustration, and insecurity, for which war offers the alternative of excitement and personal license. A third group refers to ego fulfillment: need for prestige, status, and recognition, desire to be wanted, wish for possessions. There is, finally, the not very frequently cited group of constructive factors allegedly inciting people to go to war: desire for sacrifice, neighborly love, contribution to community, sense of mission.

Other psychologists seek social rather than individual psychological causes of war. In a group the individual loses the customary social restraints, the argument runs, so that he can act aggressively against the enemy as he could not against a fellow citizen. Or, in joining a group the individual's destructive drive becomes magnified and war offers itself as an outlet. Tensions between states, even in the absence of concrete conflicts, have been blamed for the outbreak of violence. It has also been claimed that tensions and conflicts within a state are externalized for the sake of maintaining the national community and war results. Psychoanalysts have a number of explanations. They blame, for instance, remnants of man's unconscious earliest past which survive and perpetuate war as an institution. Or the fight to retain colonies has to do with the castration complex (which would make women as foreign ministers very desirable).

The protagonists of these psychological theories on the origins of war often maintain that war offers satisfaction to these psychological needs and is therefore caused by them. This conclusion of such a direct relationship is an oversimplification. Neither the facts of history nor logic bear out this relationship. Many states are militarily prepared and hostile to each other, even at the brink of war, yet war does not break out. More important: how can lengthy periods of peace be explained? When will certain neutral traits or psychological drives find outlet in war and when in more peaceful pursuits? Why did German fight German before 1870 and why not after their unification? How are these traits and drives of millions of citizens suddenly crystallized into a state of war against a given enemy at a given moment?

These human factors are undoubtedly relevant to the explanation of wars. But the question — not likely only a psychological question — is how these factors are translated into violent mass conflict involving all citizens regardless of their individual nature, and performed with the aid of a highly complex machinery constructed over a period of years for just such a purpose. There

206

is no evidence anywhere in modern times of a sudden collective impulse of a state's citizenry toward war or of a spontaneous collective demand for war.[60] The destructiveness, boredom, social responsibility of a man or a group do not by themselves turn into taxes, alliances, strategy, war matériel, and naval bases. These human traits permit wars. They may represent a readiness for war. But this is an essentially passive readiness which must be activated. Without additional impulses and intervening factors it may make wars possible but hardly cause them. What the nature of these factors and impulses might be is enormously difficult to establish, because the complexity of human nature and the environment in which it becomes effective not merely is responsible for a vast range of such possible factors and impulses, but further increases that range by allowing different factors and impulses to be effective in different situations and in different combinations. A discussion of a few complications can readily demonstrate the difficulty.

How Can Man's Traits Cause War?

Motivations for behavior cannot always be established with certainty either by outside observers or by the actor himself. The motivations may be mixed within any one individual. Or they may differ between individuals all of whom may be relevant to the outbreak of war. Those who make a decision to go to war may pretend reasons which are not the true reasons. They may believe the given reasons to be the true reasons when in fact they may not be the true reasons. Decision-makers may, after the fact, genuinely justify their actions on grounds different from those initially motivating them. Their perceptions are of utmost importance and these in turn may be very much influenced by the psyche of the decision-makers. Especially in international politics and foreign policy making, there is a tendency to see other states as at least potentially hostile, but always as being utterly selfishly motivated — which is usually a correct perception but need not apply to every act of another state! The result is a very complex cycling and recycling of psychic traits forming motivations leading to perceptions causing actions provoking reactions stimulating other psychic traits forming new motivations, etc., etc. In a collectively reached decision, different makers may be differently motivated and each may change his motivation as the war proceeds. In sum, the same war may be wanted or supported by different people for many different reasons and from many different motivations. If the cause of war

207

is to be found directly in some human motivations, all the individuals and all the groups relevant to the decision to go to war should be accounted for if adequate and justifiable conclusions are to be drawn.

A second complication in relating human traits to the outbreak of war is that man rarely appears or acts as man. He plays a role: as citizen, as a professional, a profit-seeker, as father. Depending upon his role, the war may have different relevance for him. He may want it as a profit-seeker, but will not want it as a father. In relation to his traits this means that very often these traits may be in conflict: some may drive him toward war, others against it. In the end, he is likely to "make up his mind" in some manner avoiding schizophrenia. The outcome will usually be a mixture of motives, determined by numerous internal and external factors neither whose nature nor whose effect is predictable or even knowable. While this situation is quite hopeless in regard to establishing any direct relationship between traits and war if every citizen were to be examined, it is really not much more hopeful if only those individuals are considered whose role is of considerable relevance to making decisions about war.

Some persons are obviously more important than others in creating circumstances, including making decisions, leading to war. The masses of the citizenry are most rarely if ever initiators of a process ending in war. When, for instance, India and China fought a small war in the Himalayas in 1962, over 40 percent of the Indian population was unaware of it. Once a people has been aroused, it is barely conceivable that its collective pressure will force the decision-maker to go over the brink and into war. The evidence to be gleaned from history is that the nearer a man is to the decision to go to war, the greater grows his responsibility for causing it. This is a trite observation for the highest decision-maker. It remains true in a slightly lesser degree also for those significantly influencing the highest decision-makers. But already in their case and increasingly more so as the distance between influencers and highest decision-makers grows, the influence need not be directed immediately toward war. It could be directed toward the highest decision-makers' perceptions of a situation or toward their evaluation of prevailing circumstances. In such cases, any direct connection between human traits and the outbreak of war becomes very problematical indeed, aggravated further by the difficulty of evaluating the weight of influence by all concerned on the final decision. At this point the social system becomes interesting as an indicator of a man's place in the chain of events and therefore of the importance of his personal characteristics. Thus, in the light of the varying relevance of men to the outbreak of war (e.g., as between the foreign minister and a peasant of the same country) nothing much is proved by speaking about man's traits in general, and relating them without further ado to war. It is quite meaningless, for instance, to state that aggressiveness is one of man's characteristics and then to argue that therefore wars exist, disregarding all of man's other characteristics and the station of the relevant man in the social system of the state that goes to a specific war.

This complication of which man is responsible for what aspect of a war's cause becomes ever greater when it is remembered that the final decision to go to war may be a mere formality and that the "real" cause of a war may have preceded this decision by a considerable period of time. Yet the men involved in the final decision may not be the same men involved in the "real" cause. Whose motives were then responsible for the war? When different people become responsible for different steps on the road to war, hardly more can be said than that human traits are responsible for war, which is not saying very much.

Another complication is that not only man but war also is complex. If an explanation of man as a cause of war is to be meaningful beyond the broadest generalization, war cannot any more than man be treated as a genus. There are various types of wars which cannot provide the same attraction or outlet for the same human trait. The motivations behind aggressive wars must surely be quite different from those behind defensive wars. The two types of wars would require different psychological explanations. The same point can be made about face-to-face wars in contrast to wars conducted mainly by technological means. Or about a war fought by mercenaries and professional soldiers and a war fought by drafted citizen armies. The juxtaposition of these types of wars shows that each provides quite a different total environment. Each supplies quite a different outlet for the natural traits and psychological drives of different people. In modern wars there are never enough "aggressive" or "frustrated" men flocking to the recruiting stations. On the home front high salaries for war work seem to have as great an attraction as psychic rewards from contributions to the war effort. Everywhere men are drafted into armies. The public's fighting spirit is aroused by governmental effort at great expense and not always successfully. In some armies during World War II more than half the soldiers who were supposed to shoot did not pull the trigger. At home, from ten to twenty people were required to maintain one man at the front and they were merely continuing their routine work — possibly with a slight increase in enthusiasm. Usually

209

the bellicosity of the public has to be stirred up by a propaganda campaign when a war is about to start or has started, while the stimulus of revenge or defense of the fatherland soon has to be replaced by "war aims" conjuring up visions of a beautiful peaceful future world. In the long run the more effective appeals to keep people fighting wars (and often to get them to do so in the first place) are not to aggressiveness, hatreds, and frustrations, but to a desire for lasting peace and greater welfare. The timing of appeals to the destructive impulses of man and the short span of their effectiveness make them appear to be rationalizations of wars decided on other grounds rather than causes.

A final situation may be pointed out making the direct relationship between man's traits and the outbreak of war extremely problematical. Not all factors clearly necessary to bring about a war are also sufficient factors. A distinction must be made — though it cannot always be made in practice — between general, contributing factors whose presence is indispensable to make war possible; and specific factors directly causing a given war. Once such a distinction has been made for a given war, it may prove nothing for another war. A generalization is not possible. The same factor present in two given wars may be in the one a general contributing, in the other the specific causative factor. The context in which these factors appear determines in which category they belong. A factor to be a cause requires a particular conjunction of factors not any one of which may itself be directed toward war. War is a complex of relationships developing from the interplay of innumerable factors. This interplay is unique at all times. And in the unending variations of situations created by this interplay the same factor or factors may or may not become causes of war. History teaches that roughly similar historical situations led to war in one case and not in the other. For instance, a particular kind of conflict may deteriorate into war between two states which are already in a tense relationship, and hardly affect their relationships when tension is absent. The dispute between Great Britain and France over the ownership of some tiny, uninhabited Channel islands has no ill effect whatsoever upon their relationships. Every inch of territory along the Oder-Neisse Line could serve as the cause of a major deterioration in the relations between the Soviet Union and the Western nations. The effect of these possibilities upon man's traits as a cause of war is that the same man will act differently in different situations. Different stimuli from the outside produce different decisions. A man's pugnaciousness in one context may lead him into violent behavior, in another it may not. Which should make it reasonably clear that since human traits remain the same there must be additional factors effective in triggering or not triggering war. There are thus always intervening factors between the human traits and the outbreak of war which must be considered together with the traits in any attempt at discovering the causes of war.

Interests as Causes of War

Interests may be considered to be among those intervening factors. They can codetermine in which direction (e.g., violent or nonviolent) the psyche of individuals will turn their behavior. Interests are needs and wants, or more precisely activated needs and wants. That is to say, needs and wants not merely expressed verbally or dreamed about, but actively pursued in the expectation of their fulfillment. Since collective, social interests are never organic, primary interests (like hunger), the specific behavioral form in which they appear, i.e., how the interests are formulated and the manner in which they are to be pursued, is the resultant of individual or social psychological traits. Because interests can be powerful motors of behavior, they have often been thought to be the main cause of war. Consideration of interests appears more feasible than a consideration of basic human traits. They are one step removed from these traits, to be sure, but they are also their more visible, measurable, and above all concrete expression. In fact, it is only through some such specified end product that the general spectrum of psychic traits existing in the abstract becomes socially meaningful.

The most extreme position on the possibility that special interests may cause wars is taken by the "devil theorists" of war. They hold that wars are caused by unscrupulous men having special interests and great influence with their governments. They produce violent conflicts among states or are willing to use wars to further their own interests. Such men could be statesmen with control over their people or men with economic interests controlling the foreign policy decisions of their country.

Historically, there were states so organized that a handful of individuals or a small, united elite could be instrumental in producing war. They could with some certainty calculate the risks and benefits of war and a victory could bring them personal enrichment. They could buy their armies and delimit the area of combat, and their subjects had little to do with the whole affair. Even today such possibilities cannot be entirely excluded in some parts of the world, but they do not apply to modern, highly developed

211

states — at least not on such a simple level. The devil theorists, mostly Marxists, have adapted themselves to modern conditions and their theories have become sophisticated. Very briefly, their claim is that the capitalist system enables the capitalists as the ruling class to use the state for the purpose of maintaining and enhancing their profits. They first exploit the proletariat and when growing production requires resources and markets the state cannot supply, imperialism will supply the new needs. Since all capitalist states will sooner or later go through this stage, violent clashes are bound to occur between the capitalist elites and their states as a result of competing claims to markets and resources.

The general idea that powerful, vested interests can lead a state into war is widely accepted quite independently of Marxist ideology. For many people the "military-industrial" complex is the new, or not so new, devil. Evidence of pressures upon government to serve their interests is available. In that respect, the military-industrial complex is hardly different from any other interest group lobbying for its ends. What usually makes this complex particularly suspect is that its fortunes seem so directly related to the preparation for and conduct of war. And it may be true that some members of this complex envisage the possibility of war with greater equanimity than other sections of the national public which are not potential direct beneficiaries of a war. But it remains questionable whether they actively agitate for war and can thereby become its cause. The Wisconsin cheese maker or the New England cotton goods manufacturer agitating for protective import duties and quotas may be a pacifist. Yet, as the history of the 1930s shows, he may well represent a link in the chain of events leading to the outbreak of war. There are too many items left unconsidered in the devil theory, whatever its specific shape, and its credibility is rapidly being undermined by both modern developments and counter-evidence.

The bad consequences of war are such today that no one group of the population can escape them. Even short of total destruction, the cost of war is rising for winner and loser alike. The mass character of modern wars makes it very difficult for the decision-makers to ignore the citizenry. Their support must be enlisted and to do so on some spurious grounds becomes increasingly difficult even for totalitarian states. The whole idea of "an" elite so homogeneous and unified in interests and outlook that it would agree to exert consolidated pressure toward war and could be successful is contrary to the social facts of every modern developed society. Large and important sections of the military-industrial complex are internationalized to such an extent that they might be at cross-purposes with themselves if in any one state they pressed for war. The traffic in arms — at least those arms needed for modern wars — is nowadays subject to government controls everywhere. And governments are always exposed to cross-pressures of many kinds. The struggle for markets is much more fought out in economic terms or through intervention in a foreign country's politics than on the battle field. Finally, blaming certain economic systems as causes of war is contrary to the warlike behavior of other systems. To wit: how can primitive or precapitalist wars be explained? why are Communist states engaging in violent conflict with each other? why do Communist states sell arms to non-Communist countries or engage in economic warfare? why do capitalist stock exchanges rise steeply whenever during a war peace appears to approach? and if wars are a specialty of Fascist states, what explains all the wars of history before the birth of fascism? and what about wars of states having no military-industrial complex?

All these questions are here raised not with the intention of denying the relevance of national or special interests to the origin of wars. They are raised to bring the importance of interests for the outbreak of wars into proper perspective. Special interests are likely to be among the factors contributing to war. They may be coeffective with other causes or through other causes in bringing about wars. But wars cannot be adequately explained as being caused by a particular social or economic or political system. Nor can war as the direct consequence of a special interest be convincingly demonstrated, no matter whose interest. All these devil theories do not fit the nature of modern wars with their long preparation, complicated organizational and technical machinery, and indispensable mass support. There is no evidence that the interests of those close to the making of decisions on war homogeneously point toward war. The making and conducting of wars depend upon circumstances over which no one man or one group has control — not even in the tightest of dictatorships. The willingness, for instance, of large sections of the German and Japanese people during World War II cannot satisfactorily be explained as a means to satisfy their individual interests of any material nature, and it is quite certain that the drive of some of their leaders toward war could not be explained on this ground. Modern wars require the acquiescence and cooperation of many men and groups whose personal or private interests combined with their influence upon the decision to go to war virtually never coincide to an extent assumed by the devil theory.

INTERNATIONAL POLITICS

Rational and Nonrational Causes of War

A merit of the devil theoreticians has been to draw attention to the role of interests among causes of war and to maintain that position throughout the period during which exclusively psychological explanations of the causes of war dominated the field. And that merit remains even though, as will be shown, these theoreticians argued the case of interests as causes in a manner not any more convincing than the psychologists argued their case. Whatever the causes of war may be, it is certain that they are not to be found alone either in man's psyche or man's interests for the simple reason that these two are inseparable as motors of man's behavior. The historical evidence is quite clear that modern wars never resulted from emotional outbursts or accumulated frustrations alone, either those of the decision-makers or those of their publics. War may be and has been used deliberately and rationally as an instrument of foreign policy in pursuit of a great variety of interests.

All modern wars were preceded by lengthy, careful, and cool-headed preparations. There is of course an implication in these preparations that a predisposition exists to fight wars, and such a predisposition contains emotional and sentimental elements. But the actual outbreak of war occurred only after a careful calculation of profits and losses as well as the chances of victory had made war advisable. Wars have always been fought in justification of some (alleged) definable goals. Every modern war has rationally supportable reasons, which may or may not be the real reasons. Nonrational elements enter because they are part of every rational process so that rational and nonrational factors are always coeffective, though in what proportion cannot be established with certainty. These nonrational factors enter into the actor's perceptions, interpretations, evaluations, choices, and any other of innumerable items going into the production of action. In this manner psychic traits like all other aspects of a man's nature enter into the chain of events leading to war. Needs and wants most of the time trigger actions and, depending upon what they are, they may be beyond human choice (hunger, sex) or very much the result of psychic and rational as well environmental influences. The manner of satisfying these needs and wants, especially when they are social needs and wants, is virtually always the result of choices, and this includes war.

Governments rarely justify the wars of their states on emotional grounds. Revenge may be a temporary motive. Sooner or later some interest is given either for beginning or for continuing the war. Its nature can vary from war to war, state to state, and culture to culture. The individual citizen may have his own reason for supporting a war. But in view of the mass support needed for modern wars whatever interest is advanced must be socially acceptable, and preferably attractive. Even if a war primarily favors one group, the reason for it and the benefits presumably coming from it must be formulated to satisfy a larger section of the national public. Governments habitually justify wars in terms of universal advantage: the nation's security, welfare, honor is claimed to be at stake and must be preserved. These concepts are sufficiently broad to cover conveniently whatever a government wants to do. The more the reasons and goals of war are generalized, the more broadly the "national interest" can be defined, the better can large numbers of citizens identify themselves with it and support "the cause." Widely sweeping definitions can encompass the most diversified interests. If they can also be stated in nationalistic terms, the most diverse psychological needs can find outlets in the war. The same war could then be fought by one man for his personal profit and by another as his crusade to make the world safe for democracy.

The multiple service a war can render makes it quite rational from the standpoint of those whose needs it serves. This is true not merely from a subjective standpoint but can be true objectively. In view of a particular need or want, war may indeed be the only means to satisfy it. If a form of rationality is the logical choice of means among alternatives to reach the goal in the best manner, then war may indeed be that means (and becomes a nice vindication of the theory that aggression is learned and not the dominant natural response to frustration!).

The multiple interests war can serve and the differing psychic needs it can fulfill may not only make the same war irrational for some participants and rational for others, but also complicates the discovery of a war's causes. An American war in Western Asia may be fought to contain communism; to preserve Europe's access to oil resources; to honor moral commitments to Israel; to save the investments of American oil companies; to prevent Soviet expansion; to demonstrate American might in the face of challenge; to maintain American naval predominance. Were such a war to be declared, there would be great difficulty, even for those who decided upon the war, in determining which interests and which sentiments were most instrumental in producing the declaration, and similarly in explaining why the counsel of those favoring remaining friendly with the Arab world, American withdrawal from faraway involvements, and the like did not prevent the war declaration. The tempting and politically expedient thing for the government to do would be to homogenize the various interests and emotions for some universally shared purpose such as preserving the nation and its honor. The war would then be widely accepted; the decision-makers would be spared the task of justifying their decision to themselves or the public; the opposition would be silenced; the country would be "unified." The war would possibly also be justified before an international audience, since defense of the national interest is always a just cause. The great diversity of interests and emotions to be found in every unique war situation precludes the possibility of defining any one among them as the cause. In this case, what is impossible for the unique situation is equally impossible as a generalization for all wars.

The Complex Causes of War

This examination of psychic traits, interests, and the environment in which they are located, in their relation to the outbreak of war, indicates that no one generally valid factor can be made responsible as a cause of wars. Aspects of human character and human behavior are always basically involved, of course, because human actions make war. But there are no inherent qualities in any of these aspects allowing us to point out any one as the cause. For this reason attempts at explaining wars through psychological factors alone are bound to be incomplete. Explanations concentrating on environmental, systemic, historical reasons are equally unsatisfactory. They can show up regularities in war situations or sometimes indirect, second-level causal relationships. By omitting specific reference to psychic factors, these explanations beg the question why at least the man-made part of the environment, system, etc., allows for war and why men use the permission to make war. Since the nonhuman environment exists permanently whether there are wars or not, it alone can obviously not explain the existence of war. Many of these factors can qualify as potential, contributing, necessary conditions of war. When the human factor is added to them, they may then become causative in selective conjunction. A unique combination of human and nonhuman factors then exists forming a situation in which one specific war breaks out. That the number of these combinations is enormous is evident from the multitude of psychic factors and of environmental factors. To discover the right combinations from which in general wars may result or can be predicted is totally hopeless.

There are other shortcomings in many typical attempts to find the causes of war. One is the assumption of too static a situation. A number of given characteristics of men or the environment are enumerated as having some likely relation to war and are then declared to "explain" war. What is overlooked is that peace and war are social processes. They join together certain of these characteristics which become effective in interaction over a period of time in producing peace or war. But the characteristics so joined and the nature of their interaction may vary over the period of time during which the process takes place. The uniqueness of the situation producing war lies both in the possibly continually changing combination of the specific factors and in the process which joins them. That people change their minds is notorious. They also change their feelings. That the environment is subject to change is guaranteed by the factor of time alone. All these changes can be rapid and the resultant of their varying interactions is unpredictable. So is therefore the outbreak, continuance, and end of wars to the extent that they depend upon these interactions.

The second and most important shortcoming in many attempts to explain war is their concentration on war rather than peace situations. This shortcoming might be overcome if, instead of looking for the causes of war in the unending variability of a complex of human and environmental factors, the focus were placed on peace situations. Factors might then be discovered which prevent the use of violence. Since, by definition, these factors must be absent in war situations, their absence might turn out to be not necessarily the cause of war but the reason why wars become possible. Like antibodies protecting man against attacks from viruses, these factors may protect society against violent struggles. As long as the immunization lasts, it does not matter what virus might attack a man; as long as these factors protect society against violence, it does not matter what causes for violence there might exist. One road, now to be taken, toward finding out what makes some societies relatively peaceful is to compare their (likely) relevant features with those of the international society (or other societies in which violence is prevalent).

Interests, Community, Integration, and Peace

One rather obvious result of such a comparison is that relative peacefulness in many states has not been achieved by changing human nature, altering the human psyche, or eliminating conflict. It has not even been achieved by eliminating hatreds between groups, discrimination, prejudices, biases, false stereotypes, ideological differences, economic rivalry, or incompatible interests. All these things, often assumed to be the causes of war, continue in some of the most internally peaceful states. Yet the use of mass violence as a normal and accepted behavior among citizens has disappeared. It is not among the means for solving clashes of emotions or interests. Instead, various formal and informal nonviolent arrangements exist and are used as guarantors and as consequences of peaceful behavior.

In the name of the common welfare these states provide for the citizens' security, supply machinery for the nonviolent settlement of conflicts, encourage the formation and expression of consensus, develop ways for coping with social change. Above all they guarantee a minimum of social order by organizing the satisfaction of the citizens' individual and social needs and, if necessary, by enforcing it with a superior concentration of power in the central government. Crucial questions are how men have succeeded in organizing societies for such peaceful life and why the same citizens behave peacefully on the national but violently on the international scene. England, for instance, has experienced very little mass violence internally for centuries, yet has participated in wars more than any other state. The answer to the questions is that the citizens of internally peaceful states form a community based on a widely shared interest that can be fulfilled only by the integration of the total peaceful social behavior. This answer requires elaboration.

When a state is a community, it may be recalled, the citizens share a sense of solidarity, unity, and cohesion of an affective character. These sentiments preclude violence as a means for settling conflicts. They also compensate for the disintegrating force of conflicts of whatever origin. In the case of states (in contrast to, for instance, a family) the citizens also always share common interests. These represent the other major support of the community. In interplay, the sentiments and the interests reinforce each other and form the foundation of the community. Historically, interests may be the first generators of the state (e.g., a united Italy and Germany in 1870), with community sentiments following thereafter (hence an Italian nationalist leader's statement, "now that we have created Italy we must create Italians," and the concern of almost every leader in the new states of Asia and Africa with "nation-building"). If sentiments precede interests (as, e.g., in the case of Zionists and Czechs), interests must still supplement sentiments, because large secondary groups are not likely to endure without them. When sentimental bonds and common interests coincide, the national

218

community is very strong. The citizens cherish its existence above all other social goals and refrain from doing anything endangering its existence. But to have this favorable effect on behavior, not every kind of interest can serve equally well. The interest most suitable for sustaining and binding a community must possess special qualities.

The interest must be comprehensive: a sufficiently large number of the community's members must find it relevant to all aspects of their social behavior. It must be enduring: it must cut across momentary interests and, in the case of states, it must cut across generations. It must be widely accepted: the number of members sharing the interest must be large enough to make the group dominant. Finally, the interest must be held with sufficient intensity; if individual or sectional group interests surpass the common interest, the community is likely to disintegrate. The one modern community having such an interest is the nation.

The interest in question is the maintenance of the nation itself. The express value system of a large number of citizens, and the conformist behavior pattern of even more, elevate the nation to the highest common interest to which all other social or individual interests are subordinated. Deliberate threats to the existence of the nation as such from within are very rare and are in any case resisted to the utmost. This is particularly true of violence as the greatest potential threat to the nation's survival. But, going beyond this (negative) defense of the nation against threats is the (positive) regulation of behavior designed to strengthen the survival of the nation. The whole national socialization process is directed toward that goal. The political system, more deliberately than any other subsystem of the national community, is designed to harmonize and coordinate, that is to say integrate, the behavior of the citizens with a view to the maintenance of the nation. The suppression of violence is always and everywhere the first concern of the political system.

The combined support the national community receives from the sentiments of its citizens and their overpowering interest in its existence can explain the peacefulness of many nations. In the international society (as in many new national societies) neither such sentiments nor such interest can be found.[61] The antibody neutralizing the virus causing violence is missing. Supportive sentiments are totally absent. There are shared interests, but not with community-producing qualities. They are limited either in subject matter, or in the number of states sharing them, or in duration. While they last and in regard to the states sharing them, they may serve the cause of peace. States can integrate their behavior in pursuit of such limited interests. But there may simultaneously also be clashing interests among the same states. If they are judged higher, they will undermine the integrative and peaceful effect of the shared interests.

There is no common goal in sight in the international society toward which nations would be willing to integrate all their social behavior and to which they would willingly subordinate other goals. Peace cannot serve as such a goal, for two reasons. Peace is not a goal of behavior. It is the by-product of behavior aiming toward something else. It is a quality of behavior, not an end. Second, states do not really cherish peace as their highest goal — their contrary assertions notwithstanding. They want qualified peace — peace with honor, with justice — which opens the door wide to violent behavior in order to establish that kind of peace! The universally accepted goals of the United Nations do indeed establish some peaceful integrated behavior. But all these goals are limited in every respect. They are never superior to the goal of national preservation. The integration they produce affects at most a part of total international behavior, never the overall social international behavior. With the arrival of atomic weapons just plain survival might have become a common, overpowering interest of states. That they have had a constraining influence on the behavior of their possessors is very likely. But this is not the same as having an influence toward an overall integrating influence upon the peaceful behavior of all the states of the international society. Statistics since World War II will make the convincing point that wars and their detrimental effect upon social order and peace have not disappeared with the arrival of atomic weapons.

In the absence of a community psyche and a community-producing interest, the best that can be expected from numerous shared interests is temporary, limited integration of national behaviors. The resulting peaceful situations will last until the particular interests have been satisfied or until divisive interests valued higher break up that integration. The prospect for peace improves if these temporary situations can be extended and intensified through the multiplications of many shared, though limited, interests and their overlapping in time. This possible, indeed likely, development would replicate developments in those states turning increasingly into "welfare" states. The more services the state renders, the more rational support it will have from its citizens. The bonds tying citizens through such functional interactions can compensate for the weakening of sentimental bonds which accompanies the growing size of states and depersonalization of relations between citizens. For national communities, this may mean a weakening of their cohesion.

220

For the international society, growing functional interdependence adds at least one dimension of cohesion. A multitude of shared though limited goals, overlapping in substance and time, could compensate somewhat for the lack of an intensely desired enduring overall goal and the integrated behavior it produces. The trend is toward a growing similarity between national societies and the international society, with both founded more on shared interests than bonding sentiments. The process is very long-range, and in any case social conflicts will continue. Whether violence will become more frequent within states and less frequent within the international society will depend greatly upon the volume and nature of shared interests.

The strong emphasis here on common interests, especially those relating to the maintenance of nations, as a major mover of peaceful integrated social behavior and as a substantial support of community sentiments is not new. Analysts of society, from Thucydides to Rousseau have recognized that common interests are the strongest bonds of society. Such an emphasis is not a one-cause explanation of peace and war. It does not exclude the more or less necessary contributions of other factors to peaceful, orderly social behavior. It does not ignore that the rise, perception, formulation, and common pursuit of shared interests are themselves reflections of compatible psychic constellations of the interested, who are the sources of the interests. It rests on an awareness, finally, that the growth of community sentiments, their maintenance, and their subject matter is an extremely complex but also quite obscure process.

A main point in the analysis is that the emphasis on interests is an emphasis upon human beings. They remain the center of the problem of peace and war. Any search for its solution must concentrate on man; not on man in abstract and splendid isolation, but on man in his given and self-created environment, on man playing specific roles, on man with quite definite needs and wants. As this chapter has tried to demonstrate, the more fruitful way toward the discovery of the causes of war and the conditions of peace is not to examine only what separates men and makes them violent, but to examine also what produces their orderly and peaceful social behavior. It will then be found, as this chapter has also tried to demonstrate, that pious appeals to a meaningless likeness of all men or righteous condemnation of their destructive abilities are insufficient to make men behave in a peaceful or orderly way, but that, instead, the formulation and pursuit of like and highly valued aims achievable through nonviolent cooperation are a straighter path to peace. Once these aims are defined and accepted, they will represent a powerful incentive to make the hitherto inadequate political institutions and the political behavior in the international society more adequate. For, as has been pointed out before, the inadequacy is mainly due to the summary effect of an absent community and a low valuation of any common interests. These two interrelated factors have been responsible for social and political structures, especially authority structures, supplying a weak foundation for peaceful and orderly social relations. These structures have enabled states to circumvent social controls and to ignore conflict-settling mechanisms which are not inherently inadequate in their formal existence. Ultimately, these weaknesses are mainly caused by men. When states begin to realize that an adequate political system is to their advantage and, at least eventually, feasible, it is within their capacity to create it.

But the process of creation will be very long indeed. Interaction, or even interdependence, based upon mutual needs is not in itself sufficient to produce the requisite political system for its control, though it could be the initiator. Functional cooperation may create integrated, supranational groupings of people directly concerned with the function (e.g., chemical or oil cartels), but this is not a basis for a supranational political system. Limited integration based on supranational functions is a subject matter, and is operating on rules, quite different from the political. There is no easy transferability of sentiments and behavior patterns from one to the other. The will, for instance, for economic integration does not imply the will for political integration, as the Western European example shows. Unless one assumes that the economic determines the political, an adequate political system does not have to follow from the existence of an integrated supranational economic system. Any integrated system of international functions (e.g., economic, military, religious) does not, according to experience so far, contain within itself or quickly lead to the social basis required for the construction of an adequate supranational political system. It could merely be one signal that the importance of goals hitherto pursued by people is changing, that the satisfactions hitherto provided by sovereign states can no longer be provided or are no longer the values people cherish above all else. But there is a very long step from interested people looking beyond their state for the satisfaction of specific interests to entire national populations making the international society their highest social value. Even for Western Europe, the president of the EEC Commission, Mr. Mansholt, stated early in 1973 that "there is a tendency to think of Europe of multinational corporations rather than the Europe of the peoples." The best that can be expected for a long time to come is that much functional cooperation may make violent conflict between the cooperators increasingly costly, develop therefore habits of peaceful settlement, and establish a peaceful situation not as stable as may exist in a community with a central government, but a peaceful situation of relatively long duration nevertheless.

9 Toward a More Adequate International Political System

INTERNATIONAL politics takes place in a unique milieu, not duplicated in any other social unit. Governments everywhere make their state their highest social value. They refuse to recognize any higher authority. Certain behavioral consequences follow from this choice. They give the international system and international politics their fundamental character.

In the absence of a commonly accepted organ to make and execute political decisions for the international society, states take over these functions for themselves individually. Which state will be a decision-maker in any given situation will be unknown until one succeeds in making a binding decision. The political processes are not dissimilar to those taking place in other societies. They range from cooperation to conflict, from negotiation to coercion. But there are significant differences too. These processes can be initiated arbitrarily. The means used are limited more by the capability and will of individual states than by common agreement and enforcement. The use of force and violence is customary. These special characteristics make all political processes highly uncertain and potentially anarchic. They enforce a hierarchy of interests states must pursue as members of the international society differing greatly from that pursued by individuals as members of national societies. Survival must be assured by the state itself. Building a power potential becomes a primary and overwhelming preoccupation. Extreme politicization of all social concerns becomes the inevitable consequence. Virtually all goals, internal or external, are affected by international power considerations. Ideologies and cultural achievements become the handmaidens of international politics.

With the unpredictability of the decision-maker's identity and the outcome of his decision, the performance of the political system becomes highly

224

inadequate. A reliable peace or social order cannot be accomplished. Decisions on social issues and policies are always the result of a power struggle motivated by national selfishness and unmitigated by concern for a common interest. The readily available use of violence by any member of the society defeats the normal purposes of a political system. As long as the system remains fragmented because states insist on coexistence in sovereign independence and equality, its basic features will endure. The fundamentals of the international political system have not been touched by the dynamics of the system. Nevertheless, the system is at the end of the twentieth century no longer exactly what it was at the time of its birth. It will be instructive, partly as a summary of the preceding analysis and partly as a foundation for the projection of trends toward a different future international political system, to examine which features of the system have remained quite constant and which have undergone significant changes.

Changes in the International Political System

Outstanding among the features of the system which have remained basically constant are two of its main pillars: the authority structure and the loyalty of the citizenry to their state. The main role of states has remained the same. The diffusion of power and decision-making continues. Social stratification has not been abolished and inequality in national capabilities has grown. The basic rules of international politics remain intact. Territory remains an important definer of the state. By any standard of measurement the United Nations has not had an accretion of power in twenty-five years. There is no noticeable impetus behind moves toward supranational organization. Advanced ideas about political unification await realization. Europe is still *l'Europe des Patries* which France still wishes to convert into *l'Europe de Paris*! Within COMECON the Soviet Union had to make concessions to national autonomy. In other regions of the world, mergers of states into wider political entities remain paper schemes. The incidence of war, a good measure of the success or failure of the political system, has remained unchanged in principle.

Without affecting the basic identity of the international political system many changes in detail are, however, taking place which could in their cumulative effect alter the identity in the longer run. Even now they can provide a hint regarding the direction in which the system will develop. The territorial base of the state is losing importance, which is in itself a significant fact because territory is slowly ceasing to be the prominent goal for which people are readily willing to kill or die. It is a significant fact also because the things for which territory has been symbolic are gradually diminishing in importance: prestige, patriotism, and some of the satisfactions, material and psychic, which the state used to provide, including identification. International cooperation, interaction and contacts have grown enormously. Mutual sensitivity in virtually every state to changes inside others has established linkages making a precise separation between internal and external affairs impossible. Withal the substance of sovereignty has been thinning and a revolutionary global communications system has made the separation and isolation of states extremely difficult. There is a need and a readiness hitherto unknown for states to consult with each other before they make political decisions, leading on rare occasions even to collective decision-making. The emphasis placed everywhere upon economic growth combined with mutual sensitivity to internal affairs has raised economic goals and economic methods to serious competitors with the more traditional tools of power. This in turn has affected the basis of a state's power potential and caused shifts in the rank order of the international social stratification. The diminishing majesty of the state resulting from all these changes is affecting the citizen's loyalty to the state and possibly his sense of community with fellow citizens.

For the time being, these changes have been little more than variations on the major theme of the nation-state system. The international political system has been flexible enough to cope with innovations without making concessions in principle. One difficulty of evaluating the overall results of all these changes in aspects of the system and in the mentality of the world's peoples underlying it is in the fact that these results do not all point in the same direction. A few of these changes may have effects going beyond mere adaptations of the system to innovations (e.g., the thinning substance of sovereignty). But whether they may lead to the demise of the state (as was thought of the increasing penetrability of states) or to its strengthening (as was thought of the increasing services states render to their citizens) is not easy to judge. The nearest to a fundamental change is the metamorphosis of mankind from a conglomerate of states to a global society. So far, this has not greatly affected the bases upon which the international system rests. It has only created a greater discrepancy between what the international political system is and what it should be.

In the long run this development could be seen, however, as the foundation for an eventual transformation of the basic structure of the system. It points to ever-closer relations between sections of different national publics following from growing mutual needs. It no longer sounds utopian to envisage the possibility of substantial numbers of states integrating into a new, larger statelike political unit. Nor does it sound so utopian to assume that the traditional role of states as the supreme social value of their citizens may be reduced to an administrative unit, with the political center or centers gravitating to different social groupings. Even if states continue to be the main political units and objects of their citizens' loyalties, the substance of international relations may change so much that disorder and war become increasingly unacceptable. The greater adequacy of the international political system might then result not from major structural alterations (especially not the rise of a central world government) but from such a density of transnational interactions that no state would want to or could afford to interfere violently. Indeed, by the time such density has been reached, a government would not likely be able to interfere. The politically relevant interactions would no longer be handled with such exclusivity as they now are by governments. New channels of communication will presumably have developed in which agencies other than governments have become prominent. These developments lie in the future. There is no way of predicting their exact course. The voluminous international activities of private individuals, including corporations, and of semiprivate organizations undermine the political monopoly of states. Even Communist states feel obliged to abandon their exclusivity and seclusion. Governments are beginning to realize that the mutualities between their states are matching their differences or, perhaps more correctly, that their differences and mutualities are inextricably enmeshed. They have not yet reached the point where they put the two on the same level and create a corresponding political system. Such a system is in the process of creating itself, however. In the last two decades more attention has been given to the development of methods to exploit the mutualities than of methods to settle international differences violently. It is possible to discover trends whose projection into the future may supply some ideas of how fundamental changes may come about and what international politics may be like a few decades hence.

The Conservative Nature of Social Change

The likelihood is that all changes will continue to be evolutionary, not revolutionary or abrupt. Social growth is incremental. Men do not normally create social organizations and then fill them with content. Transposing the constitution of a peaceful national community to the international society; universalizing the formal structure of one specific community to a totally different social unit, like mankind, is futile because constitutions and social structures rest on social-psychological prerequisites for their functioning. Like all social units the international society develops in response to needs. It was not created whole and in one piece. Improving technology, mainly, created the needs and simultaneously the means for their satisfaction. Each advanced the other in a process of interaction whose end is not yet in sight.

The international society more often than other modern societies has proved resistant to the disintegrating influence of innovations.[62] It has absorbed them, avoiding social disturbances and protecting national sovereignty above all else. For this reason so many blueprints for a brave new world have remained blueprints. Too often they are trying to reverse the normal process by which societies are born and grow. Social contacts, interactions, relationships grow first. Then comes the need for their organization. Blueprints may at that point provide guidelines for the most desirable or effective organization. In all probability, as the substance and volume of international relations change, the international system and international politics may adjust to these guidelines. The adjustment will be gradual, at best. For as states require new functional interrelations these are accommodated to the existing framework of the international system rather than the other way around. Presumably for this reason — among others — extreme political demands for peace and social order as they are often voiced especially by new states are evidently poorly satisfied. Even these demands may, in fact, be made for the record more than in an expectation that they will be met. No strong pressures for fundamental changes to improve the prevailing situation have come from any government. Apparently the satisfactions to be derived from the existing nation-state system and the anxieties from unforeseeable consequences of radical changes sustain a general attachment to the traditional system. The relevant publics worldwide are agreed that no fundamental changes are wanted.[63] The strongest and richest states will not readily surrender their privileged positions — and may even conspire to form an oligarchy to maintain them.

The slow tempo of social change, the resiliency of the international system to change, and the system's ability to incorporate changes within its established framework should squash the widespread hope since World War II that the historical trend of smaller social units forever growing into larger ones would continue until a world state has been established. Whether this will ever happen is unknown. Too much depends upon the interests man will value most highly in the future and upon an ability to manipulate man's psyche. There is so far no foundation for the expectation that mankind will grow into a community with a central government in an integrated political system. All that may be expected with some certainty from the changes outlined and the process of change described is an eventual basic change away from the present situation.

The prospect of a reduced use of arbitrary violence between states in the future may be taken as an important example of what may happen in and to the international political system in the not-too-distant future. The absence of war since 1945 between developed states is the result of careful and deliberate choice. The "balance of terror" has presumably a good deal to do with this. Or, as the Marxists would have it, the dominant powers have distributed the world among themselves as neocolonies and spheres of influence and they are busy fighting their wars in the Third World! There are in any case other changes bringing forth this unusual peacefulness. Highly developed states have much to lose in a war — they are very vulnerable. Territorial conquests are becoming unfashionable, perhaps in part for moral reasons, but more likely because at least well-established wealthy states have functional equivalents for conquests and spoils of war.[64] The benefits warring states sought to obtain riskily they can now obtain more securely by nonviolent means: trade; investment; financial manipulation; economic influence; or just friendly, selfish, and mutually beneficial cooperation. Any little extra benefit to be gained by violence is not worth the cost of a direct confrontation, nor even, as the biggest nations are learning, a limited or interventionist or vicarious war. A changing value system, placing economic growth and welfare above the imponderable benefits of nationalism will reinforce this development. Other examples, in fields less vital to the international society, could easily be found to show that significant changes in the behavior patterns of the international society have taken place without so far affecting the fundamental nature of the international political system. The idea that the prevention of war, for example, requires a world government has, for the time being and in relations between developed states, proved to be incorrect. It is quite possible that other mutations in the system will continue, giving birth to new behavior patterns from which a more adequate political system will arise. Such mutations are indeed already in their incipient states in regard to two major factors largely determining the nature of the international political system: the sense of community and functional relationships. They will now be examined. This should help in gaining an impression of the future character of the international political system, not what it ought to be but what it is most likely to be.

Trends in the Changes of the International Society

It appears that states are the largest communities from which psychic satisfactions through membership can be derived. The individual would presumably find identification with larger units difficult (notwithstanding the possibility that here and there some states may merge and develop a community of the new unit). The present experience is that even nations are increasingly found too large to convey a sense of community to their citizens. The growth of alienation and anomie is a widespread complaint in well-established nations. The nation-building leaders of new states find it extremely difficult to instill in their modernizing societies a sense of community whose character is totally alien to their publics.

The great size of national populations, the complexity of societies, the depersonalization of social relationships, the lack of meaning in the individual's daily activities make people feel strangers in their own environment. If people can no longer experience community in their personal immediate surroundings, they cannot transfer it to their state and, a fortiori, to mankind. The furious pace of material developments leaves people psychologically behind, without guidance from past precedents, in a situation of historical solitude. Everybody is separated from his neighbor. He is on his own. Lessons from preceding generations are largely inapplicable. The society becomes fatherless (Alexander Mitscherlich). Many individuals no longer find emotional nourishment in a nationhood that has become trivial and devoid of substance. The alienated turn away from it or find it outright objectionable. They are looking for new groups, smaller, with more inspiring items in common than those of what has to them become a meaningless nationality, and regardless of where these groups might be located across the earth. These units may become the communities in which individuals will find psychic satisfactions and identity. They may cut across state borders or lie within them and individuals may be members of more than one. Such a dissolution of national communities and their replacement by different, smaller communities means that mankind is not likely to transform itself into one community. It lacks the common features which could serve the individual as identification and form the psychological basis of a community. Mankind will remain a relatively weak society, devoid of that sense of community which is such an important foundation for the adequate political system of nations and such an important brake upon the escalation of social conflicts from peaceful to violent. Fortunately for the existence of mankind, the very same reasons leading to a decline in community bonds have produced other socially important factors exercising some comparable if less effective restraints upon social behavior. The most promising among these are concrete mutual needs.

The promise lies in the fact that the importance of states as providers of most material satisfactions is diminishing too and that citizens have to seek many satisfactions beyond national borders. This change in the sources of satisfactions applies less to large, rich states than to smaller, less self-sufficient states. But it applies in some measure to all states. Many common interests are tying groups together regardless of their members' nationalities. Functional relationships between people in many different countries cover the globe, catering to interests unrelated to any one state. The growth of international functional organizations, governmental and nongovernmental, testifies to this development which, moreover, is not likely to stand still. The growth of multinational corporations, international research organizations, academic exchange programs is illustrative of activities for which the state is at best a useful tool, at worst a hindrance.[65] The novelty of this situation — in contrast to earlier periods when functional relationships also existed — is that many of the interests involved are frequently no longer luxuries, so that it would be costlier to forgo the relationship; that the range of interests is very wide; and that the number of people directly or indirectly concerned has become enormous. Because these interests are voluminous, the functional relationships serving them make an impact on international politics. Governments cannot ignore them; they may, in the course of time, not even be able to control them because the interests of the individuals in these transnational relationships will supersede their interest in intranational relationships. The great variety of interests and the random dispersal of their consequences across the globe create connections between individuals and groups regardless of national attachments and independent of time periods (because the duration of these interests overlaps). The new functional units may also have, like the new communities, multiple and cross-cutting memberships. The possibility arises therefore that the tolerance for conflict in the absence of a community may be made up for by the opposition to conflict

231

created through the bonds tying together worldwide or at least transnational interest groups.[66] The satisfaction of their interests gives them a great stake in the avoidance of arbitrary international violence, possibly a greater stake than in the maintenance of their state at the expense of peace.

A Projection of the Consequences into the Future

The consequences growing out of these new national and international group alignments are difficult to predict. There are no precedents, at least not in the comprehensiveness of their subject matter or the number of people involved. The individual can be a member of one or more ''identity'' communities and simultaneously a member of several ''functional'' groups, with none of them coinciding either in membership or in space. For growing numbers of people the traditional identity between the boundaries circumscribing their community and their functional groupings in the form of national frontiers is disappearing. Yet the viability and strength of states rested very largely on such an identity. The state derives its strongest support from the mutual reinforcement which psychic and material satisfactions of membership in the national community lend each other. As long as such an identity prevails, the individual is spared a conflict of loyalties to his state, while the state can draw on the citizen's total personality. When this identity begins to disappear and the state provides only one or the other or none of the satisfactions, conflict can develop between the citizen's commitment to his ''identity'' (community) group and his ''functional'' group. If the state represents neither, there is bound to be diminishing commitment to it.

The present developments foreshadow new groupings within the international society. A new distribution of interests and loyalties will have telling effects upon the international social order. Groups building potential communities within and across existing states cut criss-cross over the globe. Functional groupings serving the material needs of their members also cut criss-cross over the globe, but in different patterns. These criss-cross relationships are not identical, as regards either the communities or the functional groupings. Their memberships overlap in many different ways. In the course of time an extreme pluralism may develop which is oblivious of territorial boundaries or political divisions and indifferent to any one supreme political or social unit. Very likely, instead of the often-expected integration of existing political units into larger units there will be a break-up of the presently integrated units and their replacement by a multitude of differently focused new integrated units.

232

A More Adequate Political System

In such a pluralistic situation the dominant role of the national whose emotions, interests, and behavior are focused on the state is likely to disappear. His socialization will be into transnational groups and groups smaller than the present state. He will become very pluralistic in the sense that he will perform a variety of roles in a coordinated but no-longer hierarchical order, since there will be no state demanding his supreme allegiance. The individual's membership in a great number of different but not subordinated groups will exert cross-pressures on him, pushing and pulling him in different directions and among different groups, with none dominant or demanding supremacy. The large number of individuals with memberships in these various community and interest groups makes it evident that the absolute and rigid confrontations now possible and typical of relations between states cannot occur. Conflicts there will be. But they will not, as they are in the nation-state system, sooner or later be identified with state conflicts. There will be no government making all these conflicts its own and homogenizing them into national conflicts so that conflict predictably always ends up in a confrontation between the same social units: states. The individual will not turn to his government for the solution of his conflicts; he will turn for each conflict to the particular group within whose bailiwick the interest involved is located. No one group will serve the needs of its members comprehensively enough to be able to isolate itself against any or all others. Positively, the large number of groupings, the large size of their membership, and the voluminous overlap in memberships augment the potential of interactions, deals, and trade-offs. Instead of polarization with its very limited bargaining possibilities for solving conflicts, there will be a large market with many different opportunities for combinations to solve conflicts.

There is likely to occur a great decentralization of planning and action for psychic and material satisfactions. This process will be additionally stimulated by the requirement of modern technology and economic progress of decision-making by those directly involved in and affected by them, and therefore less and less by some central governmental organ. In spite of the complaint of "Big Government" the fact is that in all modern societies crucial decisions in all spheres of social, especially economic, activity are made far below the level of government. In open societies it happens as a matter of experience, in planned closed societies as a matter of official policy. The interweaving of the pluralistic groups increasingly representing the individual's centers of interest is likely to be so complete that war between any pair of several of them not only cannot achieve any particular purpose but will become prohibitively costly by interfering with the functioning of other groupings in which the warring individuals are involved. The curious conclusion emerges — curious in the light of common assumptions — that integration of existing political units may be neither the most likely nor the most desirable path toward a peaceful world. Not likely, because there appears to be a psychological limit to the size of a community and because present trends point toward the formation of common interest rather than common sentiment groupings. Not the most desirable, because identity of sentimental and interest groupings, with mutual reinforcement, has hitherto permitted states to monopolize the conduct of conflicts and settle them by total confrontation and violence. The replacement of smaller state units by larger regional units might merely produce on a larger scale what has been happening between states in the past.

Future International Organization

What the organization of the international or transnational society will look like, i.e., how the behavior of its members will be related formally, can be discerned only most dimly. States will exist for a long time to come, although they may no longer be nations. Their role will change from crucial decision-makers to convenient coordinating administrators. With the citizens losing their intense commitment to the state, they have little reason to support political decisions by governments contravening their interests in their new community and interest groups. Indeed, the aggregation of interests as the basis for political decisions could no longer suitably be made by any one government, since those interested do not necessarily exist only within the administrative jurisdiction of any one government at all. The members of the various groups will demand decisions enabling their groups to function well within or across states. These groups will be the fountains of political decisions whose executors, if such are needed other than the groups themselves, are likely to be states, transnational agencies, or whatever new types of agencies will arise in response to needs. The bulk of global politics will be the bargaining among these various groups. Much of it can be done through direct political interaction without the intermediary of remote representatives. Some of the coordinating will remain the bailiwick of overall, society-wide agencies. The technical complications arising from such a multiplicity of decisions and from the need to possess information for making them intelligently should not represent serious problems in the computer age. The

European Economic Community can serve as an indicator of the possible direction for this development. Its whole strategy is, to cite a high German official, to break up "grand politics" into less controversial technical, economic, social questions (something the Functionalists have proposed for many years, of course) in the hope of gradually building solidarity from interweaving interests. The assignment to the governments, he continued, is then to exercise their sovereignty in common on the basis of the agreements and proposals reached on these various questions by other agencies.

The integration of each group on the basis of its common loyalties or its specific functions to cater to the members' psychic and material needs, the integration between them to the extent that they supplement each other, and their quite uncoordinated dispersion criss-cross across the globe will prevent them from relying upon any one state. The dangers of extreme politicization or bureaucratization, of subordinating interests to the ends of any one state — always present when states act as integrators or integratees — will be minimal. The use of mass violence or any other form of comprehensive mass coercion by these groupings is virtually impossible. The capabilities of any one of them for such purposes are extremely limited and, if violence were to be used within a grouping, the damage to the victim is likely to be no greater than to the victor. The use of weapons or sanctions cannot be selective because of the multiple memberships of any one individual in the most diverse groups. Moreover, it would be most difficult to see what could be gained by the use of violence or even how such violence could be organized.

Some of these considerations do not yet apply fully to poor and underdeveloped states. The reasons are mainly that their public's communities are virtually all smaller than their present states and none of them transnational, and that their interests are either so limited or narrow in scope that they do not lend themselves easily to the specialization, diversification, and criss-cross patterns forming the base of the future system. But they will themselves benefit from the projected future developments, and their own growth will gradually fit them more easily into the future patterns.

The Place of the Underdeveloped States

For the moment the underdeveloped states are often battle fields for external and mostly internal wars in which outsiders play important interventionist parts. Traditional conventional struggles for power can still take place there.

But many of these states will not remain in their low status forever. As they become more developed, they cannot as easily be used as pawns and at the same time will be able to gain more by internal and external peace. Struggles for power will, in any case, gradually assume different forms everywhere, as they have already done between developed states. As the significance of states wanes, so will the struggle for power among them. The diminishing interest which the lowest-status states will have for the higher-status states may not be an unmixed blessing. It could simply lead to a neglect of the weakest and poorest states with a resulting delay in their development. At the same time these states could develop undisturbed by outside interference. They may remain regional ghettos for some time to come. But there may be some part-solution to this problem.

The undercutting of the relevance of states is likely to proceed parallel to an increase of relevance in special qualities. The future community and interest groupings are based on specific capabilities of whoever possesses them and wherever they may be located. The totality of such qualities and capabilities, so to speak the homogenized qualities of a whole national people, which at present determine the status of states, will lose their importance. Individual and specific qualities will count more than their sum total for any given state. The present inequalities of states, based on these totalities, are likely to diminish, while a highly developed division of labor will give contributing groups high status. The homogeneity of states will break up. Specialized groups will determine future alignments and the status of these groups. Those with contributions to make will be valued and the dominant-subordinate relationship between on-the-whole rich and on-the-whole poor states will disappear. It will be replaced by a more balanced, symmetrical relationship between the various groupings cutting criss-cross over the globe. Some of the frustrations suffered by the newer, poorer, or weaker states will decrease as their people are no longer rated according to their limited overall contributions, but as groups among their people on the basis of their specialties join with groups elsewhere and make their contributions to the international society.

The North-South dividing line will at least be blurred and gradually replaced by a network of pluralistic divisions, quite dependent upon each other; just as the East-West dividing line or even Lin Piao's countryside-city division will no longer make much sense. There will still be regions in which large concentrations of members of various groupings are located, and for this reason the demise of the national state will be very slow. The United States, for instance, with its many resources and many people is bound to have a greater representation in more of the community and interest groupings than many smaller, poorly endowed regions. It would be in the interest of such regions to develop other regions, for obvious economic but also for obvious political reasons. With interests as the most powerful motivators of social action, their diffusion and dispersal would counteract that concentration of power which is now partly responsible for the inadequacy of the international political system and international politics. A highly developed pluralism across the globe is likely to diminish the significance of any one state as a political unit and is bound to make the use of violence largely self-defeating — not necessarily because higher moral considerations would proscribe it but because it would produce more damage than benefits to all concerned. Mutualities will be valued more highly than gains to be made through violent conflict.

There is a third reason why presently poor states may benefit from these possible developments. Most of these states are located in Asia and Africa. There, any tradition of formal international law, constitutionalism, systematic organization, parliamentary methods, and similar mostly Western-invented ways of arranging political relations between peoples is understood mostly by small elites. The pluralistic system as here projected and as certainly incipient in the present international system may also not be fully congenial to the cultural traditions of Asia and Africa. But it is less antagonistic to large sections of their peoples. It corresponds well to their preoccupations with problems of development. The often purely verbal respect paid to these Western institutions and practices by their statesmen and their clear preference for informal, substantive, pragmatic approaches to common problems in international organizations are indications that they would find the future system quite acceptable. Here again this vision of the future is based upon trends already discernible in the United Nations and elsewhere. The preferences of the Asian and African governments, reflecting modern needs and some local traditions, found expression first in the shift from concerns with wars and collective security to the rectification of economic and social imbalances in the world; and second in the frequent substitution of up-to-date pragmatic methods for legalistic ones or in their neglect altogether.

Perhaps the moralist will be disturbed because material interests are such powerful determinants of international politics and even more because all the improvements in the international political system appear to rest on the self-interest of individuals and groups. The fact is that whatever is favorable to peace in the contemporary political system, the modicum of order which prevails, and the likely changes in the system depending upon new ways of satisfying interests are due to selfish considerations of groups and states. The chances are that this motivation will remain the most secure foundation for the projection and manipulation of a future political system. A world order established on the basis of brotherly love and the unity of mankind would be morally more appealing. Herein lies the attraction of so many blueprints for One World. The historical evidence, however, is clearly against them. Morality is heavily outweighed by material interests in the processes of international politics. It might be a saving grace that if selfishness can improve the prospects for peace and social order, there will be more room for brotherly love.

NOTES

Notes

THE FOLLOWING NOTES relate to quantitative studies relevant to statements made in the text. For the sake of accuracy and in fairness to the authors mentioned, a word of caution is in order. For obvious reasons the notes cite only the conclusions of these studies. Taken out of context, these conclusions appear to be more definitive than their authors claim them to be, at least in most cases. Frequently these conclusions are of a preliminary nature or are claimed as valid only on a limited basis the exact nature of which is described in the body of the study. The citation of these conclusions aims merely at indicating generally the extent to which quantitative methods may support or not support conclusions reached in the text by other methods. An additional aim has been to bring together a representative sample of quantitative studies within the broad framework established in this book.

1. The growth of government machinery in every country is evidence of the need for coordination and centralization in increasingly complex modern societies. See, for instance, the growth of cabinet membership of all countries in Banks (1971, pp. 3–55). The expansion of civil services everywhere, including those of international organizations, is notorious.

2. The *Yearbook of International Organizations* (1969, p. 13) lists a total of 229 intergovernmental organizations and 2,188 nongovernmental organizations for 1968–69, whereas for 1956–57 the respective figures were 132 and 985. The growth of international organizations and their membership is described in detail by Wallace and Singer (1970). For 1815 they count 23 nations and 1 intergovernmental organization; by 1960 there were 107 states in 192 organizations. The number of diplomatic missions exchanged, the size of delegations to international organizations, and the membership in such organizations is steadily on the increase (Alger and Brams, 1967; Keohane, 1969b; Wallace and Singer, 1970). International visits have increased greatly (Brams, 1969). The journal *International Associations* supplies currently the most recent statistics on international organizations.

3. Singer (1964) found after a survey of elite publications in the Soviet Union and the United States that neither side blamed the international system for international conflicts or the use of violence. The implication was that the system would safeguard peace if it were not for some disturbing outside influences (such as national ideologies). Very similar results for a greater sample of elites were found by Vincent (1971b), and for Nehru, Nasser, and Sukarno by Choucri (1969).

4. The volume of interaction between states can be illustrated in many ways. Whichever is chosen, the result is always an increase in contacts either among state officials or among citizens in an unofficial capacity. Angell (1967) provides an accounting of travel for various purposes, foreign students in different countries, nationals serving as technical experts abroad,

241

INTERNATIONAL POLITICS

numbers of international civil servants. For tourist travel see International Union of Official Travel Organisations (1968) and Lijphart (1964). For mail flow see Russett et al. (1964, pp. 112–17). For the number of official international conferences see Shenton (1933). For interaction in the European Economic Community see Deutsch et al. (1967) and Puchala (1970). The best source for trade relations is the statistical publications of the United Nations. Hughes (1972) pointed out the difficulty of using transaction data in measuring integration because of inadequacies in the measuring process and the amorphous nature of the concept of integration.

5. The uninterest of national publics in international affairs is a cause of eternal complaint by their governments and those interested. This uninterest has been demonstrated in various ways. Uninterest in general has been demonstrated by how few people read foreign news, how little they know about foreign affairs, and what a low importance they assign to foreign affairs (Hero, 1959a, 1959b; Almond and Verba, 1965, chap. 2; Robinson, 1967). Uninterest has also been demonstrated by showing ignorance about important, acute events in international politics; see Cole and Nakanishi, n.d., and virtually all public opinion polling organizations, e.g., Indian Institute of Public Opinion, *Monthly Public Opinion Surveys*; *International Review of Public Opinion*; *The Gallup Opinion Index*; *Sondages*; *Revue Française de l'Opinion Publique*; *Jahrbuch der Öffentlichen Meinung*; *Polls*. Willick (1969) found that the "very interested" section of the public range from 27.1 percent in Germany to 4.4 percent in Italy. Damle (1955) found knowledge of international affairs in seven Indian villages at various distances from Poona to be nil. Erskine (1962) discovered that international affairs have no monopoly on being ignored; a discovery which Willick refined with his finding that there is a correlation between internal social conditions and the content of newspapers on the one hand, and public interest in politics, including international politics, on the other. Caspary (1970) in checking on Gabriel Almond's "mood theory" concluded that the American public has a strongly supportive as well as stable "passive mood" for an active American role in world affairs. To the extent that there is a public uninterest in any one or more fields of public affairs, it may well be consistent with the idea of a division of labor in society as Berelson et al. suggest (1954, pp. 196, 314).

6. Formal diplomatic relations tend to reflect substantive relations and therefore often do not supply contacts additional to those existing in regard to trade, cultural relations, etc. But memberships in international organizations provide a considerable number of contacts between states which have otherwise no diplomatic and few other contacts; see Alger and Brams (1967, pp. 654, 662). This membership is growing rapidly, as was shown by Angell (1965, p. 193).

7. Most attempts to define regions precisely have not been very successful; see Russett (1967 and 1968); Domínguez (1971). Studies in transaction flows between states have also been used to delineate regional politics. In this connection see Brams (1966) and Deutsch (1956).

8. Brams (1968, p. 94) found considerable "cosmopolitanism" of regions, i.e., they were extraregional on a number of dimensions, such as diplomatic representation, trade, etc. Russett and Lamb (1969, p. 54) found considerable overlap of groups classified as regional and seventeen nations which could not be categorized into any one region at all — even when regions were very broadly defined!

9. In western Europe, for instance, China was always considered to be a potentially powerful, i.e., high-ranking nation. This evaluation was directly related to China's growing economic development and the modernization of her weaponry (Lerner and Gorden, 1969, pp. 147–56). For the ranking of other states see Lerner and Gorden (1969, p. 158); Alcock and Newcombe (1970). In South American states industrialization and education were found to be determinants of rank (Schwartzman and Aranjo, 1966). Economic development emerges as the most important determinant of rank from several studies (Clark et al., 1971; East, 1970; Jarvad, 1968, p. 301; Kihl, 1971, p. 367; Rummel, 1971, p. 28; Sawyer, 1967; Vincent, 1971a, pp. 28–29). An inquiry among Japanese students disclosed that the economic factor was the most prominent determinant in their prestige ranking of states (Shimbori et al., 1963). An inquiry among Frenchmen showed that the French role in the world was for them the most important determinant of France's rank (Lancelot and Weill, 1969, p. 168). Wallace (1971) found tentatively a significant

Notes

association between status inconsistency or rank disequilibrium and the genesis of international wars between 1820 and 1964. He defined status inconsistency as the difference between rank on the basis of achieved status as measured by power capability and rank on the basis of ascribed diplomatic importance as measured by the number of diplomatic missions received. A related attempt to measure the rank of a state on the basis of diplomatic missions exchanged combined with the rank of the diplomats was made by Singer and Small (1966).

10. Väyrynen (1970, p. 305) found that in international organizations with great scope or high range of activities, changes in stratification between 1951 and 1966 were almost negligible, in spite of considerable changes in ranking within and between other organizations.

11. A substantial number of respondents to the question regarding the main purposes of the European Economic Community stated that they were to defend Europe's common interests, to enlarge Europe's sphere of interest, and to maintain the independence of the participating states. At one time or another almost half or more of those questioned also felt that the EEC was a counterpoise to Soviet or American influence (Lerner and Gorden, 1969, pp. 130, 139). Quite consistently, there were sizable sections of the Western European publics who agreed that it would be a "good thing" if as a result of European union American influence decreased (Merritt and Puchala, 1968, pp. 289–90, 305). The majorities shifted considerably, however, when the question related to military rather than economic matters. In that case there was greater willingness to pool resources with other, non-European states either in the Western world or in a collective security system (Merritt and Puchala, 1968, pp. 321–30; Lerner and Gorden, 1969, pp. 118, 122; Deutsch et al., 1966, p. 121). When the Association of Southeast Asian Nations was created in 1968, all participating officials stated that part of its function was to strengthen the states in the region economically and against aggression from powerful nations, especially China (Levi, 1968, pp. 60–61, 70–73).

12. Children and probably adults as well tend to judge cultural similarities and differences in terms of being "like us" or "not like us" (Lambert and Klineberg, 1959; 1967, pp. 105–8).

13. Differences in style are difficult to establish quantitatively. They have been observed empirically during negotiations with the Chinese Communists (Young, 1968; Lall, 1968). An attempt at more rigorous examination was made by Mushakoji (1968), who did discover stylistic differences on the basis of quantitative measurements. Hensley (1968) found differences in the judgments of elected justices of the International Court of Justice which he thought derived from different legal backgrounds.

14. The very few quantitative studies evaluating the impact of the culture factor on international politics reach essentially the same conclusion — that it is not very weighty. Cobb and Elder (1970, pp. 100–101) found that cultural homogeneity tends to foster mutual relevance but that its influence on politics is at best moderate. Russett (1967, p. 198) found that cultural similarity and voting behavior at best make no basic difference in the probability of conflict behavior. A difficulty in discovering the truth is that objective cultural differences may not be as relevant to international politics as accuracy or inaccuracy in perceived differences. Buchanan and Cantril (1953, pp. 12–23) discovered that citizens felt they shared many more things in common with all their fellow citizens than with individuals of comparable class and status in other countries. Montague (1963, p. 200) found that differences in attitudes according to class within a state were smaller than differences between citizens of different countries. This finding, however, had to be qualified. On nine out of twenty-two items tested, class differences within states were larger than between states.

Voting patterns of states in international organizations show no consistency regarding cultural similarities or dissimilarities. They align according to quite different criteria.

An international opinion poll in 1962 showed that at most 5 percent of the interviewees felt that cultural differences might create difficulties for the uniting of Western Europe (Gallup International, 1963, p. 110). Three successive polls in Germany between 1955 and 1962 showed that 32 percent, 16 percent, and 15 percent respectively felt that there were too many differences to allow friendship with France (Merkl, 1971, p. 460). An inquiry among Frenchmen in 1969 regarding the extension of membership in the European Economic Community indicated that their first preference was to limit the membership to the existing six because of assumed similarities

243

in the way of life of the five members with the French way. It was also clear that political inclinations affected the answer: extreme Gaullists favored the admission of Spain, while Communists favored Czechoslovakia (Lancelot and Weill, 1969, p. 150). Inglehart (1970b, p. 139) however found that "good Europeanism" goes together with a broader internationalism. Alger (1968, p. 82) concluded after a survey of work done in a committee of the United Nations that cultural differences could not effectively explain differences in national behavior between Western states and the Soviet Union. In this connection it is interesting to note that in two inquiries in Japan, spiritual and cultural factors were not rated highly as determinants in a state's prestige (Stoetzel, 1955, p. 115; Shimbori et al., 1963). Franko (1971, pp. 190–93) studied stability of joint ventures in multinational corporations and found that cultural differences were not a cause of instability. Indeed, the greatest instability was found in joint ventures of Americans and Canadians!

15. Numerous tests show that in general increasing mutual contacts and acquaintance do not necessarily lead to mutual love. But such contacts tend to break down stereotypes as a result of more accurate knowledge. Gilbert (1951) tested Princeton University students on stereotypes in 1932 and 1950. He found a striking lowering in their stereotypes about citizens of other nations and ascribed this change to improving knowledge (not in the same students but in general). Seago (1947) found no basic changes in stereotypes as a result of the war. A survey in France, however, showed that a majority of Frenchmen in 1969 considered that Germans were "now" good Europeans (Lancelot and Weill, 1969, p. 154). Meenes (1943) found no change in stereotypes among Negroes as a result of World War II except in regard to Germans, Japanese, and Chinese. That higher education and better knowledge relate to fewer stereotypes is now well established (e.g., Lambert and Klineberg, 1959). Eysenck and Crown (1948) warn that interviewers' questions may inspire stereotypes. For a survey of the literature on stereotypes, see Duijker and Frijda (1960).

16. Quantitative studies of the influence of cultural similarities or dissimilarities have remained inconclusive. While many lead to the conclusion that similarities facilitate cooperation or even integration, there is as much evidence that dissimilarities do not contribute to conflict. See Rummel (1972, p. 108); J. D. Sullivan (1972, p. 135).

17. In measuring the homogeneity of political values as a predictor of mutual relevance between states, Cobb and Elder (1970, pp. 94–95) discovered that shared values play a minor role in international interactions. Jacob (1971) and *International Studies of Values in Politics* (1971, p. 210) found many similarities in the values held by leaders in the four countries tested; many dissimilarities in the ranking of various values; and, of greatest interest here, values to be unreliable as predictors of behavior. There appears to be no empirical study producing the opposite result. The nearest to it are findings by M. P. Sullivan (1972, p. 206) to the effect that the adoption of new symbols may result in new action based upon them. Sullivan's study partly supports but also partly denies the validity of the point made in the text about the effect chronology has on the relationship between values, interests, and behavior.

18. In addition to strong positive emotional attachments to the state, there is also the social inertia making people reluctant to change their accustomed social system radically, even when, verbally, they favor substantial changes. This becomes very evident when the result of opinion polls favoring European union are compared with the actual progress of European union; or when responses favorable to the abolition of national sovereignty are compared with much less favorable responses to suggestions for the transfer of specific national prerogatives to an international authority. For relevant studies see note 21.

19. Even treaties adopted in the United Nations and other international organizations are frequently not ratified in the end by a large number of nations. The statistics on this point are disappointing even to those who hope that agreement on "functional," as opposed to "political," matters may be the best road to a more united world. See Schachter (1971, pp. 24–40, 162); Schwebel (1971).

20. This evidence can be found in the changing operations of international organizations, which are now dealing as a matter of routine with subjects formerly considered to be under purely internal, domestic jurisdiction. It can also be found in the polls asking for attitudes

toward European union in its various forms. These attitudes show a clear trend in the support of measures toward union (see note 21). It can, finally, be found also in the attempts to form regional organization in East and Southeast Asia. These attempts were totally fruitless after World War II when their aims were both utopian and very general (such as Asian Union). They began to be taken more seriously (though they remained equally unsuccessful) when later they aimed at more specific and limited goals in membership and subject matter.

21. Opinion polls on sovereignty are difficult to evaluate. There are wide discrepancies between opinions expressed on sovereignty in general and on specific items which, in their totality, amount to sovereignty. The likelihood is that the individuals questioned are not very familiar with the meaning of the sovereignty concept. While they insist on sovereignty, they also agree to the internationalization of specific aspects of sovereignty, such as a defense force or the value of the national currency. The reverse is also happening. Individuals will agree to a reduction of sovereignty and at the same time insist on retaining national control over specific items. Very likely people will give normatively motivated answers, saying what they think they ought to say rather than what they want to say. A few examples must suffice. In a poll taken in France in 1968, 53 percent favored replacement of French by European money, 43 percent favored replacement of the French by a European army; but only 25 percent favored the replacement of French by European athletic teams, and only 18 percent agreed to have the French flag replaced by a European flag (Lindberg and Scheingold, 1970, p. 255). A majority of American and Japanese high school students agreed that international cooperation was more important than the maintenance of national sovereignty, but only 25 percent were ready to transfer their loyalty to a supranational agency (Lentz, 1965, 1966). While in 1969 66 percent of interviewed Frenchmen said they wanted European unity, only 35 percent were willing to accept a diminution in the buying power of the franc if that were the price of unity (Nye, 1971, p. 45). Similarly contradictory results were found by Nye (1971, p. 45) in Africa; and by Inglehart (1967, p. 92) and Lancelot and Weill (1969) for European states. In some of the new states of Asia (and probably Africa) the attachment of the leaders to national sovereignty appears to be much stronger than that of the masses. In India, shortly after the fighting with China, a poll in 1963 among those aware of the incident showed that inviolate national sovereignty was at the bottom in a hierarchy of "national hopes" (Indian Institute of Public Opinion, October 1963). For similar indicators in other Asian states, see Levi (1968, pp. 27–48).

A British, German, and French panel in 1959 described themselves mainly as internationalist and supranationalist. Over 85 percent favored various limitations of sovereignty for various purposes, with between 20 and 50 percent favoring collective foreign policy making by a supranational authority (Lerner and Gorden, 1969, pp. 141–43, 198–99). Many data relevant to the problem at hand and related problems can be found in Lerner and Gorden (1969); Deutsch et al. (1966); Merritt and Puchala (1968); and the *Journal of Common Market Studies.*

22. Several quantitative studies show that, relatively speaking and in general, smaller states are more active and supportive of international organizations than the largest and strongest states (Clark et al., 1971; Alker, 1965; Keohane, 1969b). Väyrynen (1970, p. 294) provides figures for the "phenomenal increase" in organizational cooperation among the smaller states and also for the slight decrease in big-power domination of international organizations.

23. For some survey studies of the relationship between the age and health of a person and the making of political choices, see Gergen and Back (1965); L'Etang (1970).

24. A study of General Assembly resolutions indicated that a truly collective effort by assembled statesmen to investigate together a variety of courses of action in all their detail for the solution of an international conflict has a fair chance of success; see Lande (1971, pp. 118–29).

25. A large number of violent conflicts with international implications began as so-called internal conflicts and became international through the intervention of other states. Just how many such conflicts have occurred since the end of World War II depends upon the criteria used to define these conflicts. The point is that by any criteria there were enough such conflicts to make them a very important phenomenon in the contemporary world. For statistics and characterizations of violent conflicts since World War II, see Bloomfield (1968); Buchan (1969);

Kende (1971); Legg and Morrison (1971, p. 288); Luard (1968, pp. 62–64, 183–85); Sanger (1970); Wood (1968).

26. Many attempts have been made to measure power: Ash (1951); Dahl (1957); Deutsch (1968); Fucks (1965); German (1960); Riker (1964); Rosen (1972); Singer (1963). Studies on perception are very relevant here.

27. Jensen (1965, p. 163) found that a state's high confidence in its deterrent power leads it to negotiate less seriously than when it considers that power to be on a par with its opposite number.

28. It is impossible to calculate the proportion of its resources that a state spends on building up its power potential, since the power potential contains unmeasurable items. A calculation of military expenditures is somewhat easier, and the result shows that many of even the smallest states are devoting sizable portions of their resources to the development of a military machine. Figures on military expenditures can be found in U.S. Arms Control and Disarmament Agency; Thomson (1968); Russett et al. (1964); Hoffmann (1970); Banks (1971). The cost of war, no matter how measured, is ever increasing (Wright, 1965, Appendixes 20, 21), yet it has not kept states from fighting each other.

29. For an attempt to measure the value that less-developed states may have for the United States, see Wolf (1968).

30. In India polls show consistent and overwhelming preoccupation with national, mostly economic, problems as compared to international problems (Indian Institute of Public Opinion, 1963, November 1967, April 1968; Free, 1959, pp. 9, 10, 18). To a lesser extent this hierarchy was found in 1958 in Japan, Great Britain, and Italy (Free, 1959, pp. 34, 76, 114) and in 1968 in Malaysia and the Philippines (Indian Institute of Public Opinion, November/December 1968). In the United States there are great variations in the importance the public assigns to foreign policy as compared to other issues. Between 1935 and 1949 polls show from 7 to 81 percent believing that foreign policy problems would be the most important ones facing the United States (Almond, 1950, p. 73). Between 1936 and 1939 "neutrality" and "keeping out of war" became issues of increasing importance to the public (*Public Opinion Quarterly*, 1939a). See also note 5. In Great Britain in 1950, 20 percent of interviewees rated foreign policy among the most important national problems. In Italy in 1947, Australia in 1949, and Finland in 1950, less than 1 percent ranked foreign policy among important national problems (*International Journal of Opinion and Attitude Research*, 1947, 1949/50, 1950).

31. Innumerable tests of children show that at an early age they have views and opinions on national matters when they do not yet have any on international matters. Most of these views about their state, government, and culture are favorable (Dennis et al., 1971; Piaget and Weil, 1951; Jahoda, 1962, 1964; Weinstein, 1957; Lambert and Klineberg, 1967; Davies, 1968, and the survey of the literature there).

32. McClosky (1969, pp. 70–125) in his studies of the relation between personality and attitude to foreign policy opinion has concluded that there are definite correlations between personality characteristics and foreign policy attitudes. Although his study focuses on isolationism versus internationalism, it has relevance for nationalism as well. The same conclusion was reached by Eckhardt and Lentz (1967, pp. 23–26, 40–47) after a thorough survey of the literature, and by Levinson (1957) and Shimberg (1949). The findings of Inglehart (1970b) suggest, however, that the correlation between authoritarianism and ethnocentrism may possibly be a product of culture rather than personality.

33. Doob (1962; 1964, pp. 24–36) made an attempt to define the ingredients of nationalism quantitatively.

34. The results of studies trying to discover whether the degree of support for international organizations is related to age remain inconclusive. Some studies found that younger people are stronger supporters than older people: Abrams (1965, p. 246); Gallup International (1963, p. 120); Hero (1966, pp. 456–60, 459–62); Inglehart (1967, p. 93); Roper (1953–54). Other studies found no difference: Eckhardt and Lentz (1967, p. 33). Yet another study found older people more favorable to European organizations: Lancelot and Weill (1969, p. 147). All these and other studies agree that the level of education is a more important differentiator

246

than age. There should be no confusion between support of an organization and knowledge of its purposes and activities. These two factors do not necessarily go together, as several studies show: Cory (1957, p. 222); Gallup International (1963, pp. 102, 106); Lindberg and Scheingold (1970, pp. 76–77); Merritt and Puchala (1968, pp. 338–43); Scott and Whitey (1958, p. 252).

35. Virtually all inquiries about national priorities in all countries of the world show that items relating to economic matters, i.e., high standards of living, economic development, etc., are ranked highest (*Polls* for Australia 1967a, p. 17; for France 1967b, p. 27; for Czechoslovakia, 1968, p. 17; Indian Institute of Public Opinion, 1968, p. 5; *International Studies of Values in Politics*, 1971, p. 71). While not all respondents are necessarily nationalists, the number of respondents favoring these priorities is so great that nationalists must be among them. Wallerstein and Hechter (1970) found that in Ghana (and very likely in many other new states) the members of the highest social rank feared nationalism as a threat to their own privileged position, while the lowest-ranking groups feared that the material benefits of nationalism would not come to them.

36. An Indian poll indicated that almost half of those consulted in four major cities expressed a desire to emigrate (Indian Institute of Public Opinion, December 1967). Shortly after World War II many citizens of European states were quite willing to abandon their countries for other states with better living conditions (and many did): Buchanan and Cantril (1953, p. 30). The *International Journal of Opinion and Attitude Research* (1947, p. 142; 1948, p. 275; 1949, p. 290; 1950, p. 448) showed for France 33 percent in 1946, 28 percent in 1947, 29 percent in 1950; for Italy almost 50 percent in 1948; for Hungary 31.8 percent in 1948. A survey in Japan in 1955 showed 25–33 percent willing to emigrate, depending on age (Stoetzel, 1955, p. 122); in 1965 during the height of prosperity, another survey found only 2.6 percent willing to emigrate (Institute of Advanced Projects, p. 10). In February 1971 a Gallup Poll found willingness to emigrate among 41 percent in Great Britain, 27 percent in West Germany, 16 percent in the Netherlands; for the United States the figure was 12 percent, comparing with 6 percent in 1959 and 4 percent shortly after World War II (*Gallup Poll Index*, 1971, pp. 24–28).

37. Similar conclusions were reached on the basis of quantitative studies by Caporaso and Pelowski (1971, p. 433) and Ruggie (1972, p. 892).

38. Consultation of a French elite group showed clearly the compatibility, in their mind, of nationalist attitudes with the support of transnational institutions (Lerner and Gorden, 1969, p. 258; Lindberg and Scheingold, 1970, p. 254).

39. The evidence on differences between views and attitudes of the general public and elites regarding foreign affairs is inconclusive. Some studies show that elite opinions differ from those of the general public, the more so the more specific the issues. Other studies show very small differences, and yet others show a middle position for elites. Discovering the truth is made difficult by varying definitions of elites and by varying samples of the "general" public. For some examples see Eckhardt and Lentz (1967); Hero (1966, p. 474); Indian Institute of Public Opinion (November/December 1968); Inglehart (1970a, p. 779); Miller and Stokes (1963); Paul et al. (1963, 1968); Rogers et al. (1966); Van Wagenen (1961).

40. Miller and Stokes (1963, p. 56) concluded that in foreign policy matters the American public tends to rely upon its congressmen and they in turn rely upon the administration. This conclusion has been confirmed by many observers and is, *mutatis mutandis*, true in other states. This situation helps explain why in foreign policy matters more than in any others the administration can act and the public mainly reacts.

41. Quincy Wright (1965, vol. 1, p. 651) found that the ratio of civil to international wars was about one to three between 1480 and 1941.

42. A study by de Sola Pool et al. (1956) showed that the content of messages traveling businessmen received abroad had no specific results for their views on foreign policy; that these businessmen somewhat loosened preconceived notions and developed a greater interest in foreign policy; but that in forming their new views they used their own national reference groups, especially their government!

43. Studies of the American presidency showed that an American president can always count on strong popular support of his foreign policies, either because they are highly successful or because the people "must unite behind the President" if they lead to crises! (Polsby, 1971, p. 45; Mueller, 1970, p. 34).

44. Modelski (1970) found that a very large percentage of the world's foreign ministers share similar backgrounds, interact to the point, sometimes, of forming personal friendships, share some relevant value patterns, and possess some cohesion.

45. Modelski (1970) also found that foreign ministers have enough similarities (such as personal background, sources of information, professional interests) so that they can be classified as an elite. Keohane (1969a, p. 892) found that among the permanent representatives to the United Nations there exists a distinctive, experienced group whose socialization to the United Nations may turn them into an international elite sharing similarities in behavior patterns. Similar findings were made by Lindberg and Scheingold (1970, p. 160) for the ministers of agriculture of the European Common Market members and by Feld (1971, p. 239) for civil servants of European agencies.

46. A considerable portion of many nations' publics expects war to break out during their lifetime. For examples see Free (1959, pp. 17, 35, 76, 94, 114, 158); Indian Institute of Public Opinion (April 1968, pp. 12, 20–31); Merritt and Puchala (1968, pp. 189–200); Paul et al. (1963, 1968, vol. 1, p. 39); Stoetzel (1955, p. 129). There are many studies on perception and its effect upon the behavior of states; see, e.g., Jervis (1968); de Sola Pool and Kessler (1965); Zinnes (1968).

47. In a study critical of the idea of neo-imperialism, Miller and Bennett (1971) demonstrate the decreasing economic importance of "low-income" countries for the "high-income" countries. High-income countries are shown to be involved mainly with other high-income countries. The low-income countries, far from being threatened with neo-imperialism, may be threatened by total neglect. Arosalo (1970) shows that the massive interaction among the largest states in contrast to that among the smaller states or between larger and smaller states even among the developed states of Europe. In connection with neo-imperialism, it is interesting that Rosenau (1963, p. 221) found in a study of American national leaders that businessmen (among 14 occupational groups) were the least cordial toward foreign aid, often criticized as a major tool of American imperialism!

48. Dunn (1960) concludes that the United States is dependent upon various materials obtainable mainly or in sufficient quantities from abroad. His data also show, however, that there is a variety of suppliers to which the United States can turn for any one raw material. They show further that the United States has some resources in every one of the raw materials mentioned whose production might be increased to make the country self-sufficient.

49. The Functionalists have argued this position for a long time. Historical evidence is in their favor, foremost the success of the international public unions. Quantitative evidence is difficult to come by. Kriesberg (1968) found that in nongovernmental organizations in which the USSR and the United States participate the tendency is to create small committees for dealing with specific subjects within the overall topic of the organization. This is likely to be an attempt at "depoliticization" in order to obtain results. Jacobson (1967, p. 594) found that delegates to the International Telecommunication Union, the World Health Organization, and the International Labor Organization had a great deal of discretion in taking positions — in contrast to what is known about delegates to the more "political" organs like the General Assembly or the Security Council. Incompatible positions taken in these functional agencies are obviously not expected to lead to the "political" conflicts that comparable situations would provoke in the "political" agencies.

50. Two quantitative studies may serve as examples. Thrall and Blumberg (1963) found that among 11,300 clergymen questioned a very large number, more that half, believed that a Christian approach was no solution to the East-West conflict. Little and Strecker (1956) were told by psychiatrists in a test that they would turn a spy over to the F.B.I. even if in doing so they broke their pledge of professional secrecy.

51. Singer and Wallace (1970, p. 547) conclude that policy makers look to international

organizations as a means of reducing the incidence of war but that correlations between the outbreak and ending of wars and the existence of international organizations is very low. For some statistics of United Nations contributions to the solution of conflicts, see E. Haas (1968); Luard (1968, pp. 106, 158, 251).

52. O. Holsti (1972), in a study of the outbreak of World War I and the Cuban missile incident, concluded that in a crisis situation the decision-making statesmen too become less creative, flexible, and tolerant of ambiguity — not a state of mind conducive to exploring the possibilities offered by international organizations for the peaceful settlement of a raging conflict.

53. The influence of states upon each other or the United Nations is notoriously difficult to measure. Several attempts to do so have reached the tentative conclusion that small states can influence the politics of the United Nations only when their demands are not opposed by the larger states or when the international climate is favorable to them (Kay, 1967, 1969; Keohane, 1967; Riggs, 1958, 1967; Rowe, 1964; Rudzinski, 1951; Russett, 1965, pp. 55–105; Singer, 1963).

54. A quantitative study of the use new states make of the International Court of Justice shows that in general they share the attitudes of the older and larger states in regard either to their commitment to the court or to using it (Shihata, 1965). Once they use it they attempt to generalize legal norms and turn the court into a norm-creating agency. This strengthens them vis-à-vis strong states because they can exploit the legal equality which sovereignty guarantees them (Jarvad, 1968, pp. 310–13).

K. Holsti (1966) examined the use and success of various methods for the solution of international conflicts since 1919. The most prominent findings were that settlement by annexation or conquest has greatly diminished; that bilateral or multilateral negotiations remain the most frequently used and most frequently successful methods; and that methods involving third parties are the least popular. Luard (1968, pp. 332–36) reached similar conclusions. By December 1, 1971, 47 states had filed declarations accepting compulsory jurisdiction under the "optional clause" of Article 36 of the court's statute. Among these, only 16 had obtained their independence since 1945. An examination of the British press by Bush (1955, pp. 427–29) showed that the USA-USSR conflict was virtually never judged according to United Nations standards.

55. The growing role of smaller states as sponsors of increasing numbers of United Nations resolutions and measures might be taken as their appreciation of the United Nations' publicity value. However, the implementation of resolutions and measures agreed to is decreasing, in both the political and the economic fields (Jacobsen, 1969, p. 254). See also Kay (1969, p. 44) and Alger (1968) on this point.

56. When the impartiality of the International Court's judges was examined, the elected judges were found to be little influenced by the "national interests" of their countries. The "ad hoc" judges supplied by parties in a contentious case who have no judge of their own nationality at the court were found considerably more biased (Hensley, 1968, p. 585; Suh, 1969, p. 230).

57. Several quantitative studies have been made to establish relations between the internal attributes of states (predominant values, tensions, stability, etc.) and their aggressive international behavior. Virtually all of them found only very low correlations when behavior on the global level was examined; see Rummel (1963, 1968); M. Haas (1965, 1968); Phillips and Hall (1970); Cobb and Elder (1970, pp. 110–11); Tanter (1966); Weede (1970); Zinnes (1972, pp. 245–47). A survey of the literature is in Rummel (1969). Focusing more on international relations within certain groupings, a significant correlation between domestic stability and hostility in foreign policy was found by Wilkenfeld (1968, 1969). In studying the possible relationship between system characteristics and violence, East (1972, p. 315) found a correlation between status discrepancy and violence; see also East and Gregg (1967).

58. A listing and comparison of such wars can be found in Buchan (1969).

59. At the beginning of World War II sections of the American and British publics asserted that they were not hostile to the German people; see *Public Opinion Quarterly* (1940a, p. 99); Sargent (1943).

60. Opinion polls in the United States shortly before and early during World War II showed strong public aversion to war, indicating that a people can be engaged in war without favoring it; see *Public Opinion Quarterly* (1938, p. 388; 1939b, pp. 598, 599, 600; 1940b, pp. 102, 107, 108, 109, 111, 112; 1941, p. 477); Cantril et al. (1940a, 1940b); Dudycha (1942); Sargent (1943). In the United States half of those consulted felt that it had been a mistake to enter World War I, the Korean War, and the Vietnam War. About a third felt the same about World War II (Erskine, 1970). In Great Britain 62 percent of the men consulted in 1937 stated that they would not volunteer for the armed forces in case of war; see *Public Opinion Quarterly* (1938, p. 395). In 1939, 78 percent of British interviewees advocated that Germany should be fought rather than be allowed to regain her colonies. But, as the previous figure indicates, few wanted to do the fighting. In France, in 1947, more than half of those questioned opposed continuing fighting in Vietnam, yet the war continued; see *International Journal of Opinion and Attitude Research*, 1(1947)124.

61. Some quantitative studies provide, at best, some indirect evidence that favorable attitudes among a people toward another people are slightly correlated to favorable attitudes toward the creation of international organizations with that people. Scott (1965, p. 77) concluded from his tests that "they tend to support, at a cultural level, the psychological view that there is some degree of consistent relationship among cognitive, affective and action components" of images one people has about another. Abrams (1965) found that those sympathetic to the United States also tended to be favorable toward an inclusion of the United States in the European Economic Community. Kriesberg (1959) found that specific predispositions, such as liking or not liking the French, the British, etc., had little relation to support or not of the European Coal and Steel Community. A general predisposition toward international organizations seemed to be more significant. Deutsch and Edinger (1959, pp. 21–22, 215) and Cobb and Elder (1970, p. 95) found in general no significant correlation between affective orientations and cooperative policies. Between 1955 and 1960 about one-third of pollees in France and Germany had negative opinions about Communist China. France recognized, Germany did not recognize, the Peking regime. Great Britain had had diplomatic relations with Communist China since 1950, yet over half the British pollees had poor opinions of it.

62. Feierabend and Feierabend (1966) made a detailed study of the disturbing impact of change on the stability of political systems and the chances for aggressive behavior resulting from it.

63. A survey of Soviet and American elite attitudes showed no evidence that they considered basic changes in the international system desirable (Singer, 1964).

64. E. Haas (1969, pp. 24–27) in his tabulation of foreign policy aims since 1945 does not show territorial change once. Luard (1968, p. 64) claims that there have been no wars for the conquest of colonial territory since 1941 and only 2 out of 11 (compared to 11 out of 15 between 1915 and 1940) aiming at the conquest of adjacent territory by one of the war parties (i.e., Peru-Ecuador, India-Pakistan). K. Holsti (1966, pp. 284, 293–96) found that violent conflicts ending in conquest or annexation have greatly diminished since 1945.

65. Multinational corporations and their international political significance have lately been examined in some detail. Most of the data available relates to corporations originating in the United States. But there are many multinational corporations which had their beginnings in other states. Comprehensive data can be found in Vaupel and Curhan (1969); Feld (1970, pp. 213–17); Galloway (1970, pp. 509–15).

66. Smoker (1967) has demonstrated the growing influence of individuals and international nongovernmental agencies on the competition between escalation of hostilities and developments toward integration among states. Mitchell (1970, pp. 49–55) makes the point that cross-cutting memberships in international groupings are the result, not the cause, of integration.

Works Cited in the Notes

Abrams, M. "British Elite Attitudes and the European Common Market." *Public Opinion Quarterly*, 29(1965)236–246.

Notes

Alcock, Norman Z., and Newcombe, Alan G. "The Perception of National Power." *Journal of Conflict Resolution*, 14(1970)335–343.

Alger, Chadwick F. "Interaction in a Committee of the United Nations General Assembly." In Singer, J. David, ed., *Quantitative International Politics: Insights and Evidence*. New York: Free Press, 1968. Pp., 51–84.

———, and Brams, Steven J. "Patterns of Representation in National Capitals and Intergovernmental Organizations." *World Politics*, 19(1967)646–663.

Alker, Hayward R. "Supranationalism in the United Nations." In Peace Research Society (International), *Papers*, vol. 3, 1965, *The Chicago Conference, 1964*, pp. 197–212.

Almond, Gabriel A. *The American People and Foreign Policy*. New York: Harcourt Brace, 1950.

———, and Verba, Sidney. *The Civic Culture*. Boston: Little, Brown, 1965.

Angell, Robert C. "An Analysis of Trends in International Organizations." In Peace Research Society (International), *Papers*, vol. 3, 1965, *The Chicago Conference, 1964*, pp. 185–195.

———, "The Growth of Transnational Participation." *Journal of Social Issues*, 23(1967)108–129.

Arosalo, Uolevi. "A Model of International Interaction in Western Europe." *Journal of Peace Research*, 7(1970)247–258.

Ash, Maurice A. "An Analysis of Power, with Special Reference to International Politics." *World Politics*, 3(1951)218–237.

Banks, Arthur S., ed. *Cross-Polity Time-Series Data*. Cambridge, Mass.: M.I.T. Press, 1971.

Berelson, Bernard R., Lazarsfeld, Paul F., and McPhee, William N. *Voting*. Chicago: University of Chicago Press, 1954.

Bloomfield, Lincoln M. "Future Small Wars: Must the United States Intervene?" *Orbis*, 12(1968)669–684.

Brams, Steven J. "Transaction Flows in the International System." *American Political Science Review*, 60(1966)880–899.

———. "A Note on the Cosmopolitanism of World Regions." *Journal of Peace Research*, 1968/1, 87–95.

———. "The Structure of Influence Relationships in the International System." In Rosenau, James N., ed., *International Politics and Foreign Policy*. New York: Free Press, 1969. Pp. 583–599.

Buchan, Alastair. "Frieden und Krieg in den siebziger Jahren." *Europa Archiv*, 24(1969)305–316.

Buchanan, William, and Cantril, Hadley. *How Nations See Each Other*. Urbana: University of Illinois Press, 1953.

Bush, Henry C. "The United Nations as a Norm in British Opinion." *Public Opinion Quarterly*, 18(1955)427–429.

Cantril, Hadley. "America Faces the War: A Study in Public Opinion." *Public Opinion Quarterly*, 4(1940a)387–407.

———, Rugg, Donald, and Williams, Frederick. "America Faces the War: Shifts in Opinion." *Public Opinion Quarterly*, 4(1940b)651–656.

Caporaso, James A., and Pelowski, Alan L. "Economic and Political Integration in Europe: A Time-Series Quasi-Experimental Analysis." *American Political Science Review*, 65(1971)418–433.

Caspary, William R. "The 'Mood Theory': A Study of Public Opinion and Foreign Policy." *American Political Science Review*, 64(1970)536–547.

Choucri, Nazli. "The Perceptual Base of Non-alignment." *Journal of Conflict Resolution*, 13(1969)57–74.

Clark, John F., O'Leary, Michael K., and Wittkopf, Eugene R. "National Attributes Associated with Dimensions of Support for the United Nations." *International Organization*, 25(1971)1–25.

Cobb, Roger W., and Elder, Charles. *International Community*. New York: Holt, Rinehart and Winston, 1970.

251

INTERNATIONAL POLITICS

Cole, Allan B., and Nakanishi, Naomichi. *Japanese Opinion Polls with Socio-Political Significance, 1947–1957.* Tufts University and Roper Public Opinion Poll Research Center, n.d.

Cory, Robert H., Jr., "The Role of Public Opinion in United States Policies toward the United Nations." *International Organization*, 11(1957)220–227.

Dahl, Robert A. "The Concept of Power." *Behavioral Science*, 2(1957)201–215.

Damle, Y. B. *Communication of Modern Ideas and Knowledge in Indian Villages.* Center for International Studies, M.I.T. October 1955.

Davies, A. F. "The Child's Discovery of Nationality." *Australian and New Zealand Journal of Sociology*, 4(1968)107–125.

Dennis, Jack, Lindberg, Leon, and McCrone, Donald. "Support for Nation and Government among English Children." *British Journal of Political Science*, 1(1971)25–48.

Deutsch, Karl W. "Shifts in the Balance of International Communication Flows." *Public Opinion Quarterly*, 20(1956)143–160.

———. *The Analysis of International Relations.* Englewood Cliffs: Prentice-Hall, 1968.

———, and Edinger, Lewis J. *Germany Rejoins the Powers.* Stanford: Stanford University Press, 1959.

———, and Edinger, Lewis J., Macridis, Roy C., Merritt, Richard L. *France, Germany and the Western Alliance.* New York: Scribner, 1967.

———, and Edinger, Lewis J., Macridis, Roy C., Merritt, Richard L., and Voss-Eckermann, Helga. "French and German Elite Responses, 1964: Code Book and Data." New Haven: Yale University, Political Science Research Library, January 1966.

Domínguez, Jorge I. "Mice That Do Not Roar: Some Aspects of International Politics in the World's Peripheries." *International Organization*, 25(1971)175–208.

Doob, Leonard. "South Tyrol: An Introduction to the Psychological Syndrome of Nationalism." *Public Opinion Quarterly*, 26(1962)172–184.

———. *Patriotism and Nationalism.* New Haven: Yale University Press, 1964.

Dudycha, George J. "The Attitudes of College Students toward War and the Germans before and during the Second World War." *Journal of Social Psychology*, 15(1942)317–324.

Duijker, H. C. J., and Frijda, N. H. *National Character and National Stereotypes.* Amsterdam: North Holland Publishing Co., 1960.

Dunn, John M. "American Dependence on Materials Imports: The World-Wide Resource Base." *Journal of Conflict Resolution*, 4(1960)106–122.

East, Maurice A. "Rank-Dependent Interaction and Mobility, Two Aspects of International Stratification." In Peace Research Society (International), *Papers*, vol. 14, 1970, *The Ann Arbor Conference, 1969*, pp. 113–127.

———. "Status Discrepancy and Violence in the International System: An Empirical Analysis." In Rosenau, James N., Davis, Vincent, and East, Maurice A., eds., *The Analysis of International Politics.* New York: Free Press, 1972. Pp. 299–319.

———, and Gregg, Philip M. "Factors Influencing Cooperation and Conflict in the International System." *International Studies Quarterly*, 11(1967)244–269.

Eckhardt, William, and Lentz, Theo F. "Factors of War/Peace Attitudes." *Peace Research Reviews*, vol. 1, no. 5 (October 1967).

Erskine, Hazel G. "The Polls: The Informed Public." *Public Opinion Quarterly*, 26(1962)669–677.

———. "The Polls: Is War a Mistake?" *Public Opinion Quarterly*, 34(1970)134–150.

Eysenck, H. J., and Crown, S. "National Stereotypes: An Experimental and Methodological Study." *International Journal of Opinion and Attitude Research*, 2(1948)26–37.

Feierabend, Ivo K., and Feierabend, Rosalind L. "Aggressive Behaviors within Politics, 1948–1962: A Cross-National Study." *Journal of Conflict Resolution*, 10(1966)249–271.

Feld, Werner. "Political Aspects of Transnational Business Collaboration in the Common Market." *International Organization*, 24(1970)209–238.

———. "The National Bureaucracies of the EEC Member States and Political Integration: Preliminary Enquiry." In Jordan, Robert S., ed., *International Administration: Its*

252

Notes

Evolution and Contemporary Application. New York: Oxford University Press, 1971. Pp. 228–244.

Franko, Lawrence G. *Joint Venture Survival in Multinational Corporations.* New York: Praeger, 1971.

Free, Lloyd A. *Six Allies and a Neutral.* Glencoe: Free Press, 1959.

Fucks, Wilhelm. *Formeln zur Macht.* Stuttgart: Deutsche Verlags-Anstalt, 1965.

Galloway, Jonathan F. "Worldwide Corporations and International Integration: The Case of INTELSAT." *International Organization*, 24(1970)503–519.

The Gallup Opinion Index.

Gallup International. "Public Opinion and the European Community." *Journal of Common Market Studies*, 2(1963)101–126.

German, Clifford F. "A Tentative Evaluation of World Power." *Journal of Conflict Resolution*, 4(1960)138–144.

Gergen, Kenneth J., and Back, Kurt W. "Aging, Time Perspective, and Preferred Solutions to International Conflicts." *Journal of Conflict Resolution*, 9(1965)177–186.

Gilbert, G. M. "Stereotype Persistence and Change among College Students." *Journal of Abnormal Social Psychology*, 46(1951)245–254.

Haas, Ernst B. "Collective Security and the Future International System." In Falk, Richard A., and Hanrieder, Wolfram F., eds., *International Law and Organization.* Philadelphia: Lippincott, 1968. Pp. 299–344.

——. *Tangle of Hopes.* Englewood Cliffs: Prentice-Hall, 1969.

Haas, Michael. "Societal Approaches to the Study of War." *Journal of Peace Research*, 2(1965)307–323.

——. "Social Change and National Aggressiveness, 1900–1960." In Singer, J. David, ed., *Quantitative International Politics: Insights and Evidence.* New York: Free Press, 1968. Pp. 215–244.

Hensley, Thomas R. "National Bias and the International Court of Justice." *Midwest Journal of Political Science*, 12(1968)568–586.

Hero, Alfred O., Jr. *Mass Media and World Affairs.* Boston: World Peace Foundation, 1959a.

——. *Americans in World Affairs.* Boston: World Peace Foundation, 1959b.

——. "The American Public and the U.N., 1954–1966." *Journal of Conflict Resolution*, 10(1966)436–475.

Hoffmann, Walther G. "Der Anteil der Verteidigungsausgaben am Bruttosozialprodukt — Ein Internationaler und Intertemporaler Vergleich." *Kyklos*, 23(1970)80–97.

Holsti, K. J. "Resolving International Conflicts: A Taxonomy of Behavior and Some Figures on Procedures." *Journal of Conflict Resolution*, 10(1966)272–296.

Holsti, Ole R. *Crisis, Escalation, War.* Montreal: McGill-Queen's University Press, 1972.

Hughes, Barry B. "Transaction Data and Analysis: In Search of Concepts." *International Organization*, 26(1972)660–680.

Indian Institute of Public Opinion. *Monthly Public Opinion Surveys*, August/September 1963, nos. 95, 96, VIII, #11–12, p. 7; October 1963, no. 97, IX, #1; November 1967, no. 146, XIII, #2, p. 5; December 1967, no. 147, XIII, #3, p. 27; April 1968, no. 151, XIII, #7; November/December 1968, nos. 158, 159, XIV, #2, 3; March 1972, no. 198, XVII, #6, pp. i–xii.

Inglehart, Ronald. "An End to European Integration?" *American Political Science Review*, 61(1967)91–105.

——. "Public Opinion and Regional Integration." *International Organization*, 24(1970a) 764–795.

——. "The New Europeans: Inward or Outward Looking?" *International Organization*, 24(1970b)129–139.

International Associations.

International Journal of Opinion and Attitude Research, 1(1947)124, 140, 147; 2(1948)275; 3(1949)290; 3(1949/1950)623; 4(1950)447, 448, 449.

International Review of Public Opinion.

INTERNATIONAL POLITICS

International Studies of Values in Politics: Values and the Active Community. New York: Free Press, 1971.
International Union of Official Travel Organizations. *International Travel Statistics*. Geneva, 1968, vol. 22.
Jacob, Philip E. "The Political Ethos and Human Rights: An International Perspective." *Social Research*, 38(1971)199–216.
Jacobsen, Kurt. "Sponsorship in the United Nations." *Journal of Peace Research*, 6(1969)235–256.
Jacobson, Harold K. "Deriving Data from Delegates to International Assemblies." *International Organization*, 21(1967)592–613.
Jahoda, Gustav. "Development of Scottish Children's Ideas and Attitudes about Other Countries." *Journal of Social Psychology*, 58(1962)91–108.
———. "Children's Concepts of Nationality: A Critical Study of Piaget's Stages." *Child Development*, 35(1964)1081–1092.
Jahrbuch der Öffentlichen Meinung. Verlag für Demoskopie, Allensbach.
Jarvad, Ib Martin. "Power versus Equality." IPRA Studies in Peace Research, *Proceedings of the International Peace Research Association, Second Conference*, vol. 1. Assen: Van Gorcum, 1968. Pp. 297–314.
Jensen, Lloyd. "Military Capabilities and Bargaining Behavior." *Journal of Conflict Behavior*, 9(1965)155–163.
Jervis, Robert. "Hypotheses on Misperception." *World Politics*, 20(1968)454–479.
Journal of Common Market Studies.
Kay, David A. "The Politics of Decolonization: The New Nations and the United Nations Political Process." *International Organization*, 21(1967)786–811.
———. "The Impact of African States on the United Nations." *International Organization*, 23(1969)20–47.
Kende, Istvan. "Twenty-Five Years of Local Wars." *Journal of Peace Research*, 8(1971)5–22.
Keohane, Robert O. "The Study of Political Influence in the General Assembly." *International Organization*, 21(1967)221–237.
———. "Institutionalization in the United Nations General Assembly." *International Organization*, 23(1969a)859–896.
———. "Who Cares about the General Assembly?" *International Organization*, 23(1969b)141–149.
Kihl, Young W. "Functional Performance and Member-States Behavior in an International Organization: Test and Evaluation." *Journal of Politics*, 33(1971)337–369.
Kriesberg, Louis. "German Public Opinion and the European Coal and Steel Community." *Public Opinion Quarterly*, 23(1959)28–42.
———. "U.S. and U.S.S.R. Participation in International Non-Governmental Organizations." In Kriesberg, Louis, ed., *Social Processes in International Relations*. New York: Wiley, 1968. Pp. 466–485.
Lall, Arthur. *How Communist China Negotiates*. New York: Columbia University Press, 1968.
Lambert, W. E., and Klineberg, Otto. "A Pilot Study of the Origin and Development of National Stereotypes." *International Social Science Journal*, 11(1959)221–238.
———. *Children's Views of Foreign Peoples*. New York: Appleton, Century, Croft, 1967.
Lancelot, Alain, and Weill, Pierre. "Les Français et l'unification politique de l'Europe d'après un sondage de la SOFRES." *Revue Française de Science Politique*, 19(1969)145–170.
Lande, Gabriella Rosner. "An Inquiry into the Successes and Failures of the United Nations General Assembly." In Gordenker, Leon, ed., *The United Nations in International Politics*. Princeton: Princeton University Press, 1971. Pp. 106–129.
Legg, Keith R., and Morrison, James F. *Politics and the International System: An Introduction*. New York: Harper and Row, 1971.
Lentz, T. F. "Japan and USA: A Comparative Public Opinion Study." *Journal of Peace Research*, 3(1965)288–294.
———. "The New Generation and Peace." *Fellowship*, November 1966, pp. 27–52.

Notes

Lerner, Daniel, and Gorden, Morton. *Euratlantica*. Cambridge, Mass.: M.I.T. Press, 1969.

L'Etang, Hugh. *Pathology of Leadership*. New York: Hawthorn Books, 1970.

Levi, Werner. *The Challenge of World Politics in South and Southeast Asia*. Englewood Cliffs: Prentice-Hall, 1968.

Levinson, D. J. "Authoritarian Personality and Foreign Policy." *Journal of Conflict Resolution*, 1(1957)37–47.

Lijphart, Arend. "Tourist Traffic and Integration Potential." *Journal of Common Market Studies*, 2(1964)251–262.

Lindberg, Leon N., and Scheingold, Stuart A. *Europe's Would-Be Polity*. Englewood Cliffs: Prentice-Hall, 1970.

Little, Ralph B., and Strecker, Edward A. "Moot Questions in Psychiatric Ethics." *American Journal of Psychiatry*, 113(1956)455–460.

Luard, Evan. *Conflict and Peace in the Modern International System*. Boston: Little, Brown, 1968.

McClosky, Herbert. *Political Inquiry*. New York: Macmillan, 1969.

Meenes, Max. "A Comparison of Racial Stereotypes of 1935–1942." *Journal of Social Psychology*, 17(1943)327–336.

Merkl, Peter H. "Politico-Cultural Restraints on West German Foreign Policy." *Comparative Political Studies*, 3(1971)443–467.

Merritt, Richard L., and Puchala, Donald J. *Western European Perspectives on International Affairs*. New York: Praeger, 1968.

Miller, S. M., and Bennett, Roy. "A Neo-Imperialism Critique." New York University Center for International Studies, *Policy Papers*, vol. 4 no. 5 (1971).

Miller, Warren E., and Stokes, Donald E. "Constituency Influence in Congress." *American Political Science Review*, 57(1963)45–56.

Mitchell, John D. "Cross-Cutting Memberships, Integration and the International System." *Journal of Conflict Resolution*, 14(1970)49–55.

Modelski, George. "The World's Foreign Ministers: A Political Elite." *Journal of Conflict Resolution*, 14(1970)135–175.

Montague, Joel B., Jr. *Class and Nationality*. New Haven: College and University Press, 1963.

Mueller, John E. "Presidential Popularity from Truman to Johnson." *American Political Science Review*, 64(1970)18–34.

Mushakoji, Kinhide. "Negotiation between the West and the Non-West." IPRA Studies in Peace Research, *Proceedings of the International Peace Research Association, Second Conference*, vol. 1. Assen: Van Gorcum, 1968. Pp. 208–231.

Nye, Joseph S. *Peace in Parts*. Boston: Little, Brown, 1971.

Paul, John, and Laulicht, Jerome; Laulicht, Jerome, and Strong, George W. *In Your Opinion*. Clarkson, Ontario: Canadian Peace Research Institute, 1963, 1968.

Phillips, Warren R., and Hall, Dennis R. "The Importance of Governmental Structure as a Taxonomic Scheme for Nations." *Comparative Political Studies*, 3(1970)63–89.

Piaget, Jean, and Weil, Anne-Marie. "The Development in Children of the Idea of the Homeland and of Relations with Other Countries." *International Social Science Bulletin*, 3(1951)561–578.

Polls, 3(1967a)17; 3(1967b)27; 3(1968)17.

Polsby, Nelson. *Congress and the Presidency*. Englewood Cliffs: Prentice-Hall, 1971.

Public Opinion Quarterly, 2(1938)388, 395; 3(1939a)596; 3(1939b)598, 599, 600; 4(1940a)99; 4(1940b)102, 107, 108, 109, 111, 112; 5(1941)477.

Puchala, Donald J. "International Transactions and Regional Integration." *International Organization*, 24(1970)732–763.

Revue Française de l'Opinion Publique.

Riggs, Robert E. *Politics in the United Nations: A Study of United States Influence in the General Assembly*. Illinois Studies in the Social Sciences, vol. 41. Urbana: University of Illinois Press, 1958.

————. "The United Nations as an Influence on United States Policy." *International Organization*, 11(1967)91–109.

Riker, William H. "Some Ambiguities in the Notion of Power." *American Political Science Review*, 58(1964)341–349.

Robinson, John P. "Public Information about World Affairs." Mimeographed. Survey Research Center, University of Michigan, March 1967.

Rogers, William C., Stuhler, Barbara, and Koenig, Donald. "A Comparative Study of Informed Opinion and General Public Opinion in Minnesota on Selected Issues of U.S. Foreign Policy." Mimeographed. World Affairs Center, General Extension Division, University of Minnesota, 1966.

Roper, Elmo. "American Attitudes on World Organization." *Public Opinion Quarterly*, 17(1953–54)405–442.

Rosen, Steven. "War Power and the Willingness to Suffer." In Russett, Bruce M., ed., *Peace, War, and Numbers*. Beverly Hills: Sage Publications, 1972. Pp. 167–183.

Rosenau, James N. *National Leadership and Foreign Policy*. Princeton: Princeton University Press, 1963.

Rowe, Edward T. "The Emerging Anti-Colonial Consensus in the United Nations." *Journal of Conflict Resolution*, 8(1964)209–230.

Rudzinski, Alexander W. "The Influence of the United Nations on Soviet Policy." *International Organization*, 5(1951)282–299.

Ruggie, John G. "Collective Goods and Future International Collaboration." *American Political Science Review*, 66(1972)874–893.

Rummel, Rudolph J. "Dimensions of Conflict Behavior within and between Nations." *General Systems Yearbook*, 8(1963)1–50.

————. "The Relationship between National Attributes and Foreign Conflict Behavior." In Singer, J. David, ed., *Quantitative International Politics: Insights and Evidence*. New York: Free Press, 1968. Pp. 187–214.

————. "Dimensions of Foreign and Domestic Conflict Behavior: A Review of Empirical Findings." In Pruitt, Dean G., and Snyder, Richard C., *Theory and Research on the Causes of War*. Englewood Cliffs: Prentice-Hall, 1969. Pp. 219–228.

————. "A Status-Field Theory of International Relations." Dimensionality of Nations Project, Research Report no. 50. Mimeographed. University of Hawaii, August 1971.

————. "U.S. Foreign Relations: Conflict, Cooperation, and Attribute Distance." In Russett, Bruce M., ed., *Peace, War, and Numbers*. Beverly Hills: Sage Publications, 1972. Pp. 71–113.

Russett, Bruce M. *Trends in World Politics*. New York: Macmillan, 1965.

————. *International Regions and the International System: A Study in Political Ecology*. Chicago: Rand McNally, 1967.

————. "Delineating International Regions." In Singer, J. David, ed., *Quantitative International Politics: Insights and Evidence*. New York: Free Press, 1968. Pp. 316–352.

————, Alker, Hayward R., Deutsch, Karl W., and Lasswell, Harold D. *World Handbook of Political and Social Indicators*. New Haven: Yale University Press, 1964.

————, and Lamb, Curtis W. "Global Patterns of Diplomatic Exchanges, 1963–1964." *Journal of Peace Research*, 1969/1, pp. 37–55.

Sanger, Richard H. *Insurgent Era*. Washington, D.C.: Potomac Books, 1970.

Sargent, S. D. "Attitudes toward the War and Peace in a Midwestern Agricultural County." *Journal of Social Psychology*, 17(1943)337–345.

Sawyer, Jack. "Dimensions of Nations: Size, Wealth and Politics." *American Journal of Sociology*, 73(1967)145–172.

Schachter, Oscar, Nawaz, Mahomed, and Fried, John. *Toward Wider Acceptance of UN Treaties*. New York: Arno Press, 1971.

Schwartzman, Simon, and Mora y Aranjo, Manuel. "The Images of International Stratification in Latin America." *Journal of Peace Research*, 3(1966)225–243.

Notes

Schwebel, Stephen M., ed. *The Effectiveness of International Decisions*. Dobbs Ferry, N.Y.: Oceana Publications, 1971.

Scott, William A. "Psychological and Social Correlates of International Images." In Kelman, Herbert C., ed., *International Behavior*. New York: Holt, Rinehart, and Winston, 1965. Pp. 71–103.

————, and Whitey, Stephen B. *The United States and the United Nations: The Public View, 1945–1955*. New York: Manhattan Publishing Co., 1958.

Seago, Dorothy W. "Stereotypes Before Pearl Harbor and After." *Journal of Psychology*, 23 (1947) 55–63.

Shenton, Herbert N. *Cosmopolitan Conversations*. New York: Columbia University Press, 1933.

Shihata, Ibrahim F. I. "The Attitude of New States toward the International Court of Justice." *International Organization*, 19(1965) 203–222.

Shimberg, Benjamin. "Information and Attitudes toward World Affairs." *Journal of Educational Psychology*, 40(1949) 207–222.

Shimbori, Michiya, Ikeda, Hideo, Ishida, Tsuyoshi, and Kondo, Moto. "Measuring a Nation's Prestige." *American Journal of Sociology*, 69(1963)63–68.

Singer, J. David. "Inter-Nation Influence: A Formal Model." *American Political Science Review*, 57(1963)420–430.

————. "Soviet and American Foreign Policy Attitudes: Content Analysis of Elite Articulation." *Journal of Conflict Resolution*, 8(1964)424–485.

————, and Small, Melvin. "The Composition and Status Ordering of the International System: 1815–1940." *World Politics*, 18(1966)236–282.

————, and Wallace, Michael. "Intergovernmental Organization and the Preservation of Peace, 1816–1964: Some Bivariate Relationships." *International Organization*, 24(1970)520–547.

Smoker, Paul. "Nation State Escalation and International Integration." *Journal of Peace Research*, 4(1967)61–75.

Sola Pool, Ithiel de, Keller, Suzanne, and Bauer, Raymond A. "The Influence of Foreign Travel on Political Attitudes of American Businessmen." *Public Opinion Quarterly*, 20(1956)161–175.

————, and Kessler, Allen. "The Kaiser, the Tsar, and the Computer: Information Processing in a Crisis." *American Behavioral Scientist*, 8(1965, no. 9)31–38.

Sondages.

Stoetzel, Jean. *Without the Chrysanthemum and the Sword*. New York: UNESCO, Columbia University Press, 1955.

Suh, Il Ro. "Voting Behavior of National Judges in International Courts." *American Journal of International Law*, 63(1969)224–236.

Sullivan, John D. "Cooperating to Conflict: Sources of Informal Alignments." In Russett, Bruce M., ed., *Peace, War, and Numbers*. Beverly Hills: Sage Publications, 1972. Pp. 115–138.

Sullivan, Michael P. "Symbolic Involvement as a Correlate of Escalation: The Vietnam Case." In Russett, Bruce M., ed., *Peace, War, and Numbers*. Beverly Hills: Sage Publications, 1972. Pp. 185–212.

Tanter, Raymond. "Dimensions of Conflict Behavior within and between Nations." *Journal of Conflict Resolution*, 10(1966)41–64.

Thomson, Murray. "Militarism 1969." *Peace Research Reviews*, 2(October 1968, no. 5)8–15.

Thrall, A., and Blumberg, H. "Attitudes of the American Protestant Clergy toward Issues of War and Peace." *Fellowship*, 29(September 1, 1963)3–9.

U.S., Arms Control and Disarmament Agency. *World Military Expenditures*. Publication no. 53. Washington, D.C., 1969.

Van Wagenen, Richard. "American Defense Officials' Views on the United Nations." *Western Political Quarterly*, 14(1961)104–119.

Vaupel, James W., and Curhan, Joan P. *The Making of Multinational Enterprise*. Boston:

Division of Research, Graduate School of Business Administration, Harvard University, 1969.

Väyrynen, Raimo. "Stratification in the System of International Organizations." *Journal of Peace Research*, 7(1970)291–309.

Vincent, Jack E. "A Multivariate Analysis of Voting Patterns in the General Assembly." Paper presented to the Western Political Science Association, Albuquerque, April 1971a.

———. "Testing Some Hypotheses about Delegate Attitudes at the United Nations and Some Implications for Theory Building." Dimensionality of Nations Project, Research Report no. 52. Mimeographed. University of Hawaii, April 1971b.

Wallace, Michael D. "Power, Status, and International War." *Journal of Peace Research*, 8(1971)23–35.

———, and Singer, J. David. "Intergovernmental Organization in the Global System, 1815–1964: A Quantitative Description." *International Organization*, 24(1970)239–287.

Wallerstein, Immanuel, and Hechter, Michael. "Social Rank and Nationalism: Some African Data." *Public Opinion Quarterly*, 34(1970)360–370.

Weede, Erich. *Charakteristika von Nationen als Erklärungsgrundlage für das Internationale Konfliktverhalten.* Dissertation, Universität Mannheim, 1970.

Weinstein, Eugene A. "Development of the Concept of Flag and the Sense of National Identity." *Child Development*, 28(1957)167–174.

Wilkenfeld, Jonathan. "Domestic and Foreign Conflict Behavior within and between Nations." *Journal of Peace Research*, 5(1968)56–59.

———. "Some Further Findings Regarding the Domestic and Foreign Conflict Behavior of Nations." *Journal of Peace Research*, 6(1969)147–156.

Willick, D. H. "Public Interest in International Affairs: A Cross-National Study." *Social Science Quarterly*, 50(1969)272–285.

Wolf, Charles, Jr. "Some Aspects of the 'Value' of Less-Developed Countries to the United States." In Russett, Bruce M., ed., *Economic Theories of International Politics.* Chicago: Markham, 1968. Pp. 279–289.

Wood, David. *Conflict in the Twentieth Century.* Adelphi Papers no. 48. Institute for Strategic Studies, London, June 1968.

Wright, Quincy. *A Study of War.* 2 vols. Chicago: University of Chicago Press, 1965.

Yearbook of International Organizations.

Young, Kenneth T. *Negotiating with the Chinese Communists.* New York: McGraw-Hill, 1968.

Zinnes, Dina A. "The Expression and Perception of Hostility in Prewar Crisis: 1914." In Singer, J. David, ed., *Quantitative International Politics: Insights and Evidence.* New York: Free Press, 1968. Pp. 85–119.

———. "Some Evidence Relevant to the Man-Milieu Hypothesis." In Rosenau, James N., Davis, Vincent, and East, Maurice A., eds., *The Analysis of International Politics.* New York: Free Press, 1972. Pp. 209–251.

BIBLIOGRAPHY

Bibliography

AFTER A LIFETIME of reading the voluminous literature now available on the topic of international politics, the contributions of many authors have become homogenized in my mind. My gratitude extends to them all, for they all have had a share in the inception and formulation of the ideas expressed in this book. Their contributions have not been such as to require a footnote according to traditional standards. Indeed they have been so broad that a footnote could not do them justice. I have therefore chosen to cite only materials of a special nature which have been specifically helpful in the composition of those parts of each chapter for which they are mentioned. The literature relating to studies based on quantitative methods is cited in the Notes.

Chapter 1

On political systems:

Almond, Gabriel A., and Coleman, James S. *The Politics of Developing Areas*. Princeton: Princeton University Press, 1960.

Burton, John W. *World Society*. Cambridge: Cambridge University Press, 1972.

Easton, David. *The Political System*. New York: Knopf, 1953.

———. *A Systems Analysis of Political Life*. New York: Wiley, 1965.

Holt, Robert T., and Turner, John E. *The Political Basis of Economic Development*. Princeton: Van Nostrand, 1966.

Hopkins, Raymond F. "Securing Authority: The View from the Top." *World Politics*, 24(1972)271–292.

Kielmansegg, Peter Graf von. "Legitimität als analytische Kategorie." *Politische Vierteljahresschrift*, 12(1971)367–401.

Legg, Keith R., and Morrison, James F. *Politics and the International System: An Introduction*. New York: Harper and Row, 1971.

Schachter, Oscar. "Towards a Theory of International Obligation." In Schwebel, Stephen M., ed., *The Effectiveness of International Decisions*. Dobbs Ferry, N.Y.: Oceana Publications, 1971. Pp. 9–31.

Singer, J. David. *A General Systems Taxonomy for Political Science*. 22 pp. New York: General Learning Press, 1971.

Young, Oran R. *Systems of Political Science*. Englewood Cliffs: Prentice-Hall, 1968.

On the international system:

Faupel, Klaus. "Internationale Politik and Aussenpolitik." *Politische Vierteljahresschrift*, 10(1969, Sonderheft)11–79.

Gordenker, Leon. "The United Nations and Economic and Social Change." In Gordenker, Leon, ed., *The United Nations in International Politics*. Princeton: Princeton University Press, 1971. Pp. 151–183.
Hanrieder, Wolfram F. "The International System: Bipolar or Multibloc?" *Journal of Conflict Resolution*, 9(1965)299–308.
Horowitz, Irving L. "Consensus, Conflict, Cooperation." *Social Forces*, 41(1962)177–188.
Kaplan, Morton A. *System and Process in International Politics*. New York: Wiley, 1957.
Lindberg, Leon N. "The European Community as a Political System: Notes Toward the Construction of a Model." *Journal of Common Market Studies*, 5(1967)344–387.
Lindblom, Charles E. *The Intelligence of Democracy*. New York: Free Press, 1965.
Luard, Evan. *Nationality and Wealth*. London: Oxford University Press, 1964.
McClelland, Charles A. "Systems Theory and Human Conflict." In McNeil, Elton B., ed., *The Nature of Human Conflict*. Englewood Cliffs: Prentice-Hall, 1965. Pp. 250–273.
————. *Theory and the International System*. New York: Macmillan, 1966.
Miller, J. D. B. *The Nature of Politics*. Harmondsworth: Penguin Books, 1965.
Modelski, George. "Agraria and Industria." *World Politics*, 14(1961)118–143.
Rosenau, James N. "The Functioning of International Systems." *Background*, 7(1963)111–118.
Sievers, Burkard. "System-Organisation-Gesellschaft-Niklas Lechmanns Theorie sozialer Systeme." *Jahrbuch für Sozialwissenschaft*, 22(1971)24–57.
Spiro, Herbert J. *World Politics: The Global System*. Homewood, Ill.: Dorsey Press, 1966.
Weltman, John J. "Systems Theory in International Relations: A Critique." *Polity*, 4(1972)301–329.

On the foundation of society:

Dahrendorf, Rolf. *Class and Class Conflict in Industrial Society*. Stanford: Stanford University Press, 1959.
Lockwood, David. "Some Remarks on the Social System." *British Journal of Sociology*, 7(1956)134–143.

Chapter 2

On the nature of the international society:

Alger, Chadwick F. "Comparison of Intranational and International Politics." *American Political Science Review*, 47(1963)406–419.
Bosc, Robert. *Sociologie de la paix*. Paris: Editions Spes, 1965.
Brucan, Silviu. *The Dissolution of Power*. New York: Knopf, 1971.
Carlston, Kenneth S. *Law and Organization in World Society*. Urbana: University of Illinois Press, 1962.
König, René. "Soziologische Probleme der Internationalen Ordnung." In Nerlich, Uwe, *Krieg und Frieden im industriellen Zeitalter*. Gütersloh: C. Bertelsmann Verlag, 1966.
Landheer, Bart. *On the Sociology of International Law and International Society*. The Hague: Martinus Nijhoff, 1966.
Modelski, George. *Principles of World Politics*. New York: Free Press, 1972.
Nettle, J. P., and Robertson, Roland. *International Systems and the Modernization of Societies*. New York: Basic Books, 1968.
Rummel, Rudolph J. "Indicators of Cross-National and International Patterns." *American Political Science Review*, 63(1969)127–147.
Singer, J. David. "Man and World Politics: The Psycho-Cultural Interface." *Journal of Social Issues*, 24(1968)127–156.
Truyol y Serra, Antonio. "Genèse et structure de la société internationale." Académie de Droit International, *Recueil des Cours*, 96(1959, no. 1)557–642.

Bibliography

On regionalism:

Cantori, Louis, and Spiegel, Steven L. "The International Relations of Regions." *Polity*, 2(1969)397–425.

Connor, Walter F. "Myths of Hemispheric, Continental, Regional, and State Unity." *Political Science Quarterly*, 84(1969)555–567, 570–582.

Domínguez, Jorge I. "Mice That Do Not Roar: Some Aspects of International Politics in the World's Peripheries." *International Organization*, 25(1971)175–208.

Meyriat, Jean, ed. "Le rôle des organisations régionales dans les conflits entre leurs membres." *Revue Française de Science Politique*, 21(1971)337–381.

Nye, Joseph S. *Peace in Parts*. Boston: Little, Brown, 1971.

Russett, Bruce M. *International Regions and the International System: A Study in Political Ecology*. Chicago: Rand McNally, 1967.

Singer, J. D. "The Global System and Its Sub-Systems." In Rosenau, James N., ed., *Linkage Politics*. New York: Free Press, 1969. Pp. 21–43.

Tharp, Paul A., Jr., ed. *Regional International Organizations: Structures and Functions*. New York: St. Martin's Press, 1971.

On stratification and small states:

Aron, Raymond. *Peace and War: A Theory of International Relations*. Garden City: Doubleday, 1966.

Barrett, Carol, and Newcombe, Hanna. "Weighted Voting in International Organizations." *Peace Research Reviews*, vol. 2, no. 2 (April 1968).

Caplow, Theodore, and Finsterbusch, Kurt. "France and Other Countries: A Study in International Interaction." *Journal of Conflict Resolution*, 12(1968)1–15.

Corning, Peter. "The Biological Bases of Behavior and Some Implications for Political Science." *World Politics*, 23(1971)321–370.

East, Maurice A. "Rank Dependent Interaction and Mobility: Two Aspects of International Stratification." In Peace Research Society (International), *Papers*, vol. 14, 1970, *The Ann Arbor Conference, 1969*, pp. 113–127.

Fleiner, Thomas. *Die Kleinstaaten in den Staatenverbindungen des zwanzigsten Jahrhunderts*. Zurich: Polygraphischer Verlag, 1966.

Galtung, Johan. "A Structural Theory of Aggression." *Journal of Peace Research*, 1(1964)95–114.

————. "International Relations and International Conflicts: A Sociological Approach." International Sociological Association, *Transactions of the Sixth World Congress of Sociology*, 1966, vol. 1, pp. 121–161.

Goellner, Aladar. *Les puissances moyennes et le droit international*. Neuchâtel: Editions de la Baconnière, 1960.

Jarvad, Ib Martin. "Power and Equality." IPRA Studies in Peace Research, *Proceedings of the International Peace Research Association, Second Conference*, vol. 1. Assen: Van Gorcum, 1968. Pp. 297–314.

Keohane, Robert O. "The Big Influence of Small Allies." *Foreign Policy*, Spring 1971, no. 2, pp. 161–182.

Lagos, Gustavo. *International Stratification and Underdeveloped Countries*. Chapel Hill: University of North Carolina Press, 1963.

Ljubisavljevic, Bora. *Les problèmes de la pondération dans les institutions Européennes*. Leyden: A. W. Sijthoff, 1959.

Modelski, George. *Principles of World Politics*. New York: Free Press, 1972.

Olson, Mancur, Jr., and Zeckhauser, Richard. "An Economic Theory of Alliances." In Russett, Bruce M., ed., *Economic Theories of International Politics*. Chicago: Markham, 1968. Pp. 25–45.

Organski, A. F. K. *World Politics*. 2nd ed. New York: Random House, Knopf, 1968.

263

INTERNATIONAL POLITICS

Reinton, Per Olav. "Inequality in International Systems of Nations." In Peace Research Society (International), *Papers*, vol. 11, 1969, *The Budapest Conference, 1968*, pp. 47–55.

Riches, Cromwell A. *Majority Rule in International Organizations*. Baltimore: Johns Hopkins Press, 1940.

Rothstein, Robert L. *Alliances and Small Powers*. New York: Columbia University Press, 1968.

Rummel, Rudolph J. "A Status-Field Theory of International Relations." Dimensionality of Nations Project, Research Report no. 50. Mimeographed. University of Hawaii, 1971.

Salmore, Stephen A., and Hermann, Charles F. "The Effect of Size, Development and Accountability on Foreign Policy." Peace Research Society (International) *Papers*, vol. 14, 1970, *The Ann Arbor Conference, 1969*, pp. 15–30.

Schlupp, Friedrich, Salna, Nour, and Junne, Gerd. "Zur Theorie und Ideologie Internationaler Interdependenz." Paper presented to the Deutsche Vereinigung für Politische Wissenschaft, October 3–6, 1971, Mannheim.

Schou, August, and Brundtland, Arne O., eds. *Small States in International Relations*. Stockholm: Almqvist and Wiksell, 1971.

Schwarzenberger, Georg. *Power Politics*. New York: Praeger, 1951.

Shimbori, Michiya, et al. "Measuring a Nation's Prestige." *American Journal of Sociology*, 69(1963)63–68.

Singer, J. David, and Small, Melvin. "The Composition and Status Ordering of the International System: 1815–1940." *World Politics*, 18(1966)236–282.

Singer, Marshall R. *Weak States in a World of Powers*. New York: Free Press, 1972.

Tinbergen, Nikolaas. *Social Behavior in Animals*. New York: Wiley, 1963.

Wallace, Michael D. "Power, Status, and International War." *Journal of Peace Research*, 8(1971)23–35.

On cultural differences:

Bernard, Philippe J. "Valeurs socio-culturelles et modèles de la société globale." *Revue Française de Science Politique*, 22(1972)108–127.

Bozeman, Adda B. *Politics and Culture in International History*. Princeton: Princeton University Press, 1960.

Gantzel, Klaus. *System und Akteur*. Düsseldorf: Bertelsmann Universitätsverlag, 1972.

Glenn, Edmund S., Johnson, Robert H., Kimmel, Paul, and Wedge, Bryant. "A Cognitive Interaction Model to Analyze Culture Conflict in International Relations." *Journal of Conflict Resolution*, 14(1970)35–48.

Hveen, Helge. "'Blame' as International Behavior." *Journal of Peace Research*, 7(1970)49–67.

Levi, Werner. *Fundamentals of World Organization*. Minneapolis: University of Minnesota Press, 1950.

Luard, Evan. *Conflict and Peace in the Modern International System*. Boston: Little, Brown, 1968.

Mead, Margaret, and Metraux, Rhoda. "The Anthropology of Human Conflict." In McNeil, Elton B., ed., *The Nature of Human Conflict*. Englewood Cliffs: Prentice-Hall, 1965. Pp. 116–138.

Mushakoji, Kinhide. "Negotiation between the West and the Non-West." IPRA Studies in Peace Research, *Proceedings of the International Peace Research Association, Second Conference*, vol. 1. Assen: Van Gorcum, 1968. Pp. 208–231.

Ort, Alexandr. "Ist die Kultur ein Faktor der Entspannung in Europa?" *Europa Archiv*, 23(1968)478–484.

Vincent, Jack E. "National Attributes as Predictors of Delegate Attitudes at the United Nations." *American Political Science Review*, 62(1968)916–931.

Wright, Quincy, ed. *The World Community*. Chicago: University of Chicago Press, 1948.

Bibliography

On ideology (moral values and beliefs):

Axline, W. Andrew, and Stegenga, James A. *The Global Community*. New York: Dodd, Mead, 1972.

Frankel, Joseph. *The Making of Foreign Policy: An Analysis of Decision-Making*. London: Oxford University Press, 1963.

Good, Robert C. "National Interest and Moral Theory: The Debate among Contemporary Political Realists." In Hilsman, Roger, and Good, Robert C., eds., *Foreign Policy in the Sixties: The Issues and the Instruments*. Baltimore: Johns Hopkins Press, 1965. Pp. 271–292.

Hugo, Grant. *Appearance and Reality in International Relations*. New York: Oxford University Press, 1970.

Krakau, Knud. *Missionsbewusslsein und Völkerrechtsdoktrin in den Vereinigten Staaten von Amerika*. Frankfurt am Main: Alfred Metzner Verlag, 1967.

Levi, Werner. "The Relative Irrelevance of Moral Norms in International Politics." *Social Forces*, 44(1965)226–233.

———. "Ideology, Interests, and Foreign Policy." *International Studies Quarterly*, 14(1970)1–31.

Spiro, Herbert J. *World Politics: The Global System*. Homewood, Ill.: Dorsey Press, 1966.

Zimmermann, William. "Elite Perspectives and the Explanation of Soviet Foreign Policy." *Journal of International Affairs*, 24(1970)84–89.

On the natural environment:

Falk, Richard A. *This Endangered Planet*. New York: Random House, 1971.

Hartley, Livingston. "Challenges to the Environment: Some International Implications." *Orbis*, 14(1970)490–499.

Kaiser, Karl. "Die Umweltkrise und die Zukunft der internationalen Politik." *Europa Archiv*, 25(1970)877–890.

Kennan, George F. "To Prevent a World Wasteland: A Proposal." *Foreign Affairs*, 48(1970)401–413.

Ritchie-Calder, Lord. "Mortgaging the Old Homestead." *Foreign Affairs*, 48(1970)207–220.

Schweinfurth, Ulrich. "Umwelt und die Aufgaben der Aussenpolitik." *Aussenpolitik*, 22(1971)69–80.

Wolman, Abel. "Pollution as an International Issue." *Foreign Affairs*, 47(1968)164–175.

Chapter 3

On sovereignty:

Alker, Hayward R. "Supranationalism in the United Nations." Peace Research Society (International) *Papers*, vol. 3, 1965, *The Chicago Conference, 1964*, pp. 197–212.

Clark, John F., O'Leary, Michael K., and Wittkopf, Eugene R. "National Attributes Associated with Dimensions of Support for the United Nations." *International Organization*, 25(1971)1–25.

Politis, N. "Le problème des limitations de la souveraineté." Académie de Droit International, *Recueil des Cours, 1925, I*, 1926, pp. 5–121.

Simon, Werner von. *Die Souveränität im rechtlichen Verständnis der Gegenwart*. Berlin: Duncker and Humblot, 1965.

Skolnikoff, Eugene B. *The International Imperatives of Technology*. Berkeley: Institute of International Studies, University of California, 1972.

INTERNATIONAL POLITICS

Sullivan, David S., and Sattler, Martin J., eds. *Change and the Future International System.* New York: Columbia University Press, 1971.

On primitive societies and the international society:

Alger, Chadwick F. "Comparison of Intranational and International Politics." *American Political Science Review*, 57(1963)406–419.
Barkun, Michael. *Law without Sanctions.* New Haven: Yale University Press, 1968.
Diamond, Stanley. "The Rule of Law versus the Order of Custom." *Social Research*, 38(1971)42–72.
Masters, Roger D. "World Politics as a Primitive Political System." *World Politics*, 16(1964)595–619.

On states as actors:

Dahrendorf, Rolf. "Möglichkeiten und Grenzen einer Aussenpolitik der Europäischen Gemeinschaft." *Europa Archiv*, 26(1971)117–130.
Kay, David A. *The New Nations in the United Nations, 1960–1967.* New York: Columbia University Press, 1967.
Nye, J. S., Jr., and Keohane, Robert O. "Transnational Relations and World Politics: An Introduction," and "A Conclusion." In Keohane, Robert O., and Nye, J. S., Jr., eds., "Transnational Relations and World Politics." *International Organization*, 25(1971)329–349, 721–748.
Snyder, Richard, Bruck, H. W., and Sapin, Burton. *Foreign Policy Decision Making.* New York: Free Press, 1962.
Young, Oran R. "The United Nations and the International System." *International Organization*, 22(1968)902–922. Also in Gordenker, Leon, ed., *The United Nations in International Politics* (Princeton: Princeton University Press, 1971), pp. 10–59.
———. "The Actors in World Politics." In Rosenau, James N., Davis, Vincent, and East, Maurice A., eds., *The Analysis of International Politics.* New York: Free Press, 1972. Pp. 125–144.

On the "reality" of groups and states as actors:

Carlston, Kenneth S. *Law and Organization in World Society.* Urbana: University of Illinois Press, 1962.
Carr, Edward H. *The Twenty Years' Crisis, 1919–1939.* London: Macmillan, 1949.
Cosgrove, Carol Ann, and Twitchett, Kenneth J. *The New International Actors.* London: Macmillan, St. Martin's Press, 1970.
Frankel, Joseph. *The Making of Foreign Policy.* New York: Oxford University Press, 1967.
Landecker, Werner S. "International Relations as Intergroup Relations." *American Sociological Review*, 5(1940)335–339.
Organski, A. F. K. *World Politics.* 2nd ed. New York: Knopf, 1968.
Rosenau, James N., ed. *Linkage Politics.* New York: Free Press, 1969.
Singer, J. David, ed. *Human Behavior and International Politics.* Chicago: Rand McNally, 1965.
Sprout, Harold and Margaret. *Foundations of International Politics.* Princeton: Van Nostrand, 1962.
Warriner, Charles K. "Groups are Real: A Reaffirmation." *American Sociological Review*, 21(1956)549–554.
Wolfers, Arnold. "The Actors in International Politics." In Fox, W. T. R., ed., *Theoretical Aspects of International Relations.* Notre Dame: University of Notre Dame Press, 1959 Pp. 83–106.

Bibliography

On the treaty-making power of international organizations:

Chiu, Hungdah. *The Capacity of International Organizations to Conclude Treaties and the Special Legal Aspects of Treaties So Concluded*. The Hague: Martinius Nijhoff, 1966.

Detter, Ingrid. *Law Making by International Organizations*. Stockholm: Norstedt and Söners, 1965.

Fernandez, Daniel. *Organizacion Internacional*. Caracas: Universidad Central de Venezuela, 1965.

Jenks, C. Wilfred. *The Proper Law of International Organisations*. London: Stevens, 1962.

Schneider, Johannes W. *Treaty-Making Power of International Organizations*. Geneva: Librairie Droz, 1963.

Seidl-Hohenveldern, Ignaz von. *Das Recht der Internationalen Organisationen*. Munich: Carl Heymanns Verlag, 1967.

Yemin, Edward. *Legislative Powers in the United Nations and Specialized Agencies*. Leyden: A. W. Sijthoff, 1969.

Zemanek, K., ed. *Agreements of International Organizations and the Vienna Convention on the Law of Treaties*. Österreichische Zeitschrift für Öffentliches Recht, Supplement 1. New York: Springer-Verlag, 1971.

On linkages:

Bracher, Karl D. "Kritische Bertrachtungen über den Primat der Aussenpolitik." In Ziekura, Gilbert, ed., *Faktoren der Politischen Entscheidung*. Berlin: Walter de Gruyter, 1963. Pp. 115–148.

Faupel, Klaus. "Internationale Politik und Aussenpolitik." *Politische Vierteljahresschrift*, 10(1969, Sonderheft)11–79.

Grasser, Alfred. "Nationale und Transnationale Zusammenhänge." In Fijalkowski, Jürgen, ed., *Politologie und Soziologie*. Cologne: Westdeutscher Verlag, 1965. Pp. 85–90.

Hanrieder, Wolfram F. "Compatibility and Consensus: A Proposal for the Conceptual Linkage of External and Internal Dimensions of Foreign Policy." *American Political Science Review*, 61(1967)971–982.

———. *Foreign Policies and the International System: A Theoretical Introduction*. New York: General Learning Press, 1971.

Hessische Stiftung Friedens- und Konfliktforschung. *Die Rüstungsdynamik im Ost-West-Konflikt und die Möglichkeiten ihrer Beeinflussung*. Mitteilungen no. 4. Frankfurt, 1972.

Kaiser, Karl. "Transnationale Politik: Zu einer Theorie der Multinationalen Politik." *Politische Vierteljahresschrift*, 10(1969)80–109.

Lehmbruch, Gerhard. "Konkordanzdemokratien im Internationalen System." *Politische Vierteljahresschrift*, 10(1969)139–163.

Mendershausen, Horst. "Transnational Society versus State Sovereignty." *Kyklos*, 22(1969)251–275.

Rosenau, James N., ed. *Domestic Sources of Foreign Policy*. New York: Free Press, 1967.

———. "Comparative Foreign Policy: Fad, Fantasy or Field?" *International Studies Quarterly*, 12(1968)296–329.

———, ed. *Linkage Politics*. New York: Free Press, 1969.

Sondermann, Fred A. "The Linkage between Foreign Policy and International Politics." In Rosenau, James N., ed., *International Politics and Foreign Policy*. New York: Free Press, 1961. Pp. 8–17.

On international political processes:

Alger, Chadwick F. "Interaction in a Committee of the United Nations General Assembly." In Singer, J. David, ed., *Quantitative International Politics: Insights and Evidence*. New York: Free Press, 1968. Pp. 51–84.

Bergstraesser, Arnold. *Weltpolitik als Wissenschaft.* Cologne: Westdeutscher Verlag, 1965.
Cox, Robert W., ed. *The Politics of International Organizations.* New York: Praeger, 1970.
Gregg, Robert W., and Barkun, Michael. *The United Nations System and Its Functions.* Princeton: Van Nostrand, 1968.
Holt, Robert T., and van de Velde, Robert M. *Strategic Psychological Operations and American Foreign Policy.* Chicago: University of Chicago Press, 1960.

Chapter 4

On power:

Aron, Raymond. "The Anarchical Order of Power." In Hoffmann, Stanley H., ed., *Conditions of World Order.* Boston: Houghton Mifflin, 1968. Pp. 25–48.
Bierstedt, Robert. "An Analysis of Social Power." *American Sociological Review*, 15(1950) 730–738.
Dahl, Robert A. "The Concept of Power." *Behavioral Science*, 2(1957)201–215.
Deutsch, Karl W. *The Analysis of International Relations.* Englewood Cliffs: Prentice-Hall, 1968.
Hoffmann, Stanley H. *Contemporary Theory in International Relations.* Englewood Cliffs: Prentice-Hall, 1960.
——. *The State of War.* New York: Praeger, 1965.
——. *Gulliver's Troubles or the Setting of American Foreign Policy.* New York: McGraw Hill, 1968.
Howard, Michael. "Military Power and International Order." *International Affairs*, 40(1964)397–408.
March, James G. "An Introduction to the Theory and Measurement of Influence." *American Political Science Review*, 49(1955)431–451.
Morgenthau, Hans J. *Politics among Nations*, New York: Knopf, 1973.
Riker, William H. "Some Ambiguities in the Notion of Power." *American Political Science Review*, 58(1964)341–349.
Simon, Herbert A. "Notes on the Observation and Measurement of Political Power." *Journal of Politics*, 15(1954)500–516.
Singer, J. David. "Inter-Nation Influence: A Formal Model." *American Political Science Review*, 57(1963)420–430.
Spiro, Herbert J. *World Politics: The Global System.* Homewood, Ill.: Dorsey Press, 1966.
Walton, John. "A Methodology for the Comparative Study of Power: Some Conceptual and Procedural Applications." *Social Science Quarterly*, 52(1971)39–60.
Zoppo, Ciro Elliott. "Nuclear Technology, Multipolarity, and International Stability." *World Politics*, 18(1966)579–606.

On small states and power:

Müller, Adolf. "Die Rolle der Nation in der gegenwärtigen Politik." *Europa Archiv*, 24(1969)317–324.
Olson, Mancur, Jr., and Zeckhauser, Richard. "An Economic Theory of Alliances." In Russett, Bruce M., ed., *Economic Theories of International Politics.* Chicago: Markham, 1968. Pp. 25–45.
Paterson, William E. "Small States in International Politics." *Cooperation and Conflict*, 4(1969)119–123.
Toncic-Sorinj, Lujo. "Der Schutz der Kleinen in der Welt der Grossen." *Aussenpolitik*, 17(1966)591–598.

Bibliography

On force in international politics:

Art, Robert J., and Waltz, Kenneth N., eds. *The Use of Force*. Boston: Little, Brown, 1971.

Hassner, Pierre. "On ne badine pas avec la force." *Revue Française de Science Politique*, 21(1971)1207–1223.

Jahrbuch für Friedens-und Konfliktforschung, vol. 1, *Bedrohungsvorstellungen als Faktor der internationalen Politik*. Düsseldorf: Bertelsmann Universitätsverlag, 1971.

Rosecrance, Richard, ed. *The Future of the International Strategic System*. San Francisco: Chandler, 1972.

Senghaas, Dieter. *Abschreckung und Frieden*. Frankfurt am Main: Europäische Verlagsanstalt, 1969.

Weizsäcker, C. F. von. *Kriegsfolgen und Kriegsverhütung*. Munich: Carl Hanser Verlag, 1970.

Chapter 5

On the psychology of nationalism:

Bentheim van den Berg, Godfried van. "Contemporary Nationalism in the Western World." In Hoffmann, Stanley H., ed., *Conditions of World Order*. Boston: Houghton Mifflin, 1968.

Burton, John W. *Peace Theory*. New York: Knopf, 1962.

Doob, Leonard W. *Patriotism and Nationalism*. New Haven: Yale University Press, 1964.

Frank, Jerome D. *Sanity and Survival*. New York: Random House, 1968.

Glenn, Edmund S. "The Two Faces of Nationalism." *Comparative Political Studies*, 3(1970)347–366.

Guetzkow, Harold. "Isolation and Collaboration: A Partial Theory of International Relations." *Journal of Conflict Resolution*, 1(1957)48–68.

Haas, Ernst B. *Beyond the Nation-State*. Stanford: Stanford University Press, 1964.

Homans, George C. "Structural, Functional and Psychological Theories." In Demerath, N. S., and Peterson, Richard A., eds., *System, Change, and Conflict*. New York: Free Press, 1967. Pp. 347–366.

Katz, Daniel. "Nationalism and Strategies of International Conflict Resolution." In Kelman, Herbert C., *International Behavior*. New York: Holt, Rinehart and Winston, 1965. Pp. 354–390.

———, Kelman, Herbert C., and Flacks, Richard. "The National Role: Some Hypotheses about the Relations of Individuals to Nation in America Today." Peace Research Society (International), *Papers*, vol. 1, 1964, *The Chicago Conference, 1963*, pp. 113–127.

———, Kelman, Herbert C., and Vassilian, Vasso. "A Comparative Approach to the Study of Nationalism." Peace Research Society (International), *Papers*, vol. 14, 1970, *The Ann Arbor Conference, 1969*, pp. 1–14.

Klineberg, Otto. *The Human Dimension in International Relations*. New York: Holt, Rinehart and Winston, 1965.

Lemberg, Eugen. *Nationalismus*. Reinbach: Rowohlt Taschenbuch Verlag, 1964.

Myrdal, Gunnar. *Beyond the Welfare State*. New Haven: Yale University Press, 1960.

Ronneberger, Franz. "Nationale Integration als Ergebnis von Sozialisations-, Entkulturations- und Personalisationsprozessen." In Wurzbacher, Gerhard, ed., *Der Mensch als Soziales und Personales Wesen*. Stuttgart: Ferdinand Enke Verlag, 1963. Pp. 225–261.

Shafer, Boyd C. *Faces of Nationalism*. New York: Harcourt Brace Jovanovich, 1972.

INTERNATIONAL POLITICS

On peace settlements:

Hoffmann, Stanley H. "Obstinate or Obsolete? The Fate of the Nation-State and the Case of Western Europe." *Daedalus*, 95(1966) 455–478.

Thomson, David, Meyer, E., and Briggs, A. *Patterns of Peacemaking*. New York: Oxford University Press, 1945.

On community and society:

Cassinelli, C. W. "The National Community." *Polity*, 2(1969)14–31.

Cobb, Roger W., and Elder, Charles. *International Community*. New York: Holt, Rinehart and Winston, 1970.

Dahrendorf, Ralf. *Gesellschaft und Freiheit*. Munich: R. Piper Verlag, 1961.

Durkheim, Emile. *The Division of Labor in Society*. New York: Free Press, 1964.

Easton, David. *A Systems Analysis of Political Life*. New York: Wiley, 1965.

French, Robert M. *The Community*. Itasca, Ill.: F. E. Peacock, 1969.

Füsslein, Rudolf W. *Die Unwandelbaren Fundamente des Staates*. Hamburg: Drei Türme Verlag, 1947.

Holsti, Ole. "The Belief System and National Images." *Journal of Conflict Resolution*, 6(1962)244–252.

König, René. *The Community*. London: Routledge and Kegan Paul, 1968.

Levi, Werner. *Fundamentals of World Organization*. Minneapolis: University of Minnesota Press, 1950.

Mayntz, Renate, ed. *Theodor Geiger On Social Order and Mass Society*. Chicago: University of Chicago Press, 1969.

McWilliams, Wilson Carey. "Political Development and Foreign Policy." In Butwell, R., ed., *Foreign Policy and the Developing Nations*. Lexington: University of Kentucky Press, 1969. Pp. 13–39.

Minar, David W., and Greer, Scott. *The Concept of Community*. Chicago: Aldine, 1969.

Nisbet, Robert A. *The Quest for Community*. New York: Oxford University Press, 1953.

Rivera, Joseph H. de. *The Psychological Dimension of Foreign Policy*. Columbus, Ohio: Charles E. Merrill, 1968.

Russett, Bruce M. "Transactions, Community and International Political Integration." *Journal of Common Market Studies*, 9(1971)14–31.

Singer, Marshall R. *Weak States in a World of Powers*. New York: Free Press, 1972.

Taylor, Paul. "The Concept of Community and the European Integration Process." *Journal of Common Market Studies*, 7(1968)83–101.

Chapter 6

On social controls:

Coplin, William D. *The Functions of International Law*. Chicago: Rand McNally, 1966.

———. "International Organizations in the Future International Bargaining Process: A Theoretical Projection." In Sullivan, David S., and Sattler, Martin J., *Change and the Future International System*. New York: Columbia University Press, 1972. Pp. 81–96.

Geiger, Theodor. *Vorstudien zu einer Soziologie des Rechts*. Neuwied: Hermann Luchterhand Verlag, 1964.

Gurvitch, Georges. *Sociology of Law*. London: Routledge & Kegan Paul, 1947.

Henkin, Louis. *How Nations Behave*. London: Pall Mall Press, 1968.

Legg, Keith R., and Morrison, James F. *Politics and the International System: An Introduction*. New York: Harper and Row, 1971.

Bibliography

McIntosh, Donald S. "Power and Social Control." *American Political Science Review*, 57(1963)619–631.

Mannheim, Karl. *Man and Society in an Age of Reconstruction.* London: Kegan Paul, Trench, Trubner, 1940.

Nett, Roger. "Conformity, Deviation and the Social Control Concept." *Ethics*, 64(1953)38–43.

Parsons, Talcott, and Shils, Edward A. *Toward a General Theory of Action.* New York: Harper and Row, 1962.

Sjoberg, Gideon. "Contradictory Functional Requirements and Social Systems." *Journal of Conflict Resolution*, 4(1960)198–208.

Stone, Julius. *Social Dimensions of Law and Justice.* Stanford: Stanford University Press, 1966.

Waltz, Kenneth N. "Conflict in World Politics." In Spiegel, Steven L., and Waltz, Kenneth N., *Conflict in World Politics.* Cambridge, Mass.: Winthrop Publishers, 1971. Pp. 454–474.

On socialization and social controls:

Alger, Chadwick F. "United Nations Participation as a Learning Process." *Public Opinion Quarterly*, 26(1963)411–426.

Aron, Raymond. *Progress and Disillusion.* New York: Praeger, 1968.

Bosc, Robert. *Sociologie de la paix.* Paris: Edition Spes, 1965.

Coplin, William D. *Introduction to International Politics.* Chicago: Markham, 1971.

Etzioni, Amitai. *The Active Society.* New York: Free Press, 1968.

Fichter, Joseph, H. *Sociology.* Chicago: University of Chicago Press, 1957.

Gould, Wesley L., and Barkun, Michael. *International Law and the Social Sciences.* Princeton: Princeton University Press, 1971.

Haas, Ernest B. *The Web of Interdependence: The United States and International Organizations.* Englewood Cliffs: Prentice-Hall, 1970.

Haas, Michael. "A Functional Approach to International Organizations." *Journal of Politics*, 27(1965)498–517.

Holsti, K. J. "National Role Conceptions in the Study of Foreign Policy." *International Studies Quarterly*, 14(1970)233–309.

LeVine, Robert A. "Socialization, Social Structure and Intersocietal Images." In Kelman, Herbert C., ed., *International Behavior.* New York: Holt, Rinehart and Winston, 1965. Pp. 43–69.

Lindblom, Charles E. *The Intelligence of Democracy.* New York: Free Press, 1965.

Modelski, George. "The World's Foreign Ministers: A Political Elite." *Journal of Conflict Resolution*, 14(1970)135–175.

Schelling, Thomas C. *The Strategy of Conflict.* New York: Oxford University Press, 1963.

Treviranus, Hans-Dietrich. "Aussenpolitik and Innenpolitik." *Aussenpolitik*, 15(1964)635–644.

Visscher, Charles de. *Theory and Reality in Public International Law.* Princeton: Princeton University Press, 1957.

Wurzbacher, Gerhard, ed. *Der Mensch als Soziales und Personales Wesen.* Stuttgart: Ferdinand Enke Verlag, 1963.

On social controls and foreign policy decisions:

Bauer, Raymond A. "The Study of Policy Formation: An Introduction." In Bauer, Raymond A., and Gergen, Kenneth J., *The Study of Policy Formation.* New York: Free Press, 1968. Pp. 1–26.

Burns, Arthur L. *Of Powers and Their Politics.* Englewood Cliffs: Prentice-Hall, 1968.

Burton, J. W. *System, States, Diplomacy and Rules.* Cambridge: University Press, 1968.

Eayrs, James. *Diplomacy and Its Discontents.* Toronto: University of Toronto Press, 1971.

Farrell, R. Barry. "Foreign Policies of Open and Closed Political Societies." In Farrell, R.

INTERNATIONAL POLITICS

Barry, *Approaches to Comparative and International Politics*. Evanston: Northwestern University Press, 1966. Pp. 167–206.

Lovell, John P. *Foreign Policy in Perspective*. New York: Holt, Rinehart and Winston, 1970.

Morgan, Patrick M. *Theories and Approaches to International Politics*. San Ramon, Cal.: Consensus Publishers, 1972.

Rivera, Joseph P. *The Psychological Dimension of Foreign Policy*. Columbus, Ohio: Merrill, 1968.

Robinson, James A., and Snyder, Richard C. "Decision-Making in International Politics." In Kelman, Herbert C., *International Behavior*. New York: Holt, Rinehart and Winston, 1965. Pp. 435–463.

Rosenau, James N. "The External Environment as a Variable in Foreign Policy Analysis." In Rosenau, James N., Davis, Vincent, and East, Maurice A., eds., *The Analysis of International Politics*. New York: Free Press, 1972. Pp. 145–165.

Shapiro, Michael J., and Bonham, G. Matthew. "Cognitive Processes and Foreign Policy-Making." *International Studies Quarterly*, 17(1973)147–174.

Chapter 7

On types of conflict:

Dougherty, James E., and Pfaltzgraff, Robert L., Jr. *Contending Theories of International Relations*. Philadelphia: Lippincott, 1971.

Dahrendorf, Ralf. "Toward a Theory of Social Conflict." *Journal of Conflict Resolution*, 2(1958)170–183.

Haas, Michael. "Sources of International Conflict." In Rosenau, James N., Davis, Vincent, and East, Maurice A., *The Analysis of International Politics*. New York: Free Press, 1972. Pp. 252–277.

Mack, Raymond W., and Snyder, Richard C. "The Analysis of Social Conflict — Toward an Overview and Synthesis." *Journal of Conflict Resolution*, 1(1957)212–248.

Northedge, F. S., and Donelan, M. D. *International Disputes: The Political Aspects*. New York: St. Martin's Press, 1971.

On tension:

International Sociological Association. *The Nature of Conflict*. UNESCO Tensions and Technology Series. Paris, 1957.

Keeskemiti, Paul. "Reducing International Tension." *Commentary*, 20(1955)517–521.

Kimminich, Otto. *Rüstung und Politische Spannung*. Gütersloh: Bertelsman Verlag, 1964.

Lifton, Robert J. *History and Human Survival*. New York: Random House, 1970.

Morgenthau, Hans J. *Politics among Nations*. New York: Knopf, 1973.

Wright, Quincy. *Problems of Stability and Progress in International Relations*. Berkeley: University of California Press, 1954.

On peaceful change:

Dahrendorf, Ralf. *Gesellschaft und Freiheit*. Munich: R. Piper Verlag, 1961.

Hugo, Grant. *Appearance and Reality in International Relations*. New York: Columbia University Press, 1970.

Jenks, Wilfred C. *A New World of Law*. London: Longmans Green, 1969.

Lapierre, Jean-William. *Essai sur le fondement du pouvoir politique*. Aix-en-Provence: Université, Faculté des Lettres, 1968.

———. *Le pouvoir politique*. Paris: Presses Universitaires de France, 1970.

Bibliography

Rosenau, James N. "The External Environment as a Variable in Foreign Policy Analysis." In Rosenau, James N., Davis, Vincent, and East, Maurice A., *The Analysis of International Politics*. New York: Free Press, 1972. Pp. 145–165.

On interdependence:

Alexandrowicz-Alexander, C. H. "Vertical and Horizontal Divisions of the International Society." *Indian Yearbook of International Affairs*, 1(1952)88–96.

Cooper, Richard N. "Economic Interdependence and Foreign Policy in the Seventies." *World Politics*, 24(1972)159–81.

———. *The Economics of Interdependence: Economic Policy in the Atlantic Community*. New York: McGraw-Hill, 1968.

Erbes, Robert. *L'intégration économique internationale*. Paris: Presses Universitaires de France, 1966.

Gould, Wesley L., and Barkun, Michael. *International Law and the Social Sciences*. Princeton: Princeton University Press, 1970.

Gouldner, A. W. "The Norm of Reciprocity: A Preliminary Statement." *American Sociological Review*, 25(1960)161–178.

Haas, Ernst B. *The Web of Interdependence: The United States and International Organizations*. Englewood Cliffs: Prentice-Hall, 1970.

Krause, Lawrence B. "Why Exports Are Becoming Irrelevant." *Brookings Bulletin*, 8(1971 no. 2)7–10.

Miller, S. M., and Bennett, Roy. "A Neo-Imperialism Critique." New York University Center for International Studies, *Policy Papers*, vol. 4(1971)no. 5.

Morse, Edward L. "The Politics of Interdependence." *International Organization*, 23(1969) 311–326.

———. "The Transformation of Foreign Policies: Modernization, Interdependence, and Externalization." *World Politics*, 22(1970)371–392.

Pruitt, Dean G. "Stability and Sudden Change in Interpersonal and International Affairs." *Journal of Conflict Resolution*, 13(1969)18–38.

———, and Snyder, Richard C. *Theory and Research on the Causes of War*. Englewood Cliffs: Prentice-Hall, 1969.

Russett, Bruce M. "Interdependence and Capabilities for European Cooperation." *Journal of Common Market Studies*, 9(1970)143–150.

———, and Sullivan, John D. "Collective Goods and International Organization." *International Organization*, 25(1971)845–865.

Schelling, Thomas C. *The Strategy of Conflict*. New York: Oxford University Press, 1963.

Schlupp, Friedrich, Nour, Salna, and Junne, Gerd. "Zur Theorie und Ideologie in Internationaler Interdependenz." Paper delivered to the Tagung der Deutschen Vereinigung für Politische Wissenschaft, October 3–6, 1971.

Singer, J. David, and Wallace, Michael. "Intergovernmental Organization and the Preservation of Peace, 1816–1964: Some Bivariate Relationships." *International Organization*, 24(1970)520–547.

Skolnikoff, Eugene B. *The International Imperatives of Technology*. Institute of International Studies Research Series, no. 16, University of California, Berkeley, 1972.

———. "The International Functional Implications of Future Technology." In Sullivan, David S., and Sattler, Martin J., eds., *Change and the Future International System*. New York: Columbia University Press, 1971.

———. "Science and Technology: The Implications for International Institutions." *International Organization*, 25(1971)759–775.

Sprout, Harold, and Sprout, Margaret. *Toward a Politics of the Planet Earth*. New York: Van Nostrand Reinhold, 1971.

Stauffer, Robert. "Nation-Building in a Global Economy: The Role of the Multinational Corporation." *Philippine Journal of Public Administration*, 16(1972)3–41.

INTERNATIONAL POLITICS

Sweezy, Paul M., and Magdoff, Harry. *The Dynamics of U.S. Capitalism*. New York: Monthly Review Press, 1971.
Tudyka, Kurt P. "Transnationale Konzerne im Urteil der Gewerkschaften." *Acta Politica*, 7(1972)471–482.
Waltz, Kenneth N. "The Myth of National Interdependence." In Kindleberger, Charles P., *The International Corporation*. Cambridge, Mass.: M.I.T. Press, 1970. Pp. 205–223.
Young, Oran R. "Interdependencies in World Politics." *International Journal*, 24(1969)726–750.
Ziebura, Gilbert. "Nationales Interesse und übernationale Ordnung." In Ziebura, Gilbert, *Nationale Souveränität oder Übernationale Integration?* Berlin: Colloquium Verlag Berlin, 1966. Pp. 151–175.

On violence:

Nieburg, H. L. "Violence, Law and the Informal Policy." *Journal of Conflict Resolution*, 13(1969)192–209.

On legal and political disputes:

Kelsen, Hans, and Tucker, Robert W. *Principles of International Law*. Princeton: Princeton University Press, 1966.
Morgenthau, Hans J. *Politics among Nations*. New York: Knopf, 1973.
Visscher, Charles de. *Theory and Reality in Public International Law*. Princeton: Princeton University Press, 1957.

On the effectiveness of international law and peaceful methods:

Axline, W. Andrew. *European Community Law and Organizational Development*. Dobbs Ferry, N.Y.: Oceana Publications, 1968.
Barkun, Michael. *Law without Sanctions*. New Haven: Yale University Press, 1968.
Bozeman, Adda B. *The Future of Law in a Multicultural World*. Princeton: Princeton University Press, 1971.
Ebenstein, William. *The Pure Theory of Law*. Madison: University of Wisconsin Press, 1945.
Falk, Richard A. *The Status of Law in International Society*. Princeton: Princeton University Press, 1970.
Fisher, Roger. "Fractionating Conflict." In Fisher, Roger, ed., *International Conflict and Behavioral Science: The Craigville Papers*. New York: Basic Books, 1964. Pp. 91–109.
Franck, Thomas M. *The Structure of Impartiality*. New York: Macmillan, 1968.
Friedheim, Robert L. "The 'Satisfied' and 'Dissatisfied' States Negotiate International Law: A Case Study." *World Politics*, 18(1965)20–42.
Heller, Hermann. *Staatslehre*. Leiden: A. W. Sijthoff, 1934.
Hoffmann, Stanley. "International Systems and International Law." In Knorr, Klaus, and Verba, Sidney, eds., *The International System*. Princeton: Princeton University Press, 1961. Pp. 205–238.
———. "Introduction." In Scheinman, Lawrence, and Wilkinson, David, eds., *International Law and Political Crisis*. Boston: Little, Brown, 1968. Pp. xi–xix.
McDougal, Myres S., Lasswell, Harold D., and Miller, James C. *The Interpretation of Agreements and World Public Order*. New Haven: Yale University Press, 1967.
Nieburg, H. L. "Violence, Law, and the Informal Policy." *Journal of Conflict Resolution*, 13(1969)192–209.
Radbruch, Gustav. *Rechtsphilosophie*. Leipzig: Quelle and Meyer, 1932.
Scheingold, Stuart A. *The Law in Political Integration*. Cambridge, Mass.: Center for International Affairs, Harvard University, 1971.

Bibliography

Singer, J. David. "Escalation and Control in International Conflict: A Simple Feedback Model." *General Systems*, 15(1970)163–173.

Young, Oran R. "The United Nations and the International System." *International Organization*, 22(1968)902–922.

Chapter 8

On national conditions and war:

Buchan, Alastair. "Frieden und Krieg in den siebziger Jahren." *Europa Archiv*, 24(1969)305–316.

East, Maurice A., and Gregg, Phillip M. "Cooperation and Conflict." *International Studies Quarterly*, 11(1967)244–269.

Falk, Richard A. *Law, Morality and War in the Contemporary World*. New York: Praeger, 1963.

Feierabend, Ivo K., and Feierabend, R. L. "Aggressive Behavior within Polities, 1948–1962: A Cross-National Study." *Journal of Conflict Resolution*, 10(1966)249–271.

Haas, Michael. "Societal Approaches to the Study of War." *Journal of Peace Research*, 2(1965)307–323.

Huntington, Samuel P. "Patterns of Violence in World Politics." In Huntington, Samuel P., ed., *Changing Patterns of Military Politics*. New York: Free Press, 1962. Pp. 17–50.

Newcombe, Hanna, and Newcombe, Alan. *Peace Research Around the World*. Oakville, Manitoba: Canadian Peace Research Institute, 1969.

Rosecrance, Richard N. *Action and Reaction in World Politics*. Boston: Little, Brown, 1963.

Rosenau, James N., ed. *International Aspects of Civil Strife*. Princeton: Princeton University Press, 1964.

Rummel, Rudolph J. "The Dimensions of Conflict Behavior within and between Nations." *General Systems Yearbook*, 8(1963)1–50.

Schulte, Ludwig. "Politische Konstellation und Friedenssicherung." *Aussenpolitik*, 21(1970)9–18.

Tanter, Raymond. "Dimensions of Conflict Behavior within and between Nations." *Journal of Conflict Resolution*, 10(1966)41–64.

On biology and war:

Corning, Peter A. "The Biological Bases of Behavior: Some Implications for Political Science." *World Politics*, 23(1971)321–370.

Lorenz, Konrad. *On Aggression*. New York: Harcourt, Brace and World, 1966.

Tinbergen, Nikolaas. *Social Behaviour in Animals*. New York: Wiley, 1963.

Williams, Roger J. "The Biology of Behavior." *Saturday Review*, January 30, 1971, pp. 17–19, 61.

On sociology and war:

Aron, Raymond. *Peace and War*. Garden City: Doubleday, 1966.

Hoffmann, Stanley. *The State of War*. New York: Praeger, 1965.

Liska, George. *War and Order*. Baltimore: Johns Hopkins Press, 1968.

McNeil, Elton B., ed. *The Nature of Human Conflict*. Englewood Cliffs: Prentice-Hall, 1965.

Starke, J. G. *An Introduction to the Science of Peace (Irenology)*. Leiden: A. W. Sijthoff, 1968.

Waltz, Kenneth N. *Man, the State and War*. New York: Columbia University Press, 1959.

Wright, Quincy. *A Study of War*. 2 vols. Chicago: University of Chicago Press, 1965.

INTERNATIONAL POLITICS

On psychology and war:

Bandura, Albert. *Behavior Modification*. New York: Holt, Rinehart and Winston, 1969.
Eron, Leonard D., Walder, Leopold O., and Lebowitz, Monroe M. *Learning of Aggression in Children*. Boston: Little, Brown, 1971.
Frank, Jerome D. *Sanity and Survival*. New York: Random House, 1968.
Luard, Evan. *Conflict and Peace in the Modern International System*. Boston: Little, Brown, 1968.
Mitscherlich, Alexander. *Die Idee des Friedens und die menschliche Agressivität*. Frankfurt am Main: Suhrkamp, 1969.
Rattner, Josef. *Aggression und Menschliche Natur*. Olten-Freiburg: Walter Verlag, 1971.
Stagner, Ross. *Psychological Aspects of International Conflict*. Belmont, Cal.: Brooks/Cole Publishing Co., 1967.

On interests, integration, and peace:

De Vree, Johan K. *Political Integration: The Formation of Theory and Its Problems*. The Hague: Mouton, 1972.
Deutsch, Karl W., et al. *Political Community in the North Atlantic Area*. Princeton: Princeton University Press, 1968.
————. "Transaction Flows as Indicators of Political Cohesion." In Jacob, Philip E., and Toscano, James V., *The Integration of Political Communities*. Philadelphia: Lippincott, 1964. Pp. 75–97.
Gantzel, Klaus J. *System und Akteur*. Düsseldorf: Bertelsmann Universitätsverlag, 1972.
Haas, Ernst B. *Beyond the Nation-State: Functionalism and International Organization*. Stanford: Stanford University Press, 1964.
Hassner, Pierre. "Nationalism et relations internationales." *Revue Française de Science Politique*, 15(1965)499–528.
Huber, Ernst-Rudolf. *Nationalstaat und Verfassungsstaat*. Stuttgart: Kohlhammer Verlag, 1965.
Levi, Werner. "The Concept of Integration in Research on Peace." *Journal of Conflict Resolution*, 9(1965)111–126.
Nye, Joseph S., Jr., ed. *International Regionalism*. Boston: Little, Brown, 1968.
Perroux, François. *La coexistence pacifique*. Vol. 3. Paris: Presses Universitaires de France, 1958.
Puchala, Donald J. "International Transactions and Regional Integration." *International Organization*, 24(1970)732–763.
Sidjansky, Dusan. *Dimensions européennes de la science politique*. Paris: Librairie général de droit et de jurisprudence, 1963.
Spinelli, Altiero. *The Eurocrats*. Baltimore: Johns Hopkins Press, 1966.

Chapter 9

On the weakening of the state:

Alger, Chadwick F. "Problems in Global Organization." *International Social Science Journal*, 22(1970)691–709.
Behrendt, Richard F. *Zwischen Anarchie und Neuen Ordnungen*. Freiburg:Verlag Rombach, 1971.
Franko, Lawrence G. *Joint Venture Survival in Multinational Corporations*. New York: Praeger, 1971.
Gough, Kathleen. "The Crisis of the Nation-State." In Fisher, Roger, ed., *International Conflict and Behavioral Science: The Craigville Papers*. New York: Basic Books, 1964. Pp. 41–69.

Bibliography

Hoffmann, Stanley. "International Organization and the International System." *International Organization*, 24(1970)389–413.

Mitscherlich, Alexander. *Auf dem Weg zur Vaterlosen Gesellschaft*. Munich: R. Piper Verlag, 1963.

Singer, J. David. "Popular Diplomacy and Policy Effectiveness: A Note on the Mechanisms and Consequences." *Comparative Studies in Society and History*, 12(1970)320–326.

———— "Escalation and Control in International Conflict: A Simple Feedback Model." *General Systems*, 15(1970)163–173.

On the future of the United Nations:

Haas, Ernst B. *Collective Security and the Future International System*. Social Science Foundation, University of Denver, January 1968.

Kay, David A. *The New Nations in the United Nations, 1960–1967*. New York: Columbia University Press, 1970.

Miller, Linda B. *World Order and Local Disorder: The United Nations and Internal Conflict*, Princeton: Princeton University Press, 1967.

On pluralism:

Deutsch, Karl W., and Singer, J. David. "Multipolar Power Systems and International Stability." *World Politics*, 16(1964)390–406.

Feld, Werner J. *Nongovernmental Forces and World Politics: A Study of Business, Labor, and Political Groups*. New York: Praeger, 1972.

On transnational relations and new groupings:

Galtung, Johan. "On the Future of the International System." *Journal of Peace Research*, 4(1967)305–333.

————. "Entropy and the General Theory of Peace." In IPRA Studies in Peace Research, *Proceedings of the International Peace Research Association, Second Conference*, vol. 1. Assen: Van Gorcum, 1968. Pp. 3–37.

————. *Co-operation in Europe*. Oslo: Universitetsforlaget, 1970. Pp. 7–103.

Gregg, Robert W., and Barkun, Michael, eds. *The United Nations System and its Functions*. Princeton: Van Nostrand, 1968.

Haas, Ernst B. "The Comparative Study of the United Nations." *World Politics*, 12(1960)298–322.

Hellmann, Rainer. *The Challenge to U.S. Dominance of the International Corporation*. New York: Dunellen, 1971.

Judge, A. J. N. "Multinational Business Enterprise." *Yearbook of International Organizations*, 1968–69, pp. 1189–1214.

Kaiser, Karl. "Transnationale Politik: Zu einer Theorie der Multinationalen Politik." *Politische Vierteljahresschrift*, 10(1969)80–109. Also in *International Organization*, 25(1971)790–817.

Keohane, Robert O., and Nye, Joseph S., Jr., eds. "Transnational Relations in World Politics." *International Organization*, 25(1971)329–758.

Kindleberger, Charles P., ed. *The International Corporation: A Symposium*. Cambridge, Mass.: M.I.T. Press, 1970.

Modelski, George. "The Corporation in World Society." *Yearbook of World Affairs*, 1968, pp. 64–79.

————, ed. "Multinational Corporations and World Order." *International Studies Quarterly*, 16(1972)407–562.

INTERNATIONAL POLITICS

O'Connor, James. "International Corporations and Economic Underdevelopment." *Science and Society*, 34(1970)42–60.

Tinbergen, Jan. *International Economic Integration*. Amsterdam: Elsevier Publishing Co., 1965.

Rosecrance, Richard. *International Relations: Peace or War*. New York: McGraw Hill, 1973.

Vaupel, James W., and Curhan, Joan P. *The Making of Multinational Enterprise*. Boston: Division of Research, Graduate School of Business Administration, Harvard University, 1969.

Vernon, Raymond. "Multinational Enterprise." *Harvard Business Review*, 45(1967)157–172.

————. "The Multinational Enterprise: Power versus Sovereignty." *Foreign Affairs*, 49(1971)736–751.

INDEX

Index

281

Index

participation in, 43, 45; voting procedure in, 45, 74, 137; and morality, 56; and sovereignty, 73, 134, 138; nongovernmental organizations in, 80; and actors, 83; as social control, 149, 160, 165; future scope of, 234–235

International society: nature of, 5, 13, 23, 32–33, 140–146; change in, 5, 21, 64–66, 132, 228–232; peacefulness of, 6; quality of, 6, 8–9, 59–62; political decision-making in, 19, 27; government of, 20; inequalities in, 23, 39–45; goals of, 24, 26–27, 36, 98; power base of, 24, 106, 167; and cultural heterogeneity, 46–56, 132

International system: subjective base of, 6, 117–118; change in, 8, 225–230; efficacy of 9, 14; concept of, 11–12, 15–16; actors in, 20; and international society, 32; effect on international behavior of, 75, 156; power in, 100, and war, 201–205

Isolation: of states, 34, 70–71, 73, 123, 127, 155, 226; of regions, 92; and power, 108; and economic welfare, 126, 131

Jellinek, Georg, 74
Justice, in international system, 9, 198

Laski, Harold, 122
Lasswell, Harold D., 38
Law. *See* International law
League of Nations: as "government," 20; growth of, 21; and social change, 181
Legitimacy: of political decisions, 22–25, 30–31; of national interests, 25; of social controls, 167
Lin Piao, 236
Lindblom, Charles, 169
Linkage: of internal and international matters, 29, 65, 68, 112, 125, 131–134, 226; of private and international interests, 54; of internal and foreign policies, 153; of national conditions and war, 204
Liu Shao-ch'i, 121
Loyalty. *See* Nationalism

McIver, Robert, 93, 139
Maine, Sir Henry, 122
Mitscherlich, Alexander, 230
Morality: and community, 56–59; in international behavior, 57–58, 74; in foreign policy, 90; norms of, 95, 129, 164,

238; and power, 99; in international law, 197

Multinational groups: loyalty to, 83, 84; and pluralism, 91–92; and power, 102; and interdependence of states, 184–185

National character: disappearance of, 53–54; and nationalism, 141–142

National interests: as legitimation, 25; and peace, 27, 218–223; nature of, 35, 54, 67; subjectivity of, 39, 54, 67–68; and rank, 40, 44, 61; and morality, 57–58, 60; as symbol, 66; and sovereignty, 74, 117; and decision-making, 88–89, 92, 154; and social controls, 149; and conflict, 173–179; and interdependence, 184; and war, 211–223

Nationalism: subjective aspects of, 7, 26, 29, 63–65, 118–121, 129–131; ethnocentrism of, 26; as social bond, 38, 78; universality of, 51, 119; of multinational groups, 83; development of, 118, 121–124; behavioral aspects of, 120, 132–136, 159; changing nature of, 123–136; materialist base of, 125–129; politicization of, 135; and community, 141, 144; and interdependence of states, 186; and international law, 197; and peace, 219

Nehru, Jawaharlal, 52
Nicolson, Harold, 9

Peace: conditions of, 4, 6, 8, 27, 48, 217–223; as international value, 6, 26; subjective aspects of, 7, 10, 143; and social order, 13; and interdependence among states, 84, 183; indivisibility of, 93; and atomic weapons, 110; and community, 143, 146, 220; and international organization, 188–189

Peaceful change. *See* Social change
Pluralism: effects of, 17, 29–30, 61, 90; in decision-making, 93; and nationalism, 135; as social control, 168, 180; and interdependence of states, 183; future development of, 232–234, 237
Political processes. *See* Political system
Political system: nature of, 4, 14–15, 26, 72–73; functions of, 11–12, 16–17, 21, 25–26, 66–67; boundaries of, 13, 17–19, 20–21; decision-making in, 19–20; subject matter of, 20–21; legitimacy of, 22–23, 30–31; efficacy of, 27–31, 59–64, 89–90, 96–97, 109, 143; inequality and, 44; and cultural heterogeneity, 47–51; subjective

283